In-Home Care for Older People

Health and Supportive Services

editors

Marcia G. Ory • Alfred P. Duncker

SAGE PUBLICATIONS
The International Professional Publishers
Newbury Park London New Delhi

For information address:

SAGE Publications, Inc.
2455 Teller Road
Newbury Park, California 91320

SAGE Publications Ltd.
6 Bonhill Street
London EC2A 4PU
United Kingdom

SAGE Publications India Pvt. Ltd.
M-32 Market
Greater Kailash I
New Delhi 110 048 India

Printed in the United States of America

Library of Congress Cataloging-in-Publication Data

In-home care for older people: health and supportive services / edited by Marcia G.
    Ory, Alfred P. Duncker
        p.   cm.
    "This edited volume builds on papers originally commissioned for
an NIA/AoA In-Home Care Conference held in 1990"—P.
    Includes bibliographical references (p.   ) and Index.
    ISBN 0-8039-4413-6 (cl.)   —ISBN 0-8039-4414-4 (pb)
    1. Aged —Home care—United States. 2. Aged—Long-term care—
United States.   I. Ory, Marcia G.   II. Duncker, Alfred P.
III. NIA/AoA In-Home Care Conference (1990 : Bethesda, Md.)
RA645.35.I5   1991
362.1'6'0973—dc20   91-30887

FIRST PRINTING, 1992

Sage Production Editor: Diane S. Foster

In-Home Care for Older People

Contents

Foreword

It is the year 2000. Do we know where the millions of frail and impaired elderly are? Certainly not in nursing homes. That would be counter to their wishes in most instances and would have required a highly unlikely massive increase in nursing home beds to boot. With the number of the oldest old—those 85 and over who are most at risk of some difficulty in activities of daily living—growing at an ever increasing rate, the state of affairs by the turn of the century is no small matter for concern. According to the National Medical Expenditure Survey, close to 5 million Americans, or nearly 18% of those aged 65 or over, were in need of some help with an activity of daily living in 1987. By the year 2000, based on current population projections, 18% of the elderly would come to well over 5 million old people with some impairment that calls for the help of others. Perhaps 1.75 million, or 5% of the total, would be in nursing homes or other institutions for long-term care at any one time. What will be the fate of the some 3.5 million who need some form of long-term care but are not institutionalized?

The answer by default is that they will have to be cared for in the community. How, and by whom? It is already recognized that, just as the majority of those most often in need of help are very old women, their home care is chiefly delivered by women—whether by unpaid family members or by paid (often poorly paid) home helpers. How can such care be organized to preserve the well-being of both the frail elder and the caregiver and how can it be financed? Answers to these questions have begun to be sought as members of the gerontological, geriatric, and health service disciplines have been hit by the enormity of the problems ahead.

One approach involves reducing the need for home care. For example, the World Health Organization, through the mechanism of its Expert Committee, recently issued a report on improving the health of older people, including a section on a model of home care and day care. This effort is in line with the WHO goal of health for all by the year 2000. The American Public Health Association has set congruent health objectives for that century turning point, including the aim of reducing the number of dysfunctional life years below its current 11.7-year figure, or 16% of life expectation. Fewer dysfunctional life years translate into lower need for long-term care, whether in the community or an institution.

Other approaches address the issue of finding and paying for home care when disability and frailty preclude continued independence and self-care. The Pepper Commission report, for instance, placed major emphasis on long-term care for the elderly as an unmet need in the community but the commission could not agree on a financing mechanism. Insurance companies, recognizing a growing market, are now advertising various long-term care policies, including coverage for home health care in some instances. Numerous home and home health care agencies, also realizing that a market exists, have sprung up, some licensed and some not. Indeed, home health care is a rapidly growing industry.

In light of such ferment, this book represents a systematic and welcome attempt to define the issues involved in long-term home care and to map out a research strategy that will provide the necessary answers to the many questions that have been posed.

—Marie R. Haug

Acknowledgments

We wish to thank the many people who have contributed to our thinking about home care for an aging population. Noting the importance of home care in the continuum of care, the leadership at the National Institute on Aging (NIA) and the Administration on Aging (AoA) gave us encouragement and support to bring together a group of experts to discuss critical research and policy issues. We are especially indebted to T. Franklin Williams, Joyce Berry, and Matilda White Riley for their insights into innovative models of home and community-based care for older people.

This volume builds on the NIA/AoA-sponsored workshop on in-home and supportive service held in Bethesda, Maryland, in 1990. Special thanks to Shirley Bagley and Richard Schloss for facilitating our cross-agency interaction. Michelle Blanco and Sylvia Kniel provided able assistance in the preparation of the workshop. Marie R. Haug, the chairperson, set this workshop into the broader context of behavioral and social research on aging. Additionally the workshop speakers, reactors, and observers reviewed what was known and helped us identify a research agenda. During the preparation of this manuscript, we were assisted in editing by Sharon Ardison.

Finally, though many people worked together in producing this volume, this effort is dedicated to the millions of older people who need home care and the individuals—families, policymakers, program planners, and service workers—who are struggling to provide high-quality, affordable care for all Americans.

Introduction:
The Home Care Challenge

MARCIA G. ORY
ALFRED P. DUNCKER

The provision of long-term care services is one of our nation's greatest health care challenges. At last count approximately 7 million older Americans were dependent on others for basic tasks of daily living, and this number is expected to increase dramatically in the twenty-first century as our baby boom generation ages (The Pepper Commission, 1990). Many equate long-term care with nursing home care. However, for every person in institutional care, there are an estimated four or more persons in the community requiring some form of long-term care (U.S. Congress, Senate Special Committee on Aging, 1988).

This comes as no surprise. Most older people and their families have long expressed a distinct preference for home or community-based assistance (Commonwealth Fund, 1988; U.S. Congress, Senate Special Committee on Aging, 1988). This preference is generally endorsed by policymakers, who often view noninstitutional care as less expensive than nursing home care. Indeed the home health and supportive care industries have expanded significantly in the last decade, fueled by

AUTHORS' NOTE: This introduction was written by government employees as part of official duties; therefore the material is in the public domain and may be copied or reproduced without permission.

1

the burgeoning long-term care needs of an aging population as well as by less restrictive eligibility requirements for federal reimbursement.

During the 1980s the total number of Medicare-reimbursed home health visits more than doubled (Riley, 1989; Tsung, 1990). The 1990 Medicaid Home and Community Care Options Act (ALFAA, 1990) now provides demonstration funding for noninstitutional long-term care options, enabling more frail, lower-income older people to remain in their own homes or to move into assisted living facilities. The provision of Medicaid waivers for community care services should stimulate further growth in the assisted living industry.

Despite the overriding preference for alternatives to institutional care and the recent expansion of home health services, the American home health care system is in crisis. It is often characterized by inaccessibility, poor care, unskilled personnel, high out-of-pocket costs, and inadequate linkages to other related services (National Aging Resource Center, 1990; U.S. General Accounting Office, 1988).

Fortunately, such health care problems are not going unnoticed. National debate has and will continue to focus on reforms to the long-term care system, including in-home and community-based care. For example, the U.S. Bipartisan Commission on Comprehensive Health Care (The Pepper Commission, 1990) has reviewed the current condition of America's health care system and has issued specific recommendations for long-term care reform that address both quality and costs (The Pepper Commission, 1990). Recognizing the need for an intensified research effort to guide programmatic and policy decisions for strengthening the health care system, the commission also called for substantial increases in long-term care research. In particular, the commission highlighted the need for additional research on the implementation of home and community-based care.

Editorial Perspectives

The National Institute on Aging (NIA) and the Administration on Aging (AoA) have defined home care for older Americans as a priority area needing the attention of researchers, planners, practitioners, and policy analysts. This edited volume builds on papers originally commissioned for an NIA/AoA In-Home Care Conference held in 1990. The purpose of this volume is to summarize what is known and to identify a research agenda that highlights (a) the use of in-home services for older people with different functional needs, (b) the effectiveness of different types or packages of services for different populations, and (c) the coordination (or lack of coordination) of in-home services with traditional medical services.

This volume considers an array of formally provided services delivered in the home or community to treat, rehabilitate, or manage the disabilities of older impaired persons. The focus is on older people in need of long-term care. To be sure, those with physical and cognitive frailties requiring long-term care represent only a small portion of the older population. However, their vulnerable status is a stark profile of the fastest growing segment of the population—the oldest old (85 plus) who are widowed, alone, and poor.

The chapters recognize the significant contribution made by family and friends and the burdens that families experience in providing care. We emphasize the need for better integration across the total continuum of care and coordination of different care providers as one of the major themes in this volume. We adhere to a biosocial view of health care, arguing that in-home health and supportive services must include both medical and social components for full effectiveness.

The lack of a clear conceptualization of home and community-based long-term care services has been a major research obstacle. We point to the desirability of going beyond the traditional emphasis on cost-effectiveness as the primary area of concern. Too often reported findings have been limited by inattention to other outcomes at stake for older people and their families. Our current understanding of home care will increase only as investigators begin to specify variations in the nature and types of home care and to examine the impacts in different populations and settings of care.

Organization of the Volume

To this end the chapters in this volume provide a selected review of research on in-home health and supportive services. The first chapter, by Benjamin, provides a comprehensive overview of the need for home care by frail older persons. Defining home care as the broad array of postacute and long-term care services provided in a nonmedical residential setting, Benjamin summarizes what is known about its use, effectiveness, and organization. The context of home care is elaborated by thoughtful attention to the sociopolitical environment as well as a discussion of conceptual and methodological issues surrounding each major research area. He concludes with specific suggestions for needed research, many of which are echoed throughout the entire volume. As a companion to this excellent overview, Rappaport and Benjamin have prepared an annotated bibliography (see Appendix A).

In addition to this general overview, this volume provides three chapters that address what is known about specific types of home care. The chapter by Hughes focuses on the characteristics of different home care models and the implications of these models for effectiveness, coordination, efficiency, and quality assurance. It refines the global concept of home care by conceptualizing four distinct models of care: high-tech home care, hospice, skilled home health care, and low-tech/custodial care. Appreciating the complexity of the home care industry, Hughes calls for a better integrated home care system that would be "user friendly."

Two types of home care were singled out for special attention because of their high program and policy visibility: respite care and board and care. Despite the relative lack of information on the effectiveness of these types of care, there is popular belief that one is positive (respite care) and the other subject to abuse and scandal (board and care). In fact in both cases these public perceptions are not necessarily supported by existing research findings.

Referring to a wide range of services intended to give temporary relief to family caregivers, respite care can vary in the location or setting of care as well as in the duration or intensity of services. In the chapter on respite care, Montgomery develops a typology of respite models based on attention to the dimensions of time, place, and level of care. While there is popular advocacy for respite services, research to date offers little support for their effectiveness in reducing costs or enhancing caregiver well-being. Montgomery cautions against premature conclusions and identifies research and service delivery issues that remain unanswered. The role of critical characteristics such as financing, eligibility criteria, and staffing also need to be explored.

Even less is known about *board and care* arrangements, defined generally as nonmedical residential care that provides assistance with some activities because of physical or mental disabilities. Viewing board and care as serving marginal populations (e.g., the poor and socially isolated), Eckert and Lyon acknowledge the wide range of care environments under this general rubric that encompasses the more recently defined assisted living facility. While most research to date has focused on regulation and reimbursement issues, Eckert and Lyon identify research needed to describe the care environment and psychosocial consequences for the older residents. They are especially interested in what factors constitute a homelike environment and how to balance the growing concern for increased regulation with the encouragement of small, familylike environments. The discussion in this chapter has direct relevance for many issues currently being debated wtihin the burgeoning "Assisted Living Movement."

The next two chapters discuss cross-cutting issues. Zimmer presents a conceptual model for integrating and coordinating community services for chronically ill older persons. Particular attention is paid to three key elements that have been noted briefly in the previous chapters: case management, geriatric assessment and consultation, and quality assurance. While virtually all of the elements of the model have been examined singly, a truly comprehensive system of care has not yet been tested on a communitywide basis.

Originally the conference did not have an explicit focus on in-home care and supportive services for the mentally impaired elderly. Recognizing that glaring omission, we solicited a paper by Harper reviewing what is known about home and community-based mental health services for older people. As with physically based long-term care services, mental health services include a broad array of health and social services. An examination of the need for such services suggests that older people are especially likely to underuse mental health services. This chapter discusses the presentation of mental illness in older people, the importance of home visits for understanding environmental causes of psychopathology, and the role of the health care provider, the family, and the older patient in setting care plans. Noting the relative lack of research in this area, Harper calls for additional research on the quality and outcomes of mental health services in home and community-based programs.

Summary of Research Needs

The identification of an in-home health and supportive services re-search agenda is a major objective of this volume. To that end each contributor was asked to identify major research questions as related to the content of his or her particular chapter. Additionally during the con-ference there were breakout sessions to develop consensus about re-search needs and opportunities in three different areas: in-home health care, respite care, and board and care. The summary of these discus-sions can be found in Appendix B.

Viewed by some as a panacea for the health care problems of older people, home care is often seen as a "cost-effective" alternative to in-stitutionalized care. Yet the heterogeneity of the aging population, its complicated health care and social needs, and the complexity of the home care system defy any simplistic conclusions. Existing research on in-home care simply does not yet provide an adequate basis for policy and program development.

In this introduction we draw attention to eight cross-cutting research needs to alert the reader to the state of our current knowledge. There is an urgent need to

- obtain better baseline information on the use of in-home health and sup-portive services by older people and their families;
- specify variations in the nature and type of care services, the population, and the settings of care;
- design and evaluate models of care that link specific outcomes to particular interventions;
- develop alternative outcome measures (e.g., quality of life);
- conduct longitudinal studies to assess transitions in the need for care, use of services, and care settings;
- assess access to and utilization of care in special populations (e.g., the old-est old, minority and ethnic populations, rural elderly);
- examine the interrelations among physical health and mental disorders and their implications for the need for home and community-based care; and
- investigate how new health care policies affect the availability and quality of expanding community care options (e.g., new Medicaid waivers for as-sisted living facilities).

While much of the existing research in this area has been limited, we have gained valuable insights through our previous attempts to examine the use and effectiveness of in-home health and supportive services. Too often we have treated home care as a global concept without specifying its essential components or indicating the routes to intended benefits. The call for better conceptualization and methodological sophistication is now being heeded. Investigators are defining the most pressing research questions and identifying appropriate conceptual frameworks and methodological strategies.

Advances will come through an awareness of the need to draw upon interdisciplinary expertise in clinical, behavioral, and social aspects of health and aging. For example, current models of health care use can be expanded to include more attention to the complex interactions among medical and social influences. Similarly researchers are urged to design innovative sampling strategies to minimize typical methodological problems such as population selection bias.

Postscript

The primary purpose of this volume is to summarize what is known and to identify a research agenda on selected aspects of in-home and community-based care. The sociopolitical context that shapes our health care system and the actual workings of a particular system are also described in some of the chapters. When data are nonexistent, a comparison of lessons from other chronically ill or disabled populations (e.g., the developmentally disabled, younger adults with spinal cord or other injuries, persons with AIDS) can aid in the interpretation of research findings or in the identification of research needs.

Based on the state of current knowledge in 1990, some contributors have offered recommendations about organizational or financial changes needed to improve the structure and processes of care. In these uncertain times, predictions about the future of the long-term care system will be more tenuous than ever. We anticipate that the international crisis, coupled with economic worries, will dominate national concern for some time to come. However, we cannot imagine that the problems of the health care system will simply go away. We see this volume as providing a needed framework for future research, health care practice, and policy actions.

References

Assisted Living Facilities Association of America. Detailed Summary of the "Medicaid Home and Community Care Options ACT" S. 1942, Passed by the United States Congress on October 28, 1990. Unpublished document, 1990.

Commonwealth Fund. (1988, April). *Proceedings of the Commonwealth Fund Commission on Elderly People Living Alone, Long-Term Care Workshop* (Background Paper Series No. 11). Baltimore, MD: Author.

National Aging Resource Center. (1990). *National Aging Resource Center: Long-term care*. Waltham, MA: Brandeis University.

Pepper Commission (U.S. Bipartisan Commission on Comprehensive Health Care). (1990, March). *A call for action*. Washington, DC: Author.

Riley, P. A. (1989). *Quality assurance in home care*. Washington, DC: AARP.

Tsung, S. A. (1990). *Trends in Medicare home health benefits*. Washington, DC: AARP.

U.S. Congress, Senate, Special Committee on Aging. (1988, November). *Long-term care for the elderly, issues of need, access, and cost* (GAO/HRD-89-4). Washington, DC: General Accounting Office.

U.S. Congress, Senate, Special Committee on Aging. (1989, February). *Developments in aging: 1989* (Vol. 1). Washington, DC: Government Printing Office.

ONE

An Overview of In-Home Health and Supportive Services for Older Persons

A. E. BENJAMIN

In an era of rapid technological change in medicine, it is somewhat paradoxical that the interest of policymakers and scholars has been drawn to health and supportive services provided at home. The apparent paradox lies in traditional conceptions of home care, which tend to emphasize the informal, unskilled, and inexpensive qualities attributed to that care and thus may seem anachronistic in an era of "high technology." But of course the paradox is overdrawn because several factors have helped shift policy attention to varieties of care provided in the home and especially to care available to older persons.

The most apparent factor historically is the persistence of "the nursing home problem," which in its various forms has shaped the context in which interest in home care has grown. Since establishment of the Medicaid program in 1965 stimulated expansion of the nursing home industry in the subsequent decade, critics have pointed to problems of rising costs, inappropriate placement, inadequate care, and ineffectual

AUTHOR'S NOTE: I would like especially to thank Meryl Rappaport for providing invaluable assistance in organizing and reviewing relevant literature for this chapter. I am grateful to Carroll Estes, Dorothy Rice, Charlene Harrington, Laura Reif, Lisa Binney, Laura Reif, and Jan Wright for their insights on various aspects of home care. Special thanks also go to Gay Becker and Bob Newcomer for comments and encouragement throughout the writing process. Of course I am most grateful to Marcia Ory at the NIA for her guidance and incisive commentary throughout the preparation of the chapter.

regulation associated with the nursing home industry (Institute of Medicine, 1986; Kane & Kane, 1978; Vladeck, 1980). Because one public program, Medicaid, pays for nearly one half of all nursing home care, a primary objective of public policy in recent years has been to reduce use of these facilities through various means, including the development of alternative, community care services, especially those provided in the home.

Other factors have also drawn policy attention to home care. Widely disseminated data on demographic trends have announced the graying of the population, particularly with growth in the numbers of the oldest old (Rosenwaike, 1985; Soldo & Manton, 1985), and provided convincing arguments that the scope of the need for health care in old age will continue to increase for the foreseeable future. The impact of these demographic trends has been heightened by changes in public payment for hospital (and, soon, physician) care. The introduction of the prospective payment system (PPS) under Medicare has meant the virtual elimination of extended hospital stays for older persons with uncertain prognoses and/or uncertain posthospital care arrangements. This in turn has placed growing pressure on the organization of, delivery of, and payment for services (including intensive medical ones) for older persons at home and in other community settings (Estes et al., 1988).

In addition to these policy and demographic factors, there are some more fundamental and persistent reasons that scholarly and official interest in care at home will continue to grow and that the paradox described at the outset is more apparent than real. First, despite dramatic advances in medical technologies, the limits of curative medicine are apparent and nowhere more so than with respect to the elderly. Second, the risk of disability in basic life activities for the elderly is much larger than the risk for the nonelderly (LaPlante, 1989), and chronic disability demands long-range care strategies as well as short-term curative ones (Somers, 1982). Third, because chronic illness most often requires nonacute interventions in noninstitutional settings, most chronically ill persons spend a majority of their time in home and other community-based settings. The primary health care challenge for those concerned with the chronically ill elderly is to organize and support care in those settings. Fourth, and not to be underestimated, most older persons have established homes and a network of relationships in the community and prefer to maintain their lives at home, despite chronic illness. Often heroic home care efforts by family members and other informal caregivers attest to the depth of this commitment to living independently in the community. Finally (and here the paradox crumbles), various technological advances based upon computerization, miniaturization, and other developments have made it feasible to provide an expanding range of treatments in the home that were once confined to the hospital or clinic. This has altered the character of postacute and chronic care for older persons.

After suggesting some reasons that home care is growing in policy significance as an approach to chronic and acute conditions, a policy caveat is in order. Not long ago in-home and community-based services were considered by many policymakers to be a panacea for the health care problems of the elderly and, more recently, of other populations including persons with acquired immunodeficiency syndrome, or AIDS (Benjamin, 1988). In this scenario the overuse of hospital an l nursing home services and the subsequent escalation of health care c sts were to be eliminated by this "silver bullet" (Brecher & Knickman, 1985), which was to eliminate service delivery problems in a single shot. As the reader is well aware, the evidence with respect to the impact of home care is far more sobering and complex than these initial expectations acknowledged, and a renewed policy zeal should emanate from a foundation of empirical evidence and thoughtful inquiry.

A second, more familiar caveat is also in order, which concerns the stereotypical view of all older persons as ill or dependent. Because this chapter is concerned with the chronically ill or disabled, it may be easy to lose sight of two important perspectives: (a) There is marked variability in physical functioning within the older population, and (b) most older persons are living independently in the community and managing their health care on a daily basis without extensive medical intervention or social services (Feller, 1983; Ory & Bond, 1989; Stone, 1986). Although the focus of this chapter is on older persons with physical limitations, many of this group may be well-integrated socially, relatively independent economically, and otherwise well off. While loss of physical functioning may increase social and economic risk, the extent to which this is so is variable and needs to be judged empirically.

THE NEED FOR HOME CARE

Two dimensions of the health experience of older persons establish the context for growing interest in home care for this population. First, chronic illness affects the elderly disproportionately, so that older persons have many chronic care needs that can be addressed in home settings. Second, the elderly are relatively heavy users of hospital days and consequently have significant posthospital care needs, a growing number of which can be managed at home.

The literature on functioning in basic life activities is vast, and for our purposes only broad themes need be highlighted. Data from the 1979 and 1980 Home Care Supplement to the National Health Interview Survey indicate that 3.7 million persons of all ages who are living in the community either use equipment or need help from other persons in at least one basic physical activity, with about 60% of this group over age 65 (LaPlante, 1989). Detailed data on individual activities of daily living (ADLs) suggest that a majority of persons with functional needs require assistance in multiple activities. These findings are consistent with a process described by Katz and Aksom (1976) whereby, as persons age, loss of functioning proceeds along a hierarchy that often starts with loss of ambulation and progresses to loss of more basic physical functions. Additional evidence suggests also that, among persons with assistance needs, the elderly are more than twice as likely to be homebound (LaPlante, 1989).

Various research has suggested that, within the elderly population, assistance needs vary with age. The "oldest old" (those aged 85 and over) are much more likely to be living in the community with functional dependencies than are the younger old (Soldo & Manton, 1985), and they are more likely to have multiple assistance needs (Feller, 1983). There is also some evidence that those over age 85 have much less chance of regaining functional capacity once it is compromised than the younger old (Branch & Jette, 1984). It is important to note that, while the prevalence of functional disability is higher among the oldest old, the actual number of disabled persons is largest among the younger old (Macken, 1986).

Older persons also experience more frequent acute illness episodes and are hospitalized at a greater rate than the rest of the population. This in turn means that older persons are more frequently in need of postacute or posthospital care in community settings. While the elderly represented 12.3% of the U.S. population in 1986, they accounted for 31.3% of all hospital discharges (National Center for Health Statistics [NCHS], 1987). Again, rates of hospital use among the elderly also increase with age. While persons aged 65-74 were discharged from hospitals at a rate of 297 per 1,000 in 1986, the comparable rate for those over 75 was 470 per 1,000 (while the rate for the whole U.S. population was 143; NCHS, 1986).

DEFINING "IN-HOME HEALTH AND SUPPORTIVE SERVICES"

For our purposes the concept of "in-home health and supportive services" is defined broadly to include postacute and long-term care services provided at home. Whether postacute care should be included as a component of long-term care, rather than as a distinctive category, is debatable. The appropriate answer probably depends on the level of chronic impairment of the older person being considered. To the extent that a person is functionally disabled, postacute (medical) care should be seen as one element of chronic care. To the extent that functional impairment is absent or solely a result of acute illness, postacute care is not long-term care.

In-home health and supportive services (hereafter called "home care") have postacute and long-term care elements as well as medical and social ones, and the lines among them are often blurred. Postacute care is primarily medical and recuperative in character, while long-term care involves the delivery of medical, personal, and social services to persons with impaired functional capacities. A medical component is necessary in long-term care because many older persons have multiple chronic diseases requiring regular medical care and intermittent hospitalization. The social component is essential because the supportive care needs of the chronically ill persist long after the acute condition is controlled (Mor & Specter, 1988). Social services are often considered labor intensive and relatively unspecialized (Kane & Kane, 1987).

The concept of "home" also requires comment. In the current context this includes any residential setting in which formal medical services are not provided as part of the housing component, although supportive services may be. In other words, nursing homes are excluded but board and care homes are included. "Home" may mean a detached home, an apartment in a family member's home or a large complex, or a unit in a congregate housing arrangement with supportive services (Kane & Kane, 1987). Day care provided outside the home has not been included in the following discussion of home care, although it can be an important element of successful home care as it serves a respite function for caregivers (Pelham & Clarke, 1986; Zawadski & Eng, 1988).

Home care appropriately includes all professional and paraprofessional postacute and long-term services provided in the recipient's home. These encompass the services of physicians, nurses, and therapists, at one end of the cost-skill continuum, to housekeeping, chore, and volunteer services, at the other (Kane & Kane, 1987). This discussion of services and professions should not imply that our focus is solely on formal services. Because there is abundant evidence that most home care is provided by family members and friends and that formal care is most commonly used in conjunction with informal care (Soldo, Agree, & Wolf, 1989), for many older persons informal support must be considered the most important component of care at home.

The Policy Context

U.S. public policy regarding long-term care represents the primary context in which home care can be understood. Long-term care policy can best be described as decentralized, categorical, and limited. Implementation of federal initiatives has relied heavily on decentralized authority and state discretion, so that the study of long-term care must acknowledge that there are at least 50 care systems within our federal structure (Harrington et al., 1985). Federal funding has occurred within traditional, multiple program categories, often linked to welfare programs, ensuring fragmentation of funding and benefits (medical, social, and income) for older persons. Public long-term care reform initiatives have been limited in scope and scale, with an emphasis on eligibility limitations and cost-effectiveness rather than appropriateness and comprehensiveness.

One consequence of decentralized, categorical, and limited policy is that approximately three quarters of all disabled elderly rely, for care at home, solely on unpaid, informal care provided by family and friends and not on paid providers (Liu, Manton, & Liu, 1985; Rabin & Stockton, 1987). Another, less direct result is that, despite the enthusiasm that has generated private insurance initiatives in long-term care, home care coverage remains limited in scope and affordability. Finally, older persons who may qualify for home care services through public funding must sort through several programs that may underwrite home care services, including Medicare, Medicaid, the Older Americans Act, the Social Services Block Grant, Supplemental Security Income, and other federal programs and state-local initiatives.

MEDICARE

Medicare is the primary third-party payer (public or private) for postacute home health services. To qualify for services under Title XVIII, a beneficiary must essentially be confined to her or his residence (homebound), be under a physician's care, and need part-time (or intermittent) skilled nursing care, physical therapy, and/or speech therapy. If these conditions are met, the patient may also receive occupational therapy, medical social services, and home health aide services (Benjamin, Swan, Feigenbaum, Newcomer, & Fox, 1989). Home health services are available under Medicare Part A at no direct cost to the beneficiary, except for durable medical equipment under Part B, which is subject to 20% coinsurance (Health Care Financing Administration [HCFA], 1987). In 1986 approximately 1.5 million persons received Medicare home health services. While the prior hospitalization requirement was dropped in the Omnibus Reconciliation Act of 1980 (Public Law 96-499), most recipients still qualify for home health care benefits after a recent hospital stay. Data from 1985 indicate that about 13% of Medicare hospital discharges were referred to home health care (see Chapter 2 of this volume).

MEDICAID

Medicaid is the primary public purchaser of long-term care services for the elderly. About 3.9 million older persons qualified for Medicaid benefits in 1983, or 18.3% of recipients of all age groups. Federal law requires that states offer various mandatory services, among which are skilled nursing facility (SNF) and home health care. Combined payments for SNF and (optional) intermediate facility care represented 43.5% of all program expenditures in 1983. Expenditures for home health (including aide services) are far more modest, representing just 1% to 2% of payments. While home health spending has increased in the 1980s, recent data estimates suggest that the number of recipients has held steady between 500,000 to 600,000, about 60% of whom are elderly (Holahan & Cohen, 1986). State variations are especially significant for home health care under Medicaid. In 1988 one quarter of recipients and half of expenditures nationally were accounted for by one state, New York.

Title XIX also permits states to offer a range of optional benefits, among them personal care services. Fewer than half the states ($n = 19$) provided this benefit in 1982 (Newcomer & Bogaert-Tullis, 1985). Because Medicaid is a federal-state program and service tracking remains problematic in some states, especially for optional services, data on use of personal care services are sparse.

Far more is known about Medicaid Section 2176 waiver programs, which permit states to provide case-managed home and community-based services for clients qualified for an institutional level of care (see Laudicina & Burwell, 1988). Home care is the centerpiece of most demonstrations that attempt to show that an array of community services, mediated by case management, can substitute for nursing home care (Kane & Kane, 1987).

OLDER AMERICANS ACT

Title III of the Older Americans Act of 1965 provides funding for a variety of home and community-based services. These include home-delivered and congregate meals; transportation, outreach, information, and referral services; homemaker and home health aides; protective and day-care services; and residential repair and renovation. Title III also provides funding for the establishment of multipurpose senior centers to deliver social and nutrition services and for the organization of recreational and group activities (Rabin & Stockton, 1987).

In 1965 the Older Americans Act (OAA) was framed to provide services for all older persons, and with its implementation state and local aging agencies succeeded in addressing a wide range of service needs, despite limited funding. Because of pressures to target more funds to the frail elderly, Congress amended the objectives of the act through the 1984 OAA Amendments (Public Law 98-459) to include provision of "a comprehensive array of community-based, long-term care services adequate to appropriately sustain older people in their communities and in their homes."

Data from 1982 indicate that about half of Title III expenditures were for congregate and home-delivered meals, with most for the former.

In-home services accounted for an estimated 7% of expenditures. A survey of local aging agencies in 1985 indicated that, following implementation of PPS under Medicare, these agencies experienced a major increase in referrals of older persons requiring in-home services, including case management, home nursing, housekeeping, and personal care services (Rabin & Stockton, 1987). Approximately $858 million was allocated under Title III in 1989.

SOCIAL SERVICES BLOCK GRANT

The Social Services Block Grant (SSBG), formerly known as Title XX, has been the primary source of federal funding for social services (and nonmedical home care) since 1975. In 1984 $2.7 billion was authorized for the SSBG to be distributed to the states under very flexible federal guidelines, which, among other things, relaxed earlier requirements to target low-income persons. While data on state services expenditures are sparse, the most frequently offered services include home care (homemaker, chore aide, and home management) for children and adults. Estimates from 1981 suggest that approximately one in five recipients are elderly (Rabin & Stockton, 1987). In a few states the administration of Title III and SSBG funds is coordinated, permitting more effective targeting of services under both programs.

SUPPLEMENTAL SECURITY INCOME

The Supplemental Security Income (SSI) program (Title XVI of the Social Security Act) provides a guaranteed minimum income for the poor who are aged, blind, or disabled. Federal law also permits states to provide additional payments to SSI beneficiaries to cover the costs of congregate housing or domiciliary care (Stone & Newcomer, 1985). In 33 states SSI provides supplemental payment for persons in congregate settings (especially board and care homes) who need 24-hour supervision and personal assistance but not medical care. Board and care homes represent an important residential option for specific subsets of the vulnerable elderly population (see Chapter 4). Because SSI is the primary source of public reimbursement for board and care housing, SSI becomes an essential component of home care financing for frail older persons.

STATE AND LOCAL INITIATIVES

In addition to responding to Medicaid waiver opportunities, several states have established statewide community care networks providing services with funds from federal sources (Medicaid, Social Service Block Grant, and/or Older Americans Act) and state general revenues. Other states have established state-supported home care services programs, the largest of which is California's In-Home Supportive Services Program, which subsidizes personal care for the frail and disabled (Sabatino, 1990). Relatively little is known about the overall scope and impact of such state (and local) initiatives.

PRIVATE INSURANCE

Recent reviews (Rivlin & Weiner, 1988) and discussions with industry representatives indicate that private insurance coverage of home care is not extensive. When home care benefits are included, they frequently are restricted to the "Medicare model," meaning primarily skilled care following a hospital or nursing home stay. Private insurance with long-term care benefits can be expensive, and the price climbs rapidly with age (Rivlin & Weiner, 1988).

Use of Home Care

While it is widely recognized that older persons are disproportionately high users of health services (Lubitz & Prihoda, 1984; Waldo & Lazenby, 1984), only recently have researchers begun to examine use of home care services by persons over age 65. This research has generally been guided by two questions. First, how many older persons in the community use formal home-based services? Second, what factors distinguish those who use home care from those who do not? Underlying each of these questions is a third: What are the size and characteristics of the frail elderly population in need? There is a vast literature on the latter question, and it will be discussed here only to the extent that it highlights use issues. At the same time it is worth noting that, while estimates of use are important in themselves (e.g., to service planners and budget analysts), their meaningful interpretation depends ultimately upon estimates of need. Indeed, as Stone and Murtaugh (1988) have argued, the choice of need (functional status) criteria in recent legislative proposals dramatically affects the number of persons eligible to use home care services.

SOURCES OF DATA

Research on home care use has drawn upon national data sets as well as state and local surveys of older persons. The Home Care Supplement to the 1979 National Health Interview Survey (NHIS) as well as the Supplement on Aging to the 1984 NHIS have provided the first truly national data on home care use by all persons over 65 years of age. The National Long-Term Care Surveys of 1982 and 1986 provide detailed data on the impaired elderly and their caregivers. The Longitudinal Survey on Aging, which follows up respondents to the 1984 supplement, holds considerable promise for future analysis. Medicare claims data continue to be a rich source of Title XVIII home health service use by older persons. Other data sources include state-specific efforts, such as the statewide survey of older Virginians (Wan & Arling, 1983) and the Massachusetts Health Care Panel Study (Branch & Jette, 1983), and research on local cohorts, such as that developed by Branch and others (1988) in Boston.

LEVELS OF HOME CARE USE

Three national data sets have provided a basis for estimating actual levels of home care service use within the older population as a whole and within the subset considered functionally disabled. Analysis of the 1984 Supplement on Aging (SOA) suggests that about one in five (21.5%) older Americans used one or more community (social and health) services in the first six months of 1984 (Stone, 1986). Three fourths of this user group were senior center participants. Use of home-based services was not widespread, with 2.9% of all elderly estimated to use visiting nurse care, 1.6% home health aide services, 1.4% homemaker services, and 1.9% home-delivered meals. Nearly 80% of the elderly used no community services during this period, and more than half of those who did (11.4%) used only one service. The receipt of formal home care services by an older person is a relatively rare event (Soldo, 1985).

It is not surprising that analysis of data on service utilization by the impaired elderly reveals greater use of home care services by this subpopulation. Based upon data from the 1979 Home Care Supplement (HCS), Soldo (1985) reports that one in four older persons with functional limitations (25.1%) had received formal "community home care" services, with nearly half of these (10% overall) totally dependent upon formal services (i.e., lacking any informal care). Only 2.3% of the impaired elderly were without any help, formal or informal (Soldo, 1985).

In a related examination of the most impaired elderly living in the community, based upon data from the National Long Term Care Survey (LTCS) of 1982, Rowland (1989) and others report somewhat higher use levels: 31% of older persons with severe functional and cognitive impairments had used formal home care services (Rowland, 1989; Stone, Cafferata, & Sangl, 1987). One third of this user population had seven or more home care visits per week, and the average service user received 18 hours of care weekly. In turn, 7 out of 10 severely impaired older persons depended solely on informal care to meet their needs (Stone et al., 1987). While most public payment for home care underwrites skilled care, only one quarter of the disabled elderly using home care in 1982 received skilled services (Liu et al., 1985). In other words, market demand among frail older persons seems to be primarily for nonmedical home care.

Because Medicare continues to be the largest third-party payer for home health care, additional data are available on older persons' use of skilled, medically related services at home. In 1986 approximately 1.5 million older persons utilized home health services reimbursed by Medicare (Ruther & Helbing, 1988). Between 1981 and 1985 the percentage of all hospitalized Medicare beneficiaries receiving home health services nearly doubled—from 9.1% to 17.9%, with the largest increase occurring between 1981 and 1983, prior to the introduction of PPS (Gornick & Hall, 1988). (Another analysis, by Neu & Harrison, 1988, reports somewhat lower use rates for 1981 and 1985 and a smaller but substantial increase during that period.) The average number of visits received also grew during this period, though not as rapidly as the number of persons served. Use rates varied widely across states (Neu & Harrison, 1988) and diagnoses (Gornick & Hall, 1988; Neu & Harrison, 1988; Neu, Harrison, & Heilbrunn, 1989).

Examination of Medicare user data raises some questions about estimates of home health care use based upon national surveys. For example, based upon data from the 1984 SOA, Rowland (1989) reports that 21% of impaired elderly and 4% of all elderly used home nursing or aide services in 1984. While Medicare program data do not address the estimate for the impaired elderly, they do suggest that the Medicare use rate among all older persons was close to 5% (with 1.5 million users in 1986). These data should be interpreted in light of other evidence that unlicensed and uncertified home health providers may outnumber Medicare-certified agencies and may provide as much (or more) home health care to older persons through out-of-pocket and some private insurance payment (Grant & Harrington, 1989). There are no data available on these unlicensed providers, so we have no idea how many older persons they serve and whether they serve the same users as Medicare, a whole different subset of older persons, or, more likely, a blend of the two.

Two additional issues merit attention. First, cross-sectional survey data permit estimation of short-term home care use but reveal nothing of lifetime utilization. Without longitudinal data we have little basis for estimating use rates over time by frail older persons. Second, the survey data just discussed come from 1979 to 1984, and there are reasons to speculate that, more recently, use may have become more widespread. These reasons include (a) relaxation of prior-hospitalization requirements by Medicare and some private insurers and (b) broader experience on the part of older persons and their families in purchasing home care. On the other hand growing interest in self-care may mitigate the use of formal services at home.

PREDICTORS OF USE

A small body of research on use of home care services reflects a growing interest in understanding reasons for service use by older persons (Lubitz & Prihoda, 1983; Wolinsky, Mosely, & Coe, 1986) and, more important, indicates that home care may no longer be solely an afterthought to concerns about nursing home use. Thought on the use of home care services has been shaped foremost by the Andersen behavioral model, which posits that differential use is a function of three classes of variables: predisposing, enabling, and need (Andersen & Newman, 1973; Wan, 1989). After reviewing empirical findings from recent research, the Andersen model will be considered in more detail.

Many studies have considered a variety of demographic characteristics expected to increase the likelihood that older persons will use home
care (predisposing factors in the Andersen scheme). With some consistency, age has been found to be directly associated with home care use,
both across the age spectrum and within the elderly cohort. Whether
considering home care services, broadly defined (Shapiro, 1986; Stone,
1986; Wan & Arling, 1983), or home health services (Berk & Bernstein,
1985; Branch et al., 1988; Stone, 1986), various research indicates that,
with increasing age, the odds of home service use grow. Women also
are more likely to use home care services (Stone, 1986; Wan & Arling,
1983), and at least one study has found evidence that educational level
and urban residence are directly related to use (McAuley & Arling,
1984). Because it is widely held that age alone does not compel service
use but is associated with health and social risks that do, most analytical attention has been directed at specifying these risks.

The roles of functional, medical, and cognitive status have been assessed in several studies. Functional disability or need proves to be the
most consistent predictor of service use across these studies. Persons
with one or more limitations in activities of daily living are more likely
to use home care services than are those free of such limitations
(Berk & Bernstein, 1985; Branch et al., 1988; McAuley & Arling,
1984; Shapiro, 1986; Soldo, 1985; Wan, 1987; Wan & Arling, 1983).
A similar pattern emerges for instrumental activities of daily living
(IADLs; Shapiro, 1986; Soldo, 1985; Wan & Arling, 1983), with one
exception. McAuley and Arling (1984) present evidence from one state
that the presence of IADL limitations reduces the likelihood of service
use at home; home care users in Virginia were those with ADL problems but few IADL needs. This issue highlights a more general tendency to consider ADL and IADL levels merely statistically, in the
absence of theory or models regarding their relationships. Manton and
Soldo (1985; also see Soldo & Manton, 1985) have addressed the interaction between the presence or absence of limitations in each activity
area, the level of limitation, and the relationship of these to demographic and social characteristics of older persons. Overall relatively
little research has examined the differential effects on home services
use of numbers of ADL/IADL needs (Benjamin et al., 1989; Rowland,
1989) or level of assistance needs (Manton & Soldo, 1985).

Most use studies have addressed the role of medical status or need
in some fashion, but a variety of measures have been employed and

generalizations across studies are therefore difficult. There is both evidence and conviction nonetheless that medical status is an important predictor of home care use, whether conceptualized as number of medical care needs (Soldo, 1985), number of health disorders (Wan & Arling, 1983), self-rated health (Berk & Bernstein, 1985; Manton & Soldo, 1985; Shapiro, 1986), medical severity at index (most recent) hospitalization (Benjamin et al., 1989), or medical crisis (Kane & Kane, 1987). Soldo (1985) has argued that medical care needs play a critical role, in interaction with functional need and social factors, in shaping the decision to seek formal care. A recent study of Medicare home health use by recent hospital discharges in California reached a similar conclusion (Benjamin et al., 1989).

Evidence is mixed regarding the role of cognitive status and other mental health factors, in part because this issue has not been addressed consistently and systematically. Data from Wan (1987) and Branch et al. (1988) demonstrate that persons with more errors on the mental status questionnaire (MSQ) are heavier users of care, although these studies involve very different definitions of home care (i.e., social services, not all of which are home delivered, in Wan's research, and medical home care, in Branch's). Other studies have found only weak relationships for related mental health measures (Benjamin et al., 1989; McAuley & Arling, 1984; Shapiro, 1986). This uncertainty regarding the role of mental status is not confined to home care. It is well known that rates of dementia are much higher for persons in institutions than for community-dwellers. It has been much more difficult, however, to demonstrate consistently that mental status is a risk factor for institutionalization (Kane & Kane, 1987).

While there is growing empirical evidence to support the role of functional, medical, and other "need" factors in determining the use of home care, evidence with respect to social (or "enabling") factors is less coherent and convincing. At the same time, this state of affairs raises many interesting questions regarding relationships among social resources, care needs, and use that merit further research attention.

Studies of home care use have generally incorporated in their models measures of living arrangement, informal support availability, and level of social contact. Living arrangement helps define the social resources immediately available to assist those with care needs, and there has been much interest in sorting through its significance. While many older persons are able to live alone because they are economically and

functionally able, elderly people living alone have more difficulty remaining in the community when their ability to function independently
is impaired (Kasper, 1988). Several studies have shown that, when
functional and medical status are taken into account, older persons living alone are more likely to use home care services (Benjamin et al.,
1989; Soldo, 1985; Stone, 1986; Wan, 1987). Soldo (1985) has also
found that persons living with nonrelatives have an even greater chance
of using formal services than those living alone. On the other hand, at
least two studies have concluded that living arrangement has little or
no effect on use (Branch et al., 1988; Shapiro, 1986).

Living arrangements and informal support resources are often linked
conceptually and empirically, but we know that the former does not
determine the latter. While the evidence on informal supports is mixed
(McAuley & Arling, 1984; Wan, 1987), Soldo (1985) has argued that
the disabled older person who receives some care from her or his
informal support network is substantially less likely than others to
use formal services. Elsewhere Soldo et al. (1989) suggest that,
among informal caregivers, work status is likely to affect home care
service use. Those caregivers who also work may generate more resources to purchase formal care, have less time for informal care provision, and apply more pressure on other informal caregivers to provide
assistance. Finally, findings on social contacts have been decidedly
mixed, with evidence that contact with relatives increases the likelihood of home care use (Shapiro, 1986), while involvement with social
groups reduces the odds of service use (Branch et al., 1988).

THEMES IN USE RESEARCH

Several themes emerge from recent research on home care use that
merit our sustained attention. Though research on noninstitutional service use is in its relative infancy, we have learned enough to sharpen
our grasp of some basic issues. Several themes merit discussion here.
These include: (a) the complexity of use research, (b) definitions of
home care, (c) dominant models of home care use, (d) informal and
formal care, and (e) transitions.

Complexity. Without belaboring the obvious, it is worth noting that
research on home care use needs to be based upon complex models that
acknowledge the interaction of (a) medical, functional, and social

factors; (b) informal and formal system characteristics; (c) needs and preferences; and (d) variations in policy-service systems and "environments." There is a continuing need for model elaboration through smaller, quasi-experimental studies that in turn inform national surveys of older persons.

Fortunately the necessity for more complex models is generally understood in the field. Wan (1987) has used path analysis in an effort to specify direct and indirect effects for specific (albeit broad) service categories. Manton and Soldo (1985) have identified clusters or subsets among the frail elderly whose service use patterns vary in some systematic ways. Making sense of complexity also requires cohort analyses of longitudinal data on home care service use in the context of use of informal and other formal services (Wolinsky et al., 1986). One point merits special emphasis: The study of service use is critical to the investigation of service effectiveness and indeed to all aspects of home care. Without a foundation of theory and data on service use, the interpretation of other research issues becomes very difficult (see "Effectiveness" below). What should be avoided is a too facile transition from analysis of the "need" for home care services to one of their "effectiveness," without explicit consideration of who makes use of care and why (Kane & Kane, 1987; Wan, 1987).

Definitions of home care. It is essential to come to terms with variations in the definition of the dependent variable in home care research, a problem cited earlier. On the one hand the interaction of medical and functional need makes it necessary to cluster various home-based services to capture the complexity of the home care episode. For example, home health nursing and/or physical therapy may be accompanied by personal care services provided by a home health aide, or home health care may lead to a referral to personal care services not provided by a home health agency. On the other hand, in a medically oriented care system for older persons in which public and private payers facilitate the use of medical services at home (e.g., home health) far more than they do nonmedical services (e.g., personal care), distinct models must be developed to capture these "sector" differences. These different sets of services, often referred to as "skilled" and "unskilled," have wider ramifications for the study not only of use but also of effectiveness, quality, costs, and other themes. Finally, there is evidence that closely related services may be affected differently by given client factors. For example, Coughlin and Liu (1989) found that degree of cognitive impairment influenced levels of need for personal care, homemaker, and home health aide use.

Models of home care use. Although several alternative models have been identified for explaining complex relationships between various predictors and use of health services, including those that incorporate psychological and social variables (for example, the health belief model) to predict utilization behavior (Wan, 1987), recent research on home care use by older persons has relied primarily on the Andersen behavioral model (Andersen & Newman, 1973). The appeal of the Andersen model seems to lie less in its explanatory power than in its conceptual advantage in establishing use as a behavior that is jointly determined by individual and social factors. Various shortcomings of the model have been well documented by others (Bass & Noelker, 1987; Mechanic, 1979; Wolinsky, 1978). Of greatest salience in research relying on this model is the empirical dominance of need factors and the inadequate conceptualization of predisposing and (especially) enabling factors. The elaboration of enabling factors, which may be seen as those factors that condition both the opportunity and the choice to use given services, seems critical to expanding the explanatory power of this model and to linking it more solidly to related, but often less theoretically grounded, research in health services and policy.

Theoretical and empirical attention needs to be paid to identifying enabling factors and to linking these more solidly with broader approaches (like Andersen's) to explaining home care use. A body of research has examined the role of state and community policy environments in shaping the availability of long-term care services (Benjamin, 1986; Scanlon, 1980; Swan & Harrington, 1986). Specific attention has been given to the role of resource, supply, and practice variations across states and localities (Benjamin, 1986; Wennberg & Gittelsohn, 1973) and to the role of service substitution between nursing home and home health services (Scanlon, 1980). More study is needed on the impact of various licensing and regulatory approaches on home care access and performance.

A growing body of research on economic factors has sought to estimate the amount of out-of-pocket expenses incurred by older persons receiving services at home (Capitman, Arling, & Bowling, 1987; Kovar, 1986; Liu et al., 1985). Estimates from the 1982 NLTCS indicate that 55% of all disabled elderly who use formal services finance at least a portion of their care costs with personal funds, and slightly more than 40% pay directly for all their purchased services (Liu et al., 1985; Manton & Soldo, 1985). It can be argued that the decision to use home care (and the quantity of care demanded) will be a function of disability, income, the price of other substitutes, and the out-of-pocket costs associated with home care (Soldo, 1985). More research is needed on the economic burden of home care and the role this plays in decisions to make use of services.

Other research has emphasized the need to better understand the role of medical factors in determining the use not only of posthospital services (Benjamin et al., 1989; Kemper, 1988; Kramer, Shaughnessy, & Pettigrew, 1986) but of personal care and other community services for frail older persons (Manton & Soldo, 1985). Also, while disease-specific approaches have been criticized as inappropriate for the elderly for whom multiple chronic diseases are significant, much can be gained from elaborating the care needs associated with major diseases affecting older persons and analyzing factors associated with health care use within selected disease categories (Becker & Kaufman, 1988; Kane, 1988; Andrew Kramer, personal communication, 1990).

Effective arguments have been made for the importance of expanded attention to understanding how family needs, preferences, and expertise influence decisions to choose home care (Bass & Noelker, 1987; Seltzer, Ivry, & Litchfield, 1987). More research is needed that describes patient and family attitudes and preferences and that integrates these into a multidimensional model of service use (Becker & Kaufman, 1988; Doty, 1986; Kane & Kane, 1987). Finally, a great deal of work remains regarding the role of professional attitudes, knowledge, and referral behavior in influencing the decision to use home care. The roles of physicians and hospital discharge planners seem critical here, but over time home care nurses and personal care attendants may be important in sustaining and reinitiating service use. There is some evidence that hospitals vary with respect to posthospital referral "strategies" and their capacity or willingness to facilitate transfers to home care (Benjamin et al., 1989).

Informal and formal care. No theme related to home care has received more attention in gerontological research than the role of social supports or informal caregivers. Of special interest is research that has examined the linkages between informal care factors and the use of formal services at home. As discussed earlier, various studies have shown that formal care is most commonly used in conjunction with informal care in support of dependent older persons (Soldo et al., 1989). Data from the NLTCS of 1982, for example, showed that nearly four of five formal care users also received care from informal providers. This means that, for a majority of frail older persons, the decision to use formal services is taken (at the least) in the context of informal caregiving.

Several scholars have examined the likelihood of a "mixed helper network" for frail older persons in the community. They have argued persuasively for an expansion of Andersen's model to include the predisposing, need, and enabling characteristics of informal caregivers as well as those of care receivers (Bass & Noelker, 1987; Soldo et al., 1989). Research on mixed helper networks has also directed more precise attention to the nature of caregiving tasks, the types of expertise required, and the organization of caregiving—factors that may condition decisions to use formal care.

Transitions. For the most part research on use of home care has been concerned with the use of single service categories during relatively limited time periods. Recent research has underscored the importance of redirecting efforts to full episodes of care, involving transitions from one functional state to another, one care setting to another, and one service package to another (Koff, 1982; Ory & Bond, 1989). This perspective acknowledges the interdependence of acute and long-term care needs and permits transitions to acute care to be viewed as phases within a long-term care episode. Attention is diverted from an artificial dichotomy between acute and long-term care, or between the so-called medical and social models of care, to a more dynamic concept of health care needs and the inextricable linkages between acute and long-term care (Kane & Kane, 1987).

Those studies that have examined care for the frail elderly with an emphasis on "natural history" and transitions have given primary attention to movement between acute care and nursing homes (Kane & Kane, 1987; Lewis, Cretin, & Kane, 1985; Roos & Shapiro, 1981). An exception is Stark and Gutman (1986), who have examined the careers of impaired older persons for five years following entry into a long-term home care program in British Columbia (see also Lane, Uyeno,

Stark, Gutman, & McCashin, 1987). Lewis et al.'s (1985) success in identifying subgroups of nursing home patients on the basis of different patterns of survival and use of health care resources suggests some of the analytical possibilities in this approach. It is essential to embrace home care as well as hospital, physician, and nursing home care in such research. Because hospital and nursing home stays can be crises in the natural history of impairment in the community, it is important that studies of home care consider the transitions from hospital, nursing home, and home health care (which is normally of short duration) to home and community care.

The Impact of Home Care

Interest in assessing the impact of home care is not new, but in the last 12 to 15 years research efforts in this area have intensified as a result of profound changes in the larger health care system. Specifically, steady growth in health care expenditures and dramatic increases in nursing home use and costs led to a series of demonstration programs and evaluation efforts aimed at examining the effectiveness of home care as a substitute for expensive institutional care for frail older persons.

In recent years scholars have been attempting to digest and synthesize results from various empirical studies of home care effectiveness, and these efforts have helped account for a significant shift in perspective on the goals and impact of home-based service approaches. These attempts at research synthesis have succeeded despite some formidable barriers, especially variations in program goals, populations being served, and treatment interventions offered as well as in study goals and design. These variations are in part the result of the inherent complexity of this research area and difficulties in measuring and integrating multiple causal and conditioning factors (Shapiro & Tate, 1988; Weissert & Cready, 1989).

As suggested earlier, those supporting and conducting early research on home care not only were preoccupied with substitution goals and with reducing institutional and total care costs, but they were also generally hoping that home care would solve many of the health care problems of the elderly and the budgetary problems of public officials (Brecher & Knickman, 1985). Recently this zealousness seems to have been replaced by a more sober concern with careful specification of home care service models and with broadening perspectives on the outcomes of care. In the discussion that follows the basis for this shift in research outlook should become clear.

CONCEPTUALIZING OUTCOMES

Studies of the effectiveness of home care interventions have conceptualized outcomes within four broad categories: patient or client well-being, caregiver well-being, other service use, and costs. These will be discussed briefly.

Patient or client well-being has been conceptualized in terms of physical health, social functioning, mental health, and attitudes. Physical health outcomes have customarily included mortality or longevity and functional status; some recent studies also have measured unmet care needs (Hughes, 1989; Kemper, 1988) and adverse events like falls. Outcomes related to social functioning have included social intervention, social contacts, or relative confinement. Mental health outcomes have been conceptualized primarily in terms of cognitive functioning and, in some cases, depression. Finally, attitudinal indicators have addressed general orientation (e.g., satisfaction, contentment, morale), health (e.g., perceived physical well-being, which can also be considered a physical health outcome), and health care (e.g., confidence in receiving needed care).

Until recently caregiver-related outcomes were rarely included in effectiveness studies of home care, but this is changing (e.g., Kemper, 1988). Study outcomes have most commonly been conceptualized in terms of burden (emotional, physical, and/or financial), stress (e.g., number of potential stressful behavioral problems confronted as a caregiver), and satisfaction with care arrangements. Other caregiver indicators include level of confidence in receiving needed care and limitations on employment and personal activities.

Because the potential value of home care has been defined so persistently in terms of its impact on the use of other services, the use of formal services has been included in virtually every study of home care effectiveness. Outcomes have included hospital admissions and bed days, nursing home admissions and bed days, outpatient visits, emergency room visits, and use of other community services. Because of concern about the impact of formal home care on informal caregiving, some studies have included among outcomes the number of informal care hours provided.

Finally and often summatively, many studies define outcomes to include the total costs of formal care, including the costs of the treatment intervention (home care) and all other formal service costs. Costs are rarely imputed to informal care hours.

RESEARCH FINDINGS

Recent syntheses of research on home care (Hedrick & Inui, 1986) and community care with strong home care components (Hughes, 1985; Kane & Kane, 1987; Kemper, Applebaum, & Harrigan, 1987) have concluded that findings are equivocal but contain some lessons for future planning and research. The following discussion will echo these conclusions in reviewing a number of recent studies. Research findings are discussed in terms of the outcome categories just described. This section will emphasize the general weight of the published evidence on home care for the frail elderly rather than the details of particular studies. This approach is taken despite a measure of risk involved, because these studies have used different methods and encompass a variety of client target groups and interventions; specific findings may need to be interpreted in light of these variations. Research reported prior to 1978 has been excluded but is well covered by Hughes (1985) and Hedrick and Inui (1986).

Research findings have been mixed with respect to improvements in patient/client well-being. Virtually all studies have found that home/community care interventions yield no significant improvement in mortality or physical functioning. Exceptions are Weissert, Wan, Livieratos, and Pellegrino (1980), who demonstrate that the use of homemaker services in a randomized experiment positively affected mortality; Skellie and Coan (1980), who report reductions in mortality in a Georgia demonstration program; and Mitchell (1978), who cites improvement in physical functioning after three months of home health care. Findings with respect to cognitive status are more promising. Hicks, Raisz, Segal, and Doherty (1981) report that treatment clients with good baseline scores maintained their mental status better than controls. In a more recent study directed by Hughes (1988), the treatment group functioned significantly better cognitively at both 9- and 48-month intervals following a long-term home care intervention.

Recent studies have reported improvements in other measures of patient/client well-being. Both Kemper (1988) and Hughes (1988) present evidence of statistically significant reductions in unmet care needs for treatment groups. Kemper (1988) also reports that client confidence in receiving needed care was increased (see also Groth-Juncker, 1982). Both Kemper (1988) and Hughes (1988, 1989) report increased life satisfaction on the part of clients. Hughes (1988) describes a marked (although not significant) improvement in social contacts and perceived physical health for the treatment group, and she cites evidence from other studies that reinforce these patterns.

Research findings have been inconsistent regarding the impact of home care treatment interventions on informal caregivers, but reported evidence is suggestive. The most robust findings concern caregiver satisfaction with care and confidence in receiving needed care (Groth-Juncker, 1982; Hughes, 1989; Kemper, 1988; Zimmer, Groth-Juncker, & McCusker, 1985). In contrast to many studies, Hughes (1989) addresses the question of why caregivers were more satisfied with care. She concludes that, because the home care team intervention enhanced continuity of care and emphasized the importance of caregiver training along with supervision and monitoring of both patient and caregivers, family members were more confident and secure in their roles as caregivers.

Findings from research on the impact of home care on the use of other health services generally are not encouraging. Because nursing home use has been the primary target of most federally funded demonstrations, particular attention has been paid to this outcome relationship. Several studies have generated evidence that home and community-based care can lower nursing home use. In the National Long-Term Care (Channeling) Demonstration, nursing home use was lower within the treatment group but not significantly so (Kemper, 1988). Other studies have shown significant reductions for high-risk subgroups (Kane & Kane, 1987; Morris, Gutkin, Ruchlin, & Sherwood, 1987; Nocks, Learner, Blackman, & Brown, 1986; Skellie, Mobley, & Coan, 1982) and the terminally ill (Zimmer et al., 1985). Reviews of the evidence on use from various Medicaid and Medicare demonstration programs, however, remain skeptical. This is the case because it is not only difficult to reduce institutional use substantially, it is also necessary to demonstrate high institutional use in the control groups and to minimize the costs of home and community care. With some exceptions, these conditions often have not been met (Kane & Kane, 1987; Weissert, 1985). We will return to this in the discussion of costs.

There is relatively little evidence to support the argument that home and community-based care will reduce hospital and other medical care use. While some studies have found lower hospital use (Applebaum, Seidl, & Austin, 1980; Mitchell, 1978), the most persuasive findings involve home-based hospice care for the terminally ill and reduced hospital use (McCusker & Stoddard, 1987; Mor, 1987). In one study Hughes (1987) reported greater use of hospital days in the treatment group, but in another she found more use of lower-level hospital beds (Hughes, 1989). Hospital use differences in the channeling study were not significant (Kemper, 1988). Both Zimmer et al. (1985) and Hughes (1989) show a decline in outpatient visits for experimental home care users.

Despite some variations across studies with respect to the use of institutional care, the research evidence is overwhelmingly negative regarding the impact of home care demonstrations on the total costs of care. In some cases there was no significant difference in costs between treatment and control groups (Applebaum et al., 1980; Groth-Juncker, 1982; Papsidero, 1979). In many cases the costs of providing care to the treatment group were significantly higher than those for the controls (Hicks et al., 1981; Ruchlin et al., 1987; Vertrees, Kemper, & Adler, 1989; Weissert et al., 1980). Where institutional use declined, the high costs of community care usually offset those savings (Kane & Kane, 1987). Exceptions to this are confined to certain models of hospice care that are associated with lower overall treatment costs (McCusker & Stoddard, 1987; Mor, 1987) and to Hughes's study of a VA home care program, where treatment group costs were 10% lower, though not significantly so (Hughes, 1989).

In a recent commentary on findings from the channeling demonstration and its various predecessors, Weissert, in his usual straightforward manner, has described what he considers remarkably similar conclusions from all studies of home and community care:

> Home care is not a cost-saving substitute for nursing home care because few patients are at risk of institutionalization; reductions in institutionalization are small; home care costs exceed the small reductions in institutional costs; and patient outcome benefits are extremely limited, and sometimes even negative. (Weissert, 1988)

THEMES IN EFFECTIVENESS RESEARCH

Given this ostensibly gloomy context, in what direction should research proceed on the effectiveness of home care? Several issues merit attention: (a) reconceptualizing effectiveness, (b) respecifying populations, (c) specifying interventions, (d) understanding care settings, and (e) addressing adequacy. Each will be discussed briefly.

Reconceptualizing effectiveness. To the extent that home care research is judged solely in terms of findings on institutional use and costs, we have fallen into what Weissert has termed the "cost-effectiveness trap" (Weissert, 1985). To the extent that this research reveals relatively little about the impact of home care on client and caregiver well-being, our measures of outcomes have proved inadequate. In either case the primary research challenge is to conceptualize and develop measures for other dimensions of individual and system behavior and attitudes that may be responsive to the introduction of formal home care services.

A significant part of this challenge lies in specifying and refining the objectives of home care interventions for chronically ill older persons. Recent efforts to do this for home health interventions during the posthospital period have proven difficult despite what seems to be a more focused, postacute challenge. The task is even more demanding with respect to home care in more broad terms. The process of defining outcomes must explicitly consider a range of patient and caregiver factors, including medical diagnoses, current activity profile, cognitive status, caregiver resources and expertise, prior service experience, current service availability, and a host of other factors. A critical part of this process is understanding subpopulations and developing methodologies for assigning care goals to subsets of older persons based upon some well-grounded expectations regarding outcome feasibility.

Respecifying populations. Home care research must pay more attention to variations in populations served across studies and to the consequent likelihood that the impact of interventions will vary across subpopulations. Hughes (1985, 1989) has identified, in her own research and that of others, several instances in which important findings are only discernible when subsets of the treatment group are examined. Weissert (1988) has called for specification of "outcome subgroups," each of which has different needs and different potential to benefit from intervention. Kramer and Shaughnessy, in their research on measuring home health quality, have developed "quality indicator groups" based on a number of patient characteristics (A. Kramer, personal communication, 1990). Eckert's work on board and care reflects this same sensitivity to understanding the needs of service subpopulations (see Chapter 4 of this volume). Because older persons receiving home care are a heterogeneous lot, it is likely that subgroups benefiting in any one domain may be so small that their benefits are lost against the variance introduced by the whole study population (Weissert, 1988).

This focus on subpopulations goes well beyond the usual discussions about better targeting of community care to persons truly at risk of institutionalization. Limits on the cost-effectiveness returns from more efficient targeting have been well described (Greene, 1987; Mor, 1987; Weissert & Cready, 1989). Needed instead are, for example, diagnosis-related subgroups, as suggested by the work of Becker and Kaufman (1988), on stroke, and Mor (1987), on cancer. Outcome measures that are linked to specific diagnostic conditions and/or services as well as broad-based measures that are not so linked would be valuable.

While studies of ethnic and racial subpopulations have not been reviewed here, some significant work has been done on the use of home and community services by specific groups (e.g., Furstenberg & Mezey, 1987; Manson, 1989; Petchers & Milligan, 1987). Much more work is needed to understand how racial, ethnic, and cultural values and customs interact with need and other factors to influence service use behavior.

Specifying interventions. With respect to service interventions the task at hand seems more fundamental. With a few exceptions most studies fail to adequately describe the nature of the services being delivered and the variations in these services across the study population. The heterogeneity of the services included under home care is well known and is a result of the complexity of the needs of frail older persons. Despite this service variability, few scholars have attempted to specify service models within home care; Hughes (1985) is an exception. Fewer still have made efforts to tie their findings to analysis of the services delivered to at least speculate about what it was about those services that yielded positive (or negative) outcomes. Again Hughes (1985, 1989) is an exception. Specification of interventions should

include identification of the roles of technology in the living environment, including technologies considered "high tech" (e.g., intravenous
therapies) and "low tech" (e.g., walkers and wheelchairs) as well as
physical modifications to the living space (e.g., rails and ramps). Each
may interact with professional services in influencing the effectiveness
of home care.

The role of respite care also merits careful attention. Definitions of
the range of services associated with the respite function are broad
(Weissert et al., 1989), and controlled studies of its impact are relatively few (Lawton, Brody, & Saperstein, 1989; Montgomery, 1988).
Despite this situation the importance of respite as concept and function
is widely understood (Weissert, 1985).

Understanding care settings. Relatively little research has considered how different home settings vary with respect to populations and
resources and how setting characteristics may facilitate or constrain the
provision of care. Most work has been done regarding the impact of
living arrangements, but a broader view of care settings is needed
that encompasses congregate living arrangements (Mor, Sherwood,
& Gutkin, 1986; Oktay & Volland, 1987). Eckert's work on board and
care has described a distinctive client population and service work
force and specified a range of care issues that intersect with those associated with "traditional" home care. While the policy environment of
board and care has some distinctive features, it also mirrors broader
home care and long-term care issues. Again, characteristics of settings
and subpopulations interact to define feasible outcomes for home care.

Addressing adequacy. The concept of adequacy has received little
attention in the context of long-term care generally and home care particularly. "Adequacy" suggests a judgment regarding the fit between
the solution (proposed or actual) of a problem and the extent of that
problem. It has two dimensions: the quantity (or scale) of benefits in
relation to the magnitude of need—either individual or collective—and
the scope (or coverage) of benefits in relation to the population in need.
Current studies of the effectiveness of home care interventions have
only partially addressed adequacy themes.

The Organization of Services

In addition to addressing issues of need, use, effectiveness, and costs, a small but growing body of home care research has been concerned with questions on how to better organize, coordinate, and integrate services to meet the care requirements of frail older persons. The need to address matters of service organization is made more pressing by at least four underlying conditions. First, rising acute care costs and an uncertain societal commitment to a strong public (and especially national) role in long-term care have seriously constrained funding for chronic care services, especially the "softer," "unskilled," and social services.

Second, existing funding streams for chronic care services are multiple and fragmented, and authority for their administration is diffused (e.g., Medicaid, the Social Service Block Grant, and even the "federalized" SSI program). Third, formal care for older persons, as for nearly everyone, is centered in the hospital and physician's office, not in the home, and acute care providers have tended to limit their care domains to matters of acute rather than long-term care services. (There are notable exceptions.) Finally, reliance on a demonstration strategy in long-term care has given the illusion of widespread funding and service activity, but in fact relatively few older persons have received care under demonstration programs and, sadly, it is not yet apparent that the accumulated lessons of 15 years of demonstration have much altered the thinking or vision of policymakers regarding long-term care system development and organization.

Approaches to addressing organizational issues in home care fall roughly into three groups: refinement of delivery mechanisms, service coordination, and funding integration. Most of the following discussion will concern the last two. Refinement approaches are directed toward various treatment issues—for example, whether a team approach produces better outcomes (Zimmer et al., 1985), whether homemaker and home health aide roles can successfully be combined (Lee & Stein, 1980), whether unbundling affective and instrumental home care tasks has positive impacts (Jette et al., 1981), and what, if any, systematic differences result from home care needs assessments performed by nurses versus social workers as well as in the hospital versus in the home (Benjamin et al., 1989). More studies are needed that address delivery questions, including more of the practical kind such as those concerning how to make home care better or more efficient (Kane & Kane, 1987).

SERVICE COORDINATION

Service coordination approaches can take many forms, including interorganizational coordination among providers and client-centered service planning and management. Most community care demonstrations have used both approaches. Because it has received so much research attention, we will address the second form, which is most commonly termed "case management."

Case management services are designed to assure more appropriate and timely services for older persons and others, to reduce the coordination costs faced by older persons and their families, and to lower overall health care expenditures by ensuring that more appropriate and less costly (usually noninstitutional) services are provided (Spitz, 1987). Recent research highlights two significant paradoxes concerning the substance of this approach to health care delivery and the priorities assigned to it. First, case management continues to attract enthusiastic attention as a solution to various systemic problems in designing services for needy populations; yet there persists widespread confusion and disagreement regarding precisely what case management is and what it is intended to achieve. Second, the popularity of case management approaches has grown in proportion to its association in the eyes of policymakers with cost-containment goals, despite mounting evidence that case management increases the cost of service provision rather than reducing it.

The persistent appeal of case management is evident in the recent recommendations of the U.S. Bipartisan Commission on Comprehensive Health Care, or the Pepper Commission (1990). The commission proposes a plan for federally financed home and community-based long-term care services for the severely disabled, and local case managers are designated to assess care needs, develop individual care plans, and monitor services. Consistent with traditionally broad and frequently contradictory definitions of case management goals, the commission suggests that case managers both (a) have budgets "sufficient to provide all services needed by the patient" and (b) give "special consideration to . . . cost containment" (Pepper Commission, 1990).

Two specific issues complicate the study of case management and make interpretation of research results more difficult. First, virtually all community care demonstration programs have had case management components, and case management has proven almost impossible to study in isolation from the associated services provided (Kane & Kane, 1987; Phillips, Kemper, & Applebaum, 1988). Second, while there is general agreement that case management includes case finding, assessment, care planning, implementation, and monitoring, variation across programs in how these functions are defined is considerable (Austin, Low, Roberts, & O'Connor, 1985; Capitman et al., 1987; Pelham & Clarke, 1986).

The National Long-Term Care Demonstration, discussed earlier and known as the "channeling demonstration," was initiated in 1980 to assess the impact of comprehensive case management in allocating community services appropriately and cost-effectively to the frail elderly in need of long-term care. Results of an evaluation of these demonstration programs indicate that case management services reduce the unmet needs reported by clients, enhance client and caregiver confidence and satisfaction, and increase the use of community-based, noninstitutional services. Case management has had little impact on client health and functioning, however, and little or no effect on the use of institutional services (Kemper, 1988). Generally, provision of case management services has increased the cost of care provision without producing commensurate reductions in the use of what are considered inappropriate services, specifically hospital and nursing home care. Adding case management to an enhanced service package of home and community services does little to foster the service substitution that this package is intended to produce. Other research suggests that targeting case management resources to specific subsets of those at risk may produce some positive outcomes for patients, although the costs of care will not be reduced (Morris et al., 1987; Ruchlin et al., 1987).

Not all recent research has reported unfavorable results regarding the impact of case management (Capitman, 1988; Zawadski & Eng, 1988). One study has concluded that case managers in one state program were efficient allocators of service resources (Davidson, Moscovice, & McCaffrey, 1989). With the exception of the channeling demonstration evaluation, however, relatively little careful research on case management for the frail elderly has been reported. To remedy this it will be necessary first to standardize (and to be able to replicate) the intervention and to define its goals before meaningful research is undertaken.

In addition to a variety of substantive behavioral questions about how case managers work, what activates a case manager on a case, how they allocate their time under inevitably heavy caseloads, and how they behave under different resource constraints (Kemper, 1988), two other areas of study seem particularly promising. First, research is needed on the roles of families and other informal caregivers as partners in case management (Capitman et al., 1986; Seltzer, Simmons, Ivry, & Litchfield, 1984). Second, studies are needed on linkages between case managers and service providers, both inside and outside the sponsoring agency (Capitman et al., 1986).

FUNDING INTEGRATION

Funding integration strategies are designed to draw together disparate sources of funding into a single stream to facilitate service planning and delivery. Integration strategies differ from service coordination to the extent that the latter addresses access to services through expertise and persuasion rather than control of resources. There remains considerable overlap between these strategies, given that case management can include resource integration (e.g., the financial control model in the channeling demonstration), and integration models invariably include case management (see below). Funding integration strategies nonetheless merit separate attention and are of considerable current interest.

Such strategies are not new. One of the earliest efforts to reform long-term care delivery to the frail elderly was mounted in the early 1970s in Massachusetts. State legislation authorized the creation of a network of home care corporations (primarily through the Older Americans Act network) that used Older Americans Act, Title XX (social services), and state funds to provide case management and other contracted services, particularly home care, to frail older persons. The Massachusetts experience highlights what can be achieved by creating an operational network of programs, pooling funds, and developing a case-managed universal benefit (Kane & Kane, 1987; Piktialis & Callahan, 1986).

The most visible of current federal initiatives concerned with care of older persons is the social/health maintenance organization (S/HMO) demonstration. The S/HMO is a health plan that combines Medicare HMO coverage of hospital and physician services with chronic care benefits (e.g., personal care, homemaker services, nursing home) and other expanded benefits (e.g., prescription drugs, eyeglasses, and dental care). These acute and chronic care services are financed by Medicare through a single monthly capitated payment and premiums from health plan enrollees. The S/HMO demonstration model is being tested by organizations in four sites (Portland, Minneapolis, Long Beach, and Brooklyn) representing two types of sponsors: HMOs and long-term care organizations (Newcomer et al., 1990).

Early results of an evaluation of the S/HMO demonstration are now being published. Initial evidence has not been encouraging regarding the ability of the plans to achieve their primary objectives to manage acute care use and achieve savings to support chronic care services. Indeed, in their fourth year of operation, two of the sites continued to exceed the national average for Medicare hospital days (per 1,000 member months) for HMOs. While HMO-based plans (i.e., Portland and Minneapolis) were most successful in controlling inpatient use, all sites had sizable financial losses in the first three years and only two (Minneapolis and Long Beach) reversed this trend in the fourth year (Harrington & Newcomer, in press).

While there was substantial variation across sites in chronic care use and patterns, especially regarding nursing home and home care, there was little relationship between these and overall fiscal performance. Average chronic care expenditures per member month ($23-$30) and share of total costs (6%-10%) were relatively similar across sites (Newcomer et al., 1990). Case management costs averaged 2% to 4% of all expenditures, and case management was one of several tools (including screening prospective enrollees) to control chronic care costs (Harrington & Newcomer, in press; Newcomer et al., 1990).

A second phase of the S/HMO evaluation involves a comparison of three groups of individual Medicare beneficiaries: (a) those receiving services from traditional sources on a fee-for-service basis, (b) those enrolled in HMOs with capitated risk sharing contracts, and (c) those electing to enroll in the S/HMOs. Results of this analysis are not yet available, but this data set represents a potentially rich resource for additional research on outcomes of alternative organizational and financing arrangements.

HOME CARE PROVIDERS

In considering issues of organization of services, there are at least two other areas of home care that merit research attention. The first involves organizational providers of home care, and the second involves those individuals who deliver services in the home. Some recent studies have begun to address ways in which changes in payment systems, especially Medicare's prospective payment system, have altered (a) the market for home-based services for older persons (Estes et al., 1988), (b) incentives under which home care organizations operate (Wood & Estes, 1990), and (c) types of clients seeking care (Goldberg & Estes, 1990). Particular attention has been given to the medicalization of community-based services and its implications for frail older persons (Binney, Estes, & Ingram, in press). Other research on home care providers has begun to examine the roles of unlicensed home care agencies and issues of access and quality associated with this provider sector (Grant & Harrington, 1989). Much more research is needed on changes in federal, state, and local policy environments and their impact on home care organizations.

Additional research is also needed on home care workers and issues related to their roles, effectiveness, and career choices. Home care workers can serve as surrogate families for older persons and as important sources of respite and support for informal caregivers (Cantor, 1988). Two sets of issues seem most important. First, research is needed that examines the quality of care delivered at home and those conditions that may enhance or impede effective home care (Cantor, 1988; Donovan, 1989). Second, we need to examine broader labor market issues in home care—including issues of low pay, minimal benefits, and lack of job security that are endemic in this sector (New York City Home Care Work Group, 1989; Sabatino, 1990).

Conclusions

Evidence from research on home care use, effectiveness, and organization raises at least as many questions as it answers. Our ability to predict who will use home care services remains very limited. Various studies have provided resoundingly negative responses to claims that home care reduces institutional use and costs, but our research reveals little about ways home care interventions may affect the lives of older persons and their informal caregivers. Governments have underwritten a range of service benefits that, because they are fragmented and limited, pose serious coordination and integration challenges.

If home care research is to advance beyond the current plateau, some basic conceptual and methodological work needs to be done in three areas. First, services, populations, and settings need to be conceptualized in ways that bring some order to the diversity now included under the rubric of *home care for older persons.* Second, considerably more effort needs to be devoted to stretching the conceptual boundaries of outcomes associated with home care, so that effectiveness research can better gauge the impact of given interventions in specific settings for certain subpopulations. Third, research that focuses on factors affecting the behavior of individuals needs to incorporate relevant dimensions of local and state policy environments into study design and measurement.

In the body of this overview, various specific areas for needed research have been identified. At the risk of excluding some important topics, it seems worthwhile to suggest several areas where research is particularly needed:

1. the fit between settings and services, on the one hand, and the needs of specific subpopulations, on the other (e.g., board and care for the marginal, very frail elderly);
2. factors that initiate and sustain formal-informal linkages (i.e., mixed helper networks), including factors that support informal caregivers (e.g., various forms of respite care);
3. transitions between acute and chronic care (e.g., hospital or home health to home-based supportive services), between forms of acute care (e.g., hospital to home health), and between forms of chronic care (e.g., nursing home to home-based supportive services);
4. factors that explain heavy use of home care by a small share of the estimated one quarter of disabled older persons who use any home care (e.g., living arrangements, preferences, professional values);
5. the economic burden of home care services on afflicted older persons and their families (e.g., the direct costs of services and the indirect costs of lost caregiver productivity);
6. the relationship between alternative licensing, compensation, training, and monitoring arrangements on home care worker esteem, satisfaction, and performance;

7. models of case management that permit precise definition of the intervention and specification of anticipated patient/client and caregiver outcomes;

8. feasible models of funding and service integration that support acute and chronic care for older persons; and

9. factors that influence the behavior of home care markets, including organizational providers of home care, home care workers, and state policy.

Because of the broad scope of this background chapter, relatively little has been said about methodological issues in the study of home care. It is important to invoke what has become a familiar theme in all aging research, namely, the need for prospective, longitudinal research on chronic illness and care in the home. To enhance our understanding of the natural history of service needs and use (which provides the social and behavioral context for the study of all the research questions discussed here), we will need to make more creative use of longitudinal data sets developed to study elderly cohorts and will need to design additional data collection and analysis strategies appropriate to research on care in the home.

Home care is a centerpiece in the U.S. system of long-term care. This is apparent in recent Pepper Commission recommendations calling for federal social insurance (with copayments) to cover a wide range of home and community-based care, including skilled, personal care, and homemaker chore services at home as well as adult day and respite care. At the same time some of the thorniest long-term care issues are highlighted in the study of home care. To what extent should government intervene in matters of the family? Will informal care be undermined over time if availability of home care is expanded? Will demand for home care mushroom with improved benefits and funding? Is home care for older persons essentially custodial, or does it achieve other benefits? How much medical care is it reasonable to expect family members qua surrogate nurses to provide at home under emerging home health care models? Should family members bear more of the costs? What other consequences for older persons and their caregivers should we consider? What regulatory strategies are best able to assure quality care in home settings? As a society what should we be willing to pay? Answers to these questions will determine the policy context within which home care choices are made and the general direction of home care research. Decisions regarding specific priorities remain to be made.

References

Andersen, R., & Newman, J. (1973). Societal and individual determinants of medical care utilization in the United States. *The Milbank Quarterly, 51,* 95-124.

Applebaum, R., Seidl, F., & Austin, C. (1980). The Wisconsin Community Care Organization: Preliminary findings from the Milwaukee Experiment. *The Gerontologist, 20,* 350-355.

Applebaum, R. A., & Wilson, N. L. (1988). Training needs for providing case management for the long-term care client: Lessons from the national channeling demonstration. *The Gerontologist, 28,* 172-176.

Austin, C. D., Low, J., Roberts, E. A., & O'Connor, K. (1985). *Case management: A critical review.* Seattle: University of Washington, Pacific Northwest Long-Term Care Gerontology Center.

Bass, D. M., & Noelker, L. S. (1987). The influence of family caregivers on elders' use of in-home services: An expanded conceptual framework. *Journal of Health and Social Behavior, 28,* 184-196.

Becker, G., & Kaufman, S. (1988). Old age, rehabilitation, and research: A review of the issues. *The Gerontologist, 28,* 459-468.

Benjamin, A. E. (1986). Determinants of state variations in home health utilization and expenditures under Medicare. *Medical Care, 24,* 535-547.

Benjamin, A. E. (1988). Long-term care and AIDS: Perspectives from experience with the elderly. *The Milbank Quarterly, 66,* 415-443.

Benjamin, A. E., Swan, J. H., Feigenbaum, L., Newcomer, R. J., & Fox, P. J. (1989). *Medicare Posthospital Study: Final report* (Report to the Commonwealth Commission on Elderly People Living Alone). San Francisco: University of California, Institute for Health and Aging.

Berk, M. L., & Bernstein, A. (1985). Use of home health services: Some findings from the National Expenditure Survey. *Home Health Care Services Quarterly, 6,* 13-23.

Binney, E. A., Estes, C. L., & Ingman, S. R. (in press). Medicalization, public policy and the elderly: Social services in jeopardy. *Social Science and Medicine.*

Branch, L. G., Horowitz, A., & Carr, C. (1989). The implications for everyday life of incident self-reported visual decline among people over age 65 living in the community. *The Gerontologist, 29,* 359-365.

Branch, L. G., & Jette, A. M. (1983). Elders' use of informal long-term care assistance. *The Gerontologist, 23,* 51-56.

Branch, L. G., & Jette, A. M. (1984). Personal health practices and mortality among the elderly. *American Journal of Public Health, 74,* 1126-1129.

Branch, L. G., Wetle, T. T. et al. (1988). A prospective study of incident comprehensive medical home use among the elderly. *American Journal of Public Health, 78,* 255-259.

Brecher, C., & Knickman, J. (1985). A reconsideration of long-term care policy. *Journal of Health Politics, Policy and Law, 10,* 245-273.

Cantor, M. H. (1988). *Factors related to strain among homecare workers: A comparison of formal and informal caregivers.* Paper presented at the Gerontological Society of America, San Francisco.

Capitman, J. A. (1986). Community-based long-term care models, target groups, and impacts on service use. *The Gerontologist, 26,* 389-397.

Capitman, J. A. (1988). Case management for long-term and acute medical care. *Health Care Financing Review* (Annual Suppl.), pp. 53-55.

Capitman, J. A., Arling, G., & Bowling, C. (1987). Public and private costs of long-term care for nursing home pre-admission screening program participants. *The Gerontologist, 27,* 780-787.

Cohen, M. A., Tell, E. J., Greenberg, J. N., & Wallack, S. S. (1987). The financial capacity of the elderly to insure for long-term care. *The Gerontologist, 27,* 494-502.

Coughlin, T. A., & Liu, K. (1989). Health care costs of older persons with cognitive impairments. *The Gerontologist, 29,* 173-182.

Davidson, G., Moscovice, I., & McCaffrey, D. (1989). Allocative efficiency of case managers for the elderly. *Health Services Research, 24,* 534-554.

Donovan, R. (1989). Work stress and job satisfaction: A study of home care workers in New York City. *Home Health Care Services Quarterly, 10,* 97-114.

Doty, P. (1986). Family care of the elderly: The role of public policy. *The Milbank Quarterly, 64,* 34-75.

Eggert, G. M., & Friedman, B. (1988). The need for special interventions for multiple hospital admission patients. *Health Care Financing Review* (Annual Suppl.), pp. 57-67.

Estes, C. L., Wood, J. B., & Associates. (1988). *Organization and community responses to Medicare policy.* San Francisco: University of California, Institute for Health & Aging.

Feller, B. A. (1983). *Americans needing help to function at home* (Advance Data from Vital and Health Statistics, No. 92. DHHS Pub. No. [PHS]83-1250; National Center for Health Statistics). Hyattsville, MD: Public Health Service.

Furstenberg, A., & Mezey, M. D. (1987). Differences in outcome between Black and White elderly hip fracture patients. *Journal of Chronic Disease, 40*(10), 931-938.

Goldberg, S. C., & Estes, C. L. (in press). Medicare PPS and posthospital care for the elderly: Does out of hospital mean out of luck? *Journal of Applied Gerontology.*

Gornick, M., & Hall, M. J. (1988). Trends in Medicare use of post-hospital care. *Health Care Financing Review* (Annual Suppl.), pp. 27-38.

Grant, L. A., & Harrington, C. (1989). Quality of care in licensed and unlicensed home care agencies: A California case study. *Home Health Care Services Quarterly, 10,* 115-138.

Greene, V. L. (1987). Nursing home admission risk and the cost-effectiveness of community-based long-term care: A framework for analysis. *Health Services Research, 22,* 655-669.

Groth-Juncker, A. (1982). *Home health care team: Randomized trial of a new team approach to home care.* Rochester, NY: University of Rochester.

Harrington, C., & Newcomer, R. J. (in press). The financial performance of the Social Health Maintenance Organization Demonstration. *Health Care Financing Review.*

Harrington, C., Newcomer, R. J., Estes, C. L., & Associates. (1985). *Long term care of the elderly: Public policy issues.* Beverly Hills, CA: Sage.

Health Care Financing Administration (HCFA). (1987). *Medicare and Medicaid data book, 1986.* Washington, DC: Office of Research and Demonstrations, HCFA.

Hedrick, S. C., & Inui, T. S. (1986). The effectiveness and cost of home care: An information synthesis. *Health Services Research, 20,* 851-880.

Hicks, B., Raisz, H., Segal, J., & Doherty, N. (1981). The triage experiment in coordinated care for the elderly. *American Journal of Public Health, 71,* 991-1003.

Holahan, J., & Cohen, J. (1986). *Medicaid: The trade-off between cost containment and access to care.* Washington, DC: Urban Institute Press.

Hughes, S. L. (1985). Apples and oranges? A review of evaluations of community-based long-term care. *Health Services Research, 20,* 461-488.

Hughes, S. L. (1989). Home and community care of the elderly: System resources and constraints. In J. A. Barondess, D. E. Rogers, & K. N. Lohr (Eds.), *Care of the elderly patient: Policy issues and research opportunities* (pp. 55-61). Washington, DC: Institute of Medicine, National Academy Press.

Hughes, S. L., Conrad, K. L., Manheim, L. M., & Edelman, P. L. (1988). Impact of long-term home care on mortality, functional status, and unmet needs. *Health Services Research, 23,* 269-294.

Hughes, S. L., Cummings, J., Weaver, F., Manheim, L. M., Conrad, K. J., & Nash, K. (1989). *A randomized trial of V.A. home care for severely disabled veterans.* Evanston, IL: Northwestern University, Center for Health Services and Policy Research.

Hughes, S. L., Manheim, L. M., Edelman, P. L., & Conrad, K. J. (1987). Impact of long-term home care on hospital and nursing home use and cost. *Health Services Research, 22,* 19-47.

Institute for Health & Aging. (1990). *Long-term care public policy agenda for California.* San Francisco: University of California, Institute for Health & Aging.

Institute of Medicine. (1986). *Improving the quality of care in nursing homes.* Washington, DC: Author.

Jette, A. M. et al. (1981). Home care service diversification: A pilot investigation. *The Gerontologist, 21,* 572-579.

Kane, N. M. (1989). The home care crisis of the nineties. *The Gerontologist, 29,* 24-31.

Kane, R. A. (1988). The noblest experiment of them all: Learning from the national channeling evaluation. *Health Services Research, 23,* 189-198.

Kane, R. A., & Kane, R. L. (1987). *Long-term care: Principles, programs and policies.* New York: Springer.

Kane, R. L. (1988). *PAC: A national study of post acute care.* Minneapolis: University of Minnesota.

Kane, R. L., & Kane, R. A. (1978). Care of the aged: Old problems in need of new solutions. *Science, 200,* 913-919.

Kasper, J. D. (1988). *Aging alone: Profiles and projections* (A report of the Commonwealth Fund Commission on Elderly People Living Alone). New York: Commonwealth Fund.

Katz, S., & Aksom, A. (1976). A measure of primary sociological functions. *International Journal of Health Services, 6,* 493-507.

Kemper, P., Applebaum, R., & Harrigan, M. (1987). Community care demonstrations: What have we learned? *Health Care Financing Review, 8,* 87-100.

Kemper, P. (1988). The evaluation of the national long-term care demonstration: 10. Overview of the findings. *Health Services Research, 23,* 161-174.

Koff, T. H. (1982). *Long-term care: An approach to serving the frail elderly.* Boston: Little, Brown.

Kovar, M. G. (1986). Expenditures for the medical care of elderly people living in the community in 1980. *The Milbank Quarterly, 64,* 100-132.

Kramer, A. M., Shaughnessy, P. W., & Pettigrew, M. L. (1985). Cost-effectiveness implications based on a comparison of nursing home and health case mix. *Health Services Review, 20,* 387-405.

Lane, D., Uyeno, D., Stark, A., Gutman, G., & McCashin, B. (1987). Forecasting client transitions in British Columbia's Long-Term Care Program. *Health Services Research, 32,* 671-706.

LaPlante, M. P. (1989). Disability in basic life activities across the life span. *Disability Statistics Report, 1,* 1-42.

Laudicina, S. S., & Burwell, B. (1988). A profile of Medicaid home and community-based waivers, 1985: Findings of a national study. *Journal of Health Politics, Policy and Law, 13,* 525-546.

Lawton, M. P., Brody, E. M., & Saperstein, A. R. (1989). A controlled study of respite service for caregivers of Alzheimer's patients. *The Gerontologist, 29,* 8-16.

Lee, J. T., & Stein, M. A. (1980). Eliminating duplication in home health care for the elderly: The Guale Project. *National Association of Social Workers, 5,* 29-36.

Lewis, M. A., Cretin, S., & Kane, R. L. (1985). The natural history of nursing home patients. *The Gerontologist, 25,* 382-388.

Liu, K., Manton, K. G., & Liu, B. M. (1985). Home care expenses for the disabled elderly. *Health Care Financing Review, 7,* 51-58.

Lubitz, J., & Prihoda, R. (1984). The use and costs of Medicare services in the last two years of life. *Health Care Financing Review, 5,* 117-131.

Macken, C. L. (1986). A profile of functionally impaired elderly persons living in the community. *Health Care Financing Review, 7,* 33-49.

Manson, S. M. (1989). Long-term care in American Indian communities: Issues for planning and research. *The Gerontologist, 29,* 38-44.

Manton, K. G., & Soldo, B. J. (1985). Dynamics of health changes in the oldest old: New perspectives and evidence. *The Milbank Quarterly, 63,* 206-285.

McAuley, W. J., & Arling, G. (1984). Use of in-home care by very old people. *Journal of Health and Social Behavior, 25,* 54-64.

McCusker, J., & Stoddard, A. M. (1987). Effects of an expanding home care program for the terminally ill. *Medical Care, 25,* 373-385.

Mechanic, D. (1979). Correlates of physician utilization. *Journal of Health and Social Behavior, 20,* 387-396.

Mitchell, J. B. (1978). Patient outcomes in alternative long-term care settings. *Medical Care, 16,* 439-452.

Montgomery, R. J. V. (1988). Respite care: Lessons from a controlled design study. *Health Care Financing Review* (Annual Suppl.), pp. 133-138.

Mor, V. (1987). *Hospice care systems: Structure, process, costs, and outcome.* New York: Springer.

Mor, V., Sherwood, S., & Gutkin, C. (1986). A national study of residential care of the aged. *The Gerontologist, 26,* 405-417.

Mor, V., & Specter, W. (1988). Achieving continuity of care. *Generations, 12,* 47-52.

Morris, J. N., Gutkin, C. E., Ruchlin, H. S., & Sherwood, S. (1987). Housing and case-managed home care programs and subsequent institutional utilization. *The Gerontologist, 27,* 788-796.

Moxley, D. P., & Buzas, L. (1989). Perceptions of case management services for elderly people. *Health and Social Work, 14,* 196-203.

National Center for Health Statistics (NCHS). (1986). *Utilization of short-stay hospitals, United States, 1985 annual summary* (Vital and Health Statistics, Series 13, No. 91). Hyattsville, MD: Public Health Service.

National Center for Health Statistics (NCHS). (1987). *1986 summary: National Hospital Discharge Survey* (Advance Data, No. 145, National Center for Health Statistics). Hyattsville, MD: Public Health Service.

Netting, F. E., & Williams, F. G. (1989). Establishing interfaces between community- and hospital-based service systems for the elderly. *Health and Social Work, 14,* 134-139.

Neu, C. R., & Harrison, S. C. (1988). *Posthospital care before and after the medical prospective payment system* (Report No. R-3590-HCFA). Santa Monica, CA: Rand Corporation.

Neu, C. R., Harrison, S. C., & Heilbrunn, J. Z. (1989). *Medicare patients and post-acute care: Who goes where?* Santa Monica, CA: Rand Corporation.

Newcomer, R. J., & Bogaert-Tullis, M. P. (1985). Medicaid cost containment trials and innovations. In C. Harrington et al. (Eds.), *Long-term care of the elderly: Public policy issues.* Beverly Hills, CA: Sage.

Newcomer, R., Harrington, C., & Friedlob, A. (in press-a). Awareness and enrollment in the social/HMO. *The Gerontologist.*

Newcomer, R. J., Harrington, C., & Friedlob, A. (in press-b). Social health maintenance organizations: Assessing the initial experience. *Health Services Research.*

New York City Home Care Work Group. (1989). *Building the home care triangle: Clients and families, paraprofessionals and agencies in partnership with government.* New York: Community Service Society.

Nocks, B. C., Learner, M., Blackman, D., & Brown, T. E. (1986). The effects of a community-based long-term care project on nursing home utilization. *The Gerontologist, 26,* 151-157.

Oktay, J. S., & Volland, P. J. (1987). Foster home care for the frail elderly as an alternative to nursing home care: An experimental evaluation. *American Journal of Public Health, 77,* 1505-1510.

Ory, M. G., & Bond, K. (1989). *Aging and health care: Social science and policy perspectives.* New York: Routledge.

Papsidero, J. A. (Ed.). (1979). *Chance for change: Implications of a chronic disease module study.* East Lansing: Michigan State University.

Pelham, A. O., & Clarke, W. F. (1986). *Managing home care for the elderly: Lessons from community-based agencies.* New York: Springer.

Pepper Commission (U.S. Bipartisan Commission on Comprehensive Health Care). (1990, March). *Access to health care and long-term care for all Americans: Recommendations to the Congress.* Washington, DC: Author.

Petchers, M. K., & Milligan, S. E. (1987). Social networks and social support among Black urban elderly: A health care resource. *Social Work in Health Care, 12,* 103-117.

Phillips, B. R., Kemper, P., & Applebaum, R. A. (1988). The evaluation of the national long-term care demonstration 4: Case management under channeling. *Health Services Research, 23,* 67-81.

Piktialis, D. S., & Callahan, J. (1986). Organization of long-term care: Should there be a single or multiple focal point for long-term care coordination. In J. M. Grana & D. B. McCallum (Eds.), *The impact of technology on long-term care.* Millwood, VA: Project HOPE Center for Health Affairs.

Rabin, D. L., & Stockton, P. (1987). *Long-term care for the elderly: A factbook.* New York: Oxford University Press.

Rivlin, A. M., & Weiner, J. M. (1988). *Caring for the disabled elderly: Who will pay?* Washington, DC: Brookings Institution.

Roos, N. P., & Shapiro, E. (1981). The Manitoba Longitudinal Study on Aging: Preliminary findings on health care utilization of the elderly. *Medical Care, 19,* 644-657.

Rosenwaike, I. (1985). A demographic portrait of the oldest old. *The Milbank Quarterly, 63,* 187-205.

Rowe, J. H. (1985). Health care of the elderly. *New England Journal of Medicine, 312,* 827-835.

Rowland, D. (1989). *Help at home: Long-term care assistance for impaired elderly people.* Baltimore, MD: Commonwealth Fund, Commission on Elderly People Living Alone.

Ruchlin, H. S., Morris, J. N., Gutkin, C. E., & Sherwood, S. (1987). *Expenditures for institutional and community-based services by a cross-section of elderly living in the community.* Boston: Hebrew Rehabilitation Center for Aged.

Ruther, M., & Helbing, C. (1988). Use and cost of home health agency services under Medicare. *Health Care Financing Review, 10,* 105-108.

Sabatino, C. P. (1990). *Lessons for enhancing consumer-directed approaches in home care: Final report.* Washington, DC: American Bar Association, Commission on Legal Problems of the Elderly.

Scanlon, W. J. (1980). A theory of the nursing home market. *Inquiry, 17,* 25-41.

Seltzer, M. M., Ivry, J., & Litchfield, L. C. (1987). Family members as case managers: Partnership between the formal and informal support networks. *The Gerontologist, 27,* 722-728.

Seltzer, M. M., Krauss, M. W., Litchfield, L. C., & Modlish, N. J. K. (1989). Utilization of aging network services by elderly persons with mental retardation. *The Gerontologist, 29,* 234-238.

Seltzer, M. S., Simmons, K., Ivry, J., & Litchfield, L. (1984). Agency-family partnerships: Case management of services for the elderly. *Journal of Gerontological Social Work, 7,* 57-71.

Shapiro, E. (1986). Patterns and predictors of home care use by the elderly when need is the sole basis for admission. *Home Health Care Services Quarterly, 7,* 29-44.

Shapiro, E., & Tate, R. (1988). Who is really at risk of institutionalization. *The Gerontologist, 28,* 237-245.

Skellie, F. A., & Coan, R. E. (1980). Community-based care and mortality: Preliminary findings of Georgia's Alternative Health Services Project. *The Gerontologist, 20,* 372-379.

Skellie, F. A., Mobley, G. M., & Coan, R. E. (1982). Cost-effectiveness of community-based long-term care. *American Journal of Public Health, 72,* 353-358.

Soldo, B. J. (1985). In-home services for the dependent elderly: Determinants of current use and implications for future demand. *Research on Aging, 7,* 281-304.

Soldo, B. J., Agree, E. M., & Wolf, D. A. (1989). The balance between formal and informal care. In M. G. Ory & K. Bond (Eds.), *Aging and health care: Social science and policy perspectives.* New York: Routledge.

Soldo, B. J., & Manton, K. G. (1985). Changes in health status and service needs of the oldest old: Current patterns and future trends. *The Milbank Quarterly, 63,* 286-319.

Somers, A. R. (1982). Long-term care for the elderly and disabled: A new health priority. *New England Journal of Medicine, 307,* 221-226.

Spitz, B. (1987). National survey of medicaid care management. *Health Affairs, 6,* 61-70.

Stark, A. J., & Gutman, G. M. (1986). Client transfers in long-term care: Five years' experience. *American Journal of Public Health, 76,* 1312-1316.

Stone, R. (1986). *Aging in the eighties, age 65 years and over: Use of community services* (Advance Data, No. 124; National Center for Health Statistics). Hyattsville, MD: Public Health Service.

Stone, R., Cafferata, G. L., & Sangl, J. (1987). Caregivers of the frail elderly: A national profile. *The Gerontologist, 27,* 616-626.

Stone, R. I., & Murtaugh, C. M. (1988). *The elderly population with chronic functional limitations: Implications for home care eligibility.* Paper presented at the annual meeting of the American Public Health Association, Boston.

Stone, R., & Newcomer, R. J. (1985). The state role in board and care housing. In C. Harrington et al. (Eds.), *Long-term care of the elderly: Public policy issues.* Beverly Hills, CA: Sage.

Swan, J. H., & Harrington, C. (1986). Estimating undersupply of nursing home beds in states. *Health Services Research, 21,* 57-83.

Tennstedt, S. L., McKinlay, J. B., & Sullivan, L. M. (1989). Informal care for frail elders: The role of secondary caregivers. *The Gerontologist, 29,* 677-683.

Vertrees, J. C., Manton, K. G., & Adler, G. S. (1989). Cost effectiveness of home and community-based care. *Health Care Financing Review, 10,* 65-78.

Vladeck, B. C. (1980). *Unloving care: The nursing home tragedy.* New York: Basic Books.

Waldo, D. R., & Lazenby, H. C. (1984). Demographic characteristics and health care use and expenditures by the aged in the United States: 1977-1984. *Health Care Financing Review, 6,* 1-49.

Wan, T. T. H. (1987). Functionally disabled elderly: Health status, social support, and use of health services. *Research on Aging, 9,* 61-78.

Wan, T. T. H. (1989). The behavioral model of health care utilization by older people. In M. G. Ory & K. Bond (Eds.), *Aging and health care: Social science and policy perspectives.* New York: Routledge.

Wan, T. T. H., & Arling, G. (1983). Differential use of health services among disabled elderly. *Research on Aging, 5,* 411-431.

Wan, T. T. H., Weissert, W. G., & Livieratos, B. B. (1980). Geriatric day care and home-maker services: An experimental study. *Journal of Gerontology, 35,* 256-274.

Weissert, W. G. (1985). Home and community-based care: The cost-effectiveness trap. *Generations, 10,* 47-50.

Weissert, W. G. (1988). The national channeling demonstration: What we knew, know now, and still need to know. *Health Services Research, 2,* 175-187.

Weissert, W. G., & Cready, C. M. (1989). Toward a model for improved targeting of aged at risk of institutionalization. *Health Services Research, 24,* 485-510.

Weissert, W. G., Elston, J. J., Bolda, E. J. et al. (1989). Models of adult day care: Findings from a national survey. *The Gerontologist, 29,* 640-649.

Weissert, W. G., Wan, T. H., Livieratos, B. B., & Pellegrino, J. (1980). Cost-effectiveness of homemaker services for the chronically ill. *Inquiry, 17,* 230-243.

Wennberg, J., & Gittelsohn, A. (1973). Small area variations in health care delivery. *Science, 182,* 1102-1108.

Wolinsky, F. (1978). Assessing the effects of predisposing, enabling, and illness-morbidity characteristics on health services utilization. *Journal of Health and Social Behavior, 19,* 384-396.

Wolinsky, F. D., Mosely, R. R., & Coe, R. M. (1986). A cohort analysis of the use of health services by elderly Americans. *Journal of Health and Social Behavior, 27,* 209-219.

Wolock, I., Schlesinger, E., Dinerman, M., & Seaton, R. (1987). The posthospital needs and care of patients: Implications for discharge planning. *Social Work in Health Care, 12,* 61-76.

Wood, J. B. (1989). The emergency of adult day care as post-acute care agencies. *Journal of Aging and Health, 1,* 521-539.

Wooldridge, J., & Schore, J. (1988). Effects of channeling on use of nursing home, hospitals and other medical services. *Health Services Research, 23,* 119-128.

Zawadski, R. T., & Eng, C. (1988). Case management in capitated long-term care. *Health Care Financing Review* (Annual Suppl.), pp. 75-81.

Zimmer, J. G., Groth-Juncker, A., & McCusker, J. (1985). A randomized controlled study of a home health care team. *American Journal of Public Health, 75,* 134-141.

TWO

Home Care:
Where We Are and Where We Need to Go

SUSAN L. HUGHES

Until very recently the term *home care* was used loosely by the uninitiated to refer to a broad array of services that could be provided by a variety of different organizations and personnel. Frequently these services are funded by different payors and have different eligibility criteria. As a result they may be targeted toward the same or different clients.

Table 2.1 displays 20 different kinds of services that might be needed and provided in the home today, ranging from "high-tech" enteral and parenteral nutrition services to chore/housekeeping help and home-delivered meals. Although this list is probably incomplete, it indicates the complexity and variety of home care services that are possible across clients.

Most industrial designers adhere to the adage that, in product design, form should follow function. In the home care industry one could interpret this to mean that the mix of home care services provided should

AUTHOR'S NOTE: I would like to acknowledge the assistance provided by Judith Sangl and Charles Helbing of the Health Care Financing Administration, Robert Hoyer of the National Association for Home Care, Colleen Noland of the National Home Caring Council, Ann Rooney of JCAHO, Wanda Ryan, President of the Illinois Home Care Association, and Delores Perteet of the Region V Health Care Financing Administration office in providing background information for this chapter. Their help is greatly appreciated.

TABLE 2.1. Home Care Services by Degree of Skilled Care Intensity

Enteral/parenteral
  nutrition
Ventilation/respirator
  therapy
Antibiotic therapy
Chemotherapy
Renal dialysis

Skilled nursing
Physical therapy
Occupational therapy
Speech therapy

Medical social services
Nutrition services
Case management
Full-time (24-hour) personal
  care attendants

Home health aide/personal care
Homemaker
Chore/housekeeping
Respite care
Home-delivered meals

Pharmaceuticals
Durable medical equipment

reflect the care needs of the client and the informal care resources available in the client's family network.

In this case the funding and the organization of services would be designed to facilitate the development of individualized home care service packages that would be highly responsive to client needs at baseline and to changes in those needs over time. Unfortunately, evidence suggests that our current ability to respond to home care needs is greatly hampered by the complexity of existing funding sources and resulting divergent eligibility criteria for different types of home care services.

Models of Care

This chapter examines four distinct models of home care that have evolved in the United States as a largely unintentional effect of our system of financing: (a) high-tech home care, (b) hospice, (c) skilled home health care, and (d) low-tech/custodial care. Each of these models is described and the implications of this complex mix of services for achieving effectiveness, coordination, efficiency, and quality of care are then addressed.

HIGH-TECH HOME CARE

Beginning with the most technologically sophisticated model, "high-tech" home care has grown astronomically over the last decade. In 1968 patients without functioning digestive organs were sustained for the first time through total parenteral nutrition provided intravenously. These treatments initially required 24-hour-a-day hospital care. The invention of pumps in the early 1970s permitted more rapid infusion of solutions, freeing patients from tubes and bottles for up to 16 hours a day. The logical next step was the transfer of this technology outside of the hospital, where it now enables persons to maintain normal lives, including, in some cases, resumption of employment. In 1983 approximately 2,500 patients received parenteral nutrition therapy at home at a cost of $150-$250 a day, or about $200 million a year (Donlan, 1983). Currently, high-tech services include respirator/ventilation, IV antibiotic, chemotherapy treatments, and home-based renal dialysis in addition to enteral and parenteral nutrition. Major providers are large corporations like Baxter, Inc.'s Caremark division and other large pharmaceutical or hospital supply corporations. Recently hospitals and home health care providers have begun forming joint ventures with each other and with pharmaceutical/medical supply companies to provide these services.

Original projections of growth in high-tech home care were glowing. The American Society for Parenteral and Enteral Nutrition estimated in 1983 that 150,000 to 200,000 home parenteral patients alone would be treated in 1990, at expenditures of up to $1.6 billion per year (Donlan, 1983).

More recent examinations of total sales of high-tech services and products have yielded estimates of $1.2 billion in 1985, projected to increase by 17% to $1.4 billion in 1990, accounting for roughly 21% of the medical home care market (Kane, 1989). According to the National Association for Home Care (NAHC), market research firms estimate that the core home care services industry accounted for expenditures of $5 billion in 1986, with high-tech services and products accounting for an additional $1.2 billion, estimated to increase to $2.3 billion by 1991 (Foundation for Home and Hospice Care, 1988). Analysts believe that growth in high-tech expenditures could have been higher in recent years but have been constrained by Medicare and private insurance payors who have subjected claims to intense utilization review, resulting in extreme payment delays (Foundation for Home and Hospice Care, 1988; Selz, 1990).

It is generally believed that high-tech services are less likely than other types of home care services to be used by elderly persons. However, it is certainly possible to envision instances where "young-old" persons, between the ages of 65 and 80, could be active consumers of home-based antibiotic, chemotherapy, and ventilator therapy or renal dialysis. Currently, high-tech home care services can be provided by unlicensed, uncertified providers. As a result the quality of care provided is unknown, and it is not clear who is ultimately responsible for quality of care among the multiple providers involved.

HOSPICE

Hospice programs are discussed next because, although the antithesis of high-tech care in philosophy, hospice programs serve gravely ill elderly who have a prognosis of less than six months' life expectancy. Thus, although hospice programs provide palliative rather than curative care, the illness severity level of patients served is very high. The Medicare hospice benefit was implemented in 1983 with 6 providers fully certified to participate in the program. By 1987 this number had grown to 443, representing 25% of the 1,700 operational hospices nationwide. The largest number of medicare-certified programs (6% of existing programs) are located in Florida, with more than half of all Medicare-certified hospices located in 11 of the 50 states.

Many home care agencies were cautious about applying for Medicare hospice certification because the conditions of participation include a cap on average aggregated patient payment and a 210-day benefit period limit. The 210-day limit could theoretically expose providers to risk if patient survival were longer than estimated. Given that determination of remaining months of life is less than an exact science and given that the original hospice benefit also contained a "sunset" provision, which could have terminated the program in 1986, many eligible providers are believed to have elected not to participate in the hospice program. In addition, beneficiaries who elect to use the hospice benefit must waive Medicare benefits for curative or duplicative services during three 90- and 30-day benefit periods. Medicare beneficiaries may revoke hospice care at any time but in doing so lose any other medicare benefit during that election period. Services covered under the Medicare hospice benefit include nursing care, medical social services, physician services, counseling, short-term inpatient care, medical appliances and supplies, home health aide services, and physical, occupational, and speech therapy.

Not all certified hospices are home care providers. However, the Health Care Financing Administration (HCFA) estimates that the majority of Medicare-certified hospices are home health agencies. Half of all hospices operated by a home health agency were Medicare certified in 187, compared with 21% of independent hospices and 14% of hospital- and SNF-based hospices. It is expected that more home care agencies will enroll in the program because (a) the sunset provision has been lifted, (b) existing certified providers have not had difficulty meeting expenditure caps, and (c) expansion of days covered may occur as a result of a bill recently introduced in Congress that seeks to restore expanded days of hospice care as covered in the repealed catastrophic care benefit.

SKILLED HOME HEALTH CARE

According to the NAHC, in December 1987 10,848 home health agencies, accounting for expenditures of $5.8 billion, were identified to exist in the United States (Foundation for Hospice and Home Care, 1988). Of these 53% were Medicare certified, accounting for expenditures of $2.7 billion. Nationally there is a great deal of variation in the distribution of home care agencies, which ranges from a low of 27 in Alaska, Maine, and Vermont to highs of 821 in New York, 806 in Texas, and 730 in California. The proportion of Medicare-certified agencies also varies widely by state from a low of 21% of all home care agencies in New York to a high of 96% in Tennessee. The smallest number of

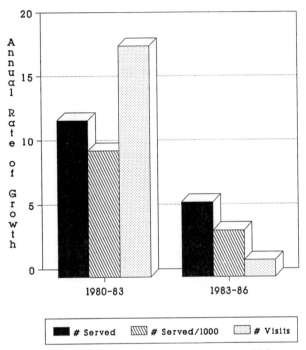

Figure 2.1. Growth in Medicare Home Care Pre- and Post-PPS

certified home care agencies is 8, in Alaska, compared with 356 in California and 454 in Texas.

Growth over time. The number of home health care agencies that participate in Medicare has grown steadily since the passage of the Medicare legislation in 1966. Growth was especially rapid from 1981 to 1986 but appears to have stabilized in recent years (see Figure 2.1) as a result of more stringent interpretation of regulations by fiscal intermediaries.

Medicare home care agencies provide skilled nursing care or physical, speech, or occupational therapy. Home health aide personal care and household assistance are provided if the patient is also receiving skilled treatment. The aide service is thus viewed as an adjunct to that skilled care. Need for skilled care must be certified by a physician, who over time recertifies continued need for home skilled nursing care and physical, speech, or occupational therapy. Claims for payment are reviewed by designated fiscal intermediaries in eight regions of the country. The intermediaries allow payment for care until a beneficiary has reached his or her "maximum feasible rehabilitation potential." At that point claims are disallowed and patients are given the option of paying for care privately, or they may be referred for supportive maintenance care to a low-tech home care program. The status of patients at discharge from Medicare home care is largely unknown and is a topic that requires further study.

Until 1981 Medicare home care services were only reimbursed by Part A of Medicare if they were prescribed following acute care hospitalization. The Omnibus Reconciliation Act of 1980 (ORA) removed that requirement, effective July 1, 1981, as well as the 100-visit limit. ORA also allowed proprietary home care agencies in states without licensure laws to participate in the Medicare program for the first time (Hughes, 1986). A corresponding jump in the number of agencies can be seen beginning in 1981-1983, preceding prospective payment (PPS), which was not implemented until 1983.

The impact of PPS and ensuing concerns about "quicker and sicker" discharges of Medicare patients have been the subject of some controversy. Analyses of this issue conclude that the growth in home care agencies largely predates PPS and reflects the expansion of home care regulations under the 1980 ORA (Ruther & Helbing, 1988). Analyses of patients admitted to Medicare home health care agencies by Guterman, Eggers, Riley, Greene, and Terrell (1988) have shown that the impact of PPS on case mix severity was mixed. Specifically the proportion of patients discharged to home health agencies with the two highest levels of severity, according to Medisgroup measures, dropped by 5% from 1982 to 1985. The proportion of discharges with the highest levels of disability also decreased by 5.1% and 0.5%, respectively (Guterman et al., 1988). Finally it may be possible that PPS had more of an impact on nursing home use than home health care insofar as Guterman et al. point out that PPS increased the percentage of patients receiving HHA visits within 7 days of discharge by 14% but increased SNF admissions as a percentage of hospital discharges by 65%.

Substituting for institutional care. It seems probable that both home health care and skilled nursing home care have substituted for more costly short-stay hospital care during the period following PPS. Specifically, patients discharged from hospitals with large length of stay reductions in 1982-1984 increased their use of SNF care from 1981 to 1985 by 83%, compared with 58% for patients discharged from hospitals with small length of stay reductions. Similar figures for home health agencies were 102% and 148%, indicating that increased home care referrals achieved reduction in both long- and short-term hospital stays of the elderly.

Examination of use rates by census region indicates that home care may also be substituting for nursing home care in some areas. Medicare enrollees per home health care nurse have been noted to vary from a low of 529 in New England to a high of 917 in the east north central region (Guterman et al., 1988). It seems more than coincidental that skilled nursing home use was also lowest in the northeast region (9 SNF admissions per 1,000 enrollees) and highest in the north central region (14 SNF admissions per 1,000 enrollees; Gornick & Hall, 1988).

However, national data also suggest that SNF and HHA users differ in terms of diagnosis. Specifically, in 1984-1985 three DRGs (number 14, stroke; 210, hip and femur procedures; and 209, major joint and limb reattachment procedures) accounted for nearly 40% of total covered SNF charges (Neu & Harrison, 1988). Stroke and major joint and limb reattachment were also the first and third DRG categories for home health agencies (HHAs). However, these two conditions accounted for only 11% of HHA charges with the second ranked DRG, number 127, heart failure and shock, accounting for an additional 5.8% of total covered HHA charges.

It is also important to remember that the rate of Medicare enrollees who use SNF care is very small at a steady 10-11 per 1,000 enrollees during 1981 to 1985, compared with a rate of 35-50 per 1,000 enrollees using home care over the same period (Gornick & Hall, 1988). The fact that a much larger pool of enrollees uses home care may help explain why home care users are more heterogeneous in terms of diagnoses. Also, as Guterman et al. (1988) point out, because SNF and HHA services are positively correlated at the state level, there does not seem to be much substitutability of one type of care for the other across states. Rather it could be that individuals with similar diagnoses are differentially referred for SNF or HHA care on the basis of a combination of severity of illness within a DRG category and the presence of particular sets of comorbidities and/or as a result of inadequate informal supports.

Because Medicare agencies are publicly certified and reimbursed, more is known about these agencies and their staffing, services, and clientele than about any other segment of the home care industry. We know, for example, that Medicare home health care providers have changed considerably over time. In 1969 visiting nurse and public health home care agencies dominated the industry, accounting for 89% of all providers (Hughes, 1986). By 1987 their combined share dropped to 28%, with hospital-based agencies accounting for 25% and proprietary agencies accounting for 32%, respectively, of all certified agencies (Foundation for Home and Hospice Care, 1988).

Just as the composition of providers by type has changed, so too has the composition of service visits. Initially, skilled nursing visits constituted the great majority of home care visits. During the 12-year period of 1974 to 1986, however, skilled nursing visits declined from more than two thirds of all visits to slightly more than half (50.6), with a concomitant increase in the proportion of home health aide and physical therapy visits.

Currently the core Medicare home care services are (a) skilled nursing, provided directly by 100% of agencies; (b) home health aides, provided directly by 97% of agencies; (c) physical therapy, provided directly by 89% of agencies; and (d) speech therapy, medical social services, and occupational therapy, which also are provided directly by more than half of all certified agencies.

Correlates of use. Analyses indicate that use of Medicare skilled home care increases sharply by age and sex, with persons over age 75 constituting 63% of all aged beneficiary users, visits, and reimbursements. Although the rate of persons served per 1,000 enrollees was 26 for persons 65-66 years of age in 1986, it increased to 97 per 1,000 for those 85 years or over—an increase of 273%. Similarly, number of visits per 1,000 enrollees increased from 578 for persons 65-66 years old to 2,352 for persons 85 years and older—an increase of 307%. In contrast, visits and reimbursements per person increased only slightly with age (Ruther & Helbing, 1988).

Branch and colleagues confirmed these findings in a prospective study of incident use of home care by a cohort of 3,706 elderly in East Boston during 1982 to 1985. For both men and women incidence use rates among those 85 and older were 12 times the rates of those aged 65 to 74. Multivariate predictors of use included receiving help with at least one activity of daily living, dependency in Rosow-Breslau functional health areas, homebound status, increased mental status errors, and no involvement in social groups (Branch et al., 1988).

It is interesting that older users do not appear to use more visits than younger users; however, their overall incidence of home care use is substantially higher. Female aged beneficiaries account for 56% of users and 69% of reimbursements, probably reflecting their higher prevalence in older, higher-incidence age categories (Ruther & Helbing, 1988).

Unfortunately, little is known about the functional status of Medicare home care users at entry to care. Similarly, little is known about their social supports. Therefore, we currently do not know how many of the 1.5 million elderly Americans with two or more ADL impairments are currently receiving medicare home care.

As indicated earlier, diagnosis alone is a poor predictor of Medicare home health care use. Specifically, the 10 leading principal diagnoses for persons using HHA services accounted for only 25% of all users and 26% of total charges and reimbursements. The most frequent circulatory system principal diagnoses were acute, ill-defined cerebrovascular disease (5.7%), followed by congestive heart failure (4.8%) and acute myocardial infarction—unspecified site. Current studies that may shed some light on these issues include the Longitudinal Study on Aging, which will link demographic and functional status data with Medicare use data, and the Kane postacute care study. Although the postacute care study will provide valuable data on Medicare and non-Medicare home care use for postacute patients, it will not provide data on home care use by nonhospitalized elderly. Thus important gaps will continue to exist in our knowledge of the case mix of clients served by Medicare home care, including their functional status and unmet service needs at both entry to and discharge from care.

LOW-TECH HOME CARE

Characteristics of providers. In comparison to the relative wealth of statistics currently available on Medicare-reimbursed home care, very little is known about low-tech home care, which is sometimes also described as long-term home care or maintenance or custodial home care. As the name implies these agencies provide paraprofessional homemaker and chore/housekeeping services to persons of all ages.

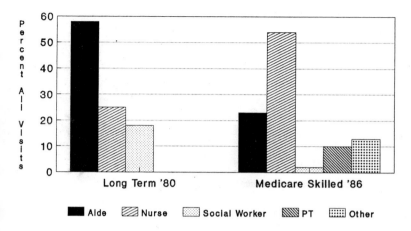

Figure 2.2. Home Health Agency Visits by Type: Long-Term Versus Medicare Home Health Care

These services may be the only formal services provided to a given client, or they may be provided in combination with high-tech, hospice, or Medicare skilled home care. As Figure 2.2 demonstrates, the mix of services provided by long-term or low-tech home care differs markedly from that provided by skilled care programs. Specifically, skilled nursing visits predominate in skilled home care programs, whereas home health aide/homemaker services predominate in at least one low-tech home care program studied in Chicago (Hughes, 1986).

As previous data indicated, 45% of home care agencies identified by the NAHC as existing in 1989 do not participate in the Medicare program. These agencies may form the lower bound estimate of low-tech agencies, which some have estimated to be as many as 30,000 to 45,000 in number.

The majority of low-tech providers are believed to be proprietary, which in many cases means publicly held multiunit proprietary chains (Kane, 1989). Low-tech services are reimbursed by a variety of sources including Medicaid 2176 waivers, state block grants, Older Americans Act Title III funds, state and local revenues, and private out-of-pocket payment. Although Medicaid funding for community care has increased substantially over the past decade, Title XX and Administration on Aging (AoA) funds have remained constant (Hughes, 1989).

In cases where states pool funding streams to finance expanded community-based long-term care, clients must meet certain criteria for care. For example, in Illinois, State Community Care clients must receive a certain score on a determination of need assessment instrument designed to target services to those at greatest risk of nursing home admission. The score in this case represents a combination of functional impairments, availability of informal help, and residual unmet needs for maintenance care.

Correlates of use. Just as little is known about low-tech providers, little is known across states about users. Currently it is estimated nationally that, of the nearly 3 million persons aged 85 and older, 32% need some type of personal care assistance (Scanlon & Feder, 1984). It is estimated that 5% to 10% of these individuals must rely totally on paid formal care and that an additional 16% to 25% require formal care to supplement services provided by informal caregivers (Scanlon & Feder, 1984). According to the U.S. General Accounting Office (GAO), 46% of Medicare home care users must purchase additional services beyond those that Medicare and informal caregivers provide (U.S. GAO, 1987). As Liu, Manton, and Liu and Soldo have confirmed, the great majority of care that is purchased out of pocket is unskilled (Liu et al., 1985; Soldo, 1985).

Recent data are available regarding the demographic characteristics of 29,000 elderly clients served by the Illinois State Community Care Program in September 1988. These data indicate that use increases with age (61% of users are aged 75 or above), sex (81% are female), and marital status (84% are single; U.S. GAO, 1989). If we assume that the greatest demand for low-tech home care exists among the very old, impaired elderly, the outlook for these needs being met in the future may be cloudy. First, Kane's analysis of the profitability of seven of the country's largest low-tech home care chains indicates that five of the seven operated at a loss during 1984 to 1986 (Kane, 1989). Reasons for this include the lower economic status of the average client, described as a disabled 77-year-old woman who had previously been hospitalized, and the fact that 53% of persons over age 75 have cash and income benefits equal to only twice the poverty level. As a result many are ill-equipped to afford the average $164 per month paid for low-tech care in 1982 (U.S. GAO, 1986).

State programs that pool Medicaid and other funding streams often establish cost-based hourly rates for care, cap overhead allowable costs, and take 50 to 150 days to process claims. Much of the effort to curb overhead is thought ultimately to result in shorter service hours for homemakers and fewer benefits. As a result of the limited resources currently being devoted to low-tech home care, the field is generally believed to be unattractive for entry by either providers or unskilled workers, many of whom can earn higher pay and benefits in other service industries such as fast-food chains.

As a result the field currently is believed to be characterized by high worker turnover, low morale, and questionable quality of care. Currently only 200 of existing providers voluntarily participate in quality assurance programs offered by the Homecaring Council of the Foundation for Hospice and Home Care and/or by the National League for Nursing (Hughes, 1989). The AoA recently awarded grants to 10 states in an effort to promote state-level quality assurance for low-tech home care. Findings from these efforts will be available in 1990 and 1991 and may shed some light on this important sector of the home care industry.

AN INTEGRATED HOME CARE SYSTEM: DIRECTIONS FOR CHANGE

As this overview of the home care industry demonstrates, home care today encompasses a complex array of providers, services, and users. Appreciation of this complexity is necessary if we are to develop policies that encourage the development of an adequate supply of home care services and a financing and delivery system that encourages appropriate access to and use of home care services. Ideally an integrated home care system in the future will be accessible—with access based on need for care—and will be affordable, efficient, and effective. Care will also be appropriate, of high quality, and responsive, to the extent possible, to consumer preferences.

The achievement of these goals depends upon our ability to learn from past research on home care and to shape an appropriate, highly targeted research agenda that can answer these questions within a relatively short time frame—ideally the next 5 to 10 years. It is important that the question at hand at this point is not whether home care should be part of the long-term care picture; rather the question concerns what mix of services should be provided to whom, within what funding and reimbursement system, and using what type of delivery system?

ACCESS

Scanlon has estimated that 7 million elderly, or 24% of the total elderly population, need some long-term care assistance. Only 22% of this population reside in institutions. The remaining 78% live in the community with a spouse, with others, or alone (Scanlon, 1988). We need to understand what portion of this population is already receiving care and then enable the remainder to access appropriate types and levels of community care. We also must recognize the fact that impairment levels and consequent service needs are subject to change over time. Longitudinal studies now in the field, such as the Longitudinal Survey on Aging (NCHS) and the EPESE (NIA) studies, should provide more information about transitions in functional status for different elderly subgroups. Awareness of these transitions should help us, as a society, to develop a service system that will facilitate transitions across service levels as an individual's needs increase or decrease. Our understanding of these issues would be greatly enhanced by better data on the case-mix characteristics of elderly persons currently receiving different types of home care as well as by some sense of who the under- or unserved are and what barriers prevent their access to care.

EFFECTIVENESS

Previous research on home care effectiveness has focused on the impact of home care on institutional use and quality of life. Community care in most of these studies was ill-defined at best and could encompass any of the four home care models described in this chapter as well as additional community care services, such as adult day care. Figure 2.3 illustrates theoretical models of home care use. As the figure demonstrates, different populations can be expected to use different home care models, with different care outcomes being likely. The heterogeneity of services, users, and plausible outcomes is crucial to understand and illustrates the urgent need for theoretical underpinnings in future research on home care (Hughes, 1985).

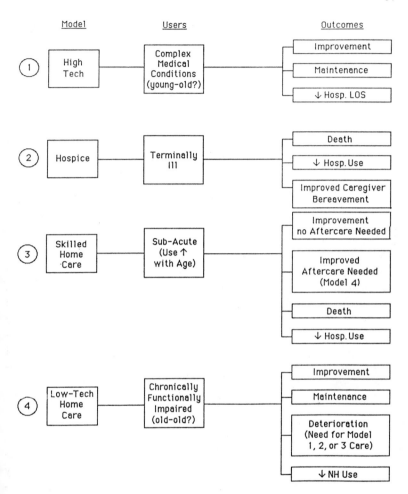

Figure 2.3. Theoretical Models of Home Care Use

In the past we have focused heavily on the substitutability of home care services for hospital and nursing home care. The results with respect to nursing home care are mainly disappointing (Kemper, Applebaum, & Harrigan, 1988; Weissert, Cready, & Pawelak, 1988). However, largely as a result of these studies, we now have a much more realistic understanding of predictors of nursing home use. Continued examination of this particular line of inquiry may not be warranted for two reasons. First, there does not seem to be much overlap in impaired elderly who are equally likely to use nursing home or home care. Statistics indicate that nursing home use increases as a function of severity of impairment—with those impaired in all ADLs and IADLs being much more likely to receive nursing home care—and as a function of impoverishment in social support. Most elderly persons prefer to receive care at home and resist nursing home entrance as long as possible.

Furthermore, data on nursing homes indicate that many are already operating at capacity, with average occupancy levels of 91% in 1985. Other evidence on the impact of PPS, presented earlier in this chapter, suggests that the case mix of the nursing home population is becoming more severely impaired over time. As a result there may be very little, if any, fat in the nursing home sector, and a more appropriate research question may be this: What is happening to persons with lower impairment levels who used to be able to access sheltered and intermediate nursing home care? Examination of low-tech home care users, and of the unmet needs for care of Medicare home care users at discharge, could shed light on this important issue.

Similarly, given statistics presented earlier on post-PPS hospital length of stay reductions attributable to increased nursing home and home care referrals, the ability of Medicare skilled home care, hospice, and high-tech home care to further reduce hospital stays seems limited. Absent major new technological advances to enable safe treatment for conditions that now require hospital care, it appears that we have eliminated much, if not all, of the inefficiency of hospital care from the system.

In any case, if home care is to substitute for nursing home or hospital care, it stands to reason that home care providers must be in a position to exercise gatekeeping authority over these other forms of care. For example, we recently completed a randomized trial of a VA hospital-based home care (HBHC) program that targeted services to severely disabled (two or more ADL impairments) or terminally ill veterans. This VA home care model is directed by a physician who has the capacity to case-manage care inside and outside of the hospital, including optional use of a hospital step-down unit (Hughes et al., 1990). Figure 2.4 demonstrates that HBHC services were far more comprehensive than those provided under the existing Medicare model to patients in the control group. Although more comprehensive, services were also

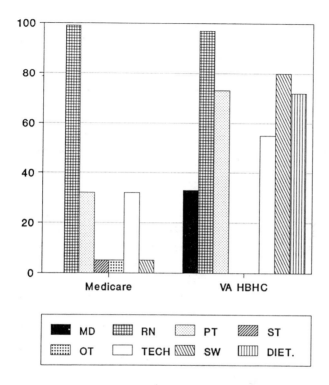

Figure 2.4. Percentages of Patients Using Home Care Services: Medicare Versus VA HBHC

less intensive and were provided over a more continuous time period. HBHC services ultimately provided a 13% net cost savings—largely due to significantly lower hospital costs—as well as significantly higher patient and caregiver satisfaction with care (Cummings et al., 1990).

This leaves the impact of care on patient and caregiver outcomes as suitable topics for continued research. However, it is important to understand what home care can reasonably be expected to achieve in these areas. First, we need a clearer understanding of who home care users are, including standardized age, functional status, diagnosis, social supports, and unmet need data across the spectrum of home care models. Second, given a clear understanding of the characteristics and service needs of users, we need to posit reasonable outcomes that reflect case mix and service intensity. One outcome that seems unsuitable for continued examination is life satisfaction, which is far too global and distal an outcome to be appropriate. Similarly the inclusion of ADL improvement as an outcome is only appropriate in those specific instances in which a prognosis indicates that improvement is plausible *and* substantial amounts of physical therapy or occupational therapy are provided. In contrast, we urgently need to develop valid indicators of satisfaction with care.

To date, satisfaction with care has been viewed as a "soft" outcome by many. In acute care research, however, this same outcome is highly regarded as a desirable indicator of quality of care. The fact that the home care literature repeatedly demonstrates high satisfaction levels for clients and caregivers (even when 60% of comparison groups are also receiving some type of home care) suggests that something more systematic than a Hawthorne effect is operating and deserves closer scrutiny.

Finally, another area that also needs attention is the development of quantifiable intermediate treatment goals and plans for home care users that would enable the more proximal measurement of outcomes. Such plans and goals might include the determination that previously unmet needs are now being met appropriately and well, for example, special diets are being maintained and the client is clean, well-fed, and well-nourished and functioning in a reasonably clean and safe environment of his or her choosing.

AFFORDABILITY

Data on various types of users and their probable use patterns over time are needed to provide reliable estimates of cost. Similarly, demonstrations entailing different levels of cost sharing by users would be useful. Preliminary findings from the GAO indicate that users of Title III and Medicaid 2176 community care services in three states are already copaying for services without adverse effects (U.S. GAO, 1989). However, more systematic research on this topic is needed.

QUALITY

Quality of home care services currently is receiving a fair amount of attention. As a result of OBRA 1987, HCFA has funded two large-scale studies by Shaughnessy and Kane, respectively, regarding the quality of Medicare skilled home care.

The AoA has also funded studies on improved quality assurance for low-tech home care services in 10 states. This research on quality assurance is badly needed and should provide valuable information. A hallmark of some of these studies is a new concern for the value of consumer and provider input in defining quality care and helping to measure it. For example, our current research with the Illinois Department on Aging (one of the ten AoA quality of care studies) has included 20 focus groups with clients, informal caregivers, workers, supervisors, and administrators of low-tech in-home services in urban/suburban and rural areas of Illinois to identify the key attributes of high-quality care and measures that can be used to assure it. This effort and many others currently ongoing are attempts to introduce reasonable process and outcome measures into the assessment of the quality of low-tech services.

Our overall understanding of quality is limited, however, by the fragmentation of the home care industry. Because many high- and low-tech providers are unlicensed, no information currently exists about their clients or services. While one hesitates to recommend licensure for low-tech providers, this step may be needed if we are to have any meaningful way in the future to assess the adequacy of our home care supply and the quality of care provided.

Continuity of Care/Need for Better Delivery Systems

As this review demonstrates, older persons in the United States who are disabled have difficulty accessing appropriate care across multiple levels and types of home care providers. Our current "system" is not user friendly, often by design, as a result of fears about runaway costs if services were more readily available. It appears that we now have the tools needed to target services to those most in need. Uniform need assessments coupled with sliding scale copayments based on income and service intensity could be used in demonstrations to link different types of home care services and promote transitions across levels of care as needed. These demonstrations could use Medicare/Medicaid waivers to encourage home care providers to become full-service, one-stop providers to the extent possible. This shift in *promoting* access to care would represent an absolute turnaround in our current community care policy—one that many believe is badly needed. The effects of this policy shift could be tested in various communities under controlled conditions with the outcomes being cost, appropriateness, comprehensiveness (degree to which needs are met), and quality of care, including client and caregiver satisfaction and caregiver burden. Both brokered and consolidated case management models could be tested, with both types of providers placed at risk through "capped" capitation rates. Alternatively, or simultaneously, we could also test the attractiveness and effectiveness of vouchers that would enable elderly persons and their families to be their own case managers, a scenario that is likely to evolve if benefits for community care increase under private long-term care insurance policies. Both research topics would address the question of who is in charge of community care—a question currently begging for an answer.

Conclusion

We have come a long way in our understanding of the complexity of home care users, services, costs, and outcomes. We have the technology to progress much further—if we are willing to devote incremental resources to this important issue. In these terms the top priorities for future research include the following:

- a systematic inventory of users, providers, provider characteristics, service use patterns, and outcomes across the four types of home care providers (e.g., survey research);
- the development of theoretical models of home care that posit appropriate populations, processes, and outcomes of care, and;
- the development and testing of different service models that integrate care options at reasonable cost and quality.

Better data in these three areas are essential if we, as a society, are to provide the high-quality home care that older Americans will need and want in the twenty-first century.

References

Branch, L. G., Wetle, T. T., Scherr, P. A., Cook, N. B., Evans, D. A., Hebert, L. E., Nasland, E. N., Keough, N. E., & Taylor, J. O. (1988). A prospective study of incident comprehensive medical home care use among the elderly. *American Journal of Public Health, 78,* 255-259.

Cummings, J., Hughes, S. L., Weaver, F., Manheim, L., Conrad, K., Nash, K., Braun, B., & Adelman, J. (1990). Cost-effectiveness of V.A. hospital-based home care: A randomized clinical trial. *Archives of Internal Medicine, 150,* 1274-1280.

Donlan, T. (1983, March 21). No place like home. *Barron's,* pp. 6-32.

Foundation for Home and Hospice Care. (1988). *Basic home care statistics: The industry.* Washington, DC: Author.

Gornick, M., & Hall, M. J. (1988). Trend in Medicare use of post-hospital care. *Health Care Financing Review* (Annual Suppl.), pp. 27-38.

Guterman, S., Eggers, P. W., Riley, G., Greene, T. F., & Terrell, S. A. (1988). Special report: The first 3 years of Medicare prospective payment—an overview. *Health Care Financing Review, 9*(1), 67-77.

Hing, E. (1987). *Use of nursing homes by the elderly: Preliminary data from the 1985 National Nursing Home Survey* (Advance Data from Vital and Health Statistics, No. 135, DHHS Pub. No. [PHS] 87-1250, National Center for Health Statistics). Hyattsville, MD: Public Health Service.

Hughes, S. L. (1985). Apples and oranges? A review of evaluations of community-based long-term care. *Health Services Research, 20,* 461-488.

Hughes, S. L. (1986). *Long term care: Options in an expanding market.* Rockville, MD: Aspen.

Hughes, S. L. (1989). Home and community care of the elderly: System resources and constraints. In J. A. Barondess, D. E. Rogers, & K. N. Lohr (Eds.), *Care of the elderly patient: Policy issues and research opportunities* (pp. 55-61). Washington, DC: Institute of Medicine, National Academy Press.

Hughes, S. L., Cummings, J., Weaver, F., Manheim, L., Conrad, K., & Nash, K. (1990). Randomized trial of VA home care for severely disabled veterans. *Medical Care, 28*(2), 135-145.

Kane, M. (1989). The home care crisis of the nineties. *The Gerontologist, 22,* 24-31.

Kemper, P. R., Applebaum, R., & Harrigan, M. (1988). Community care demonstrations: What have we learned? *Health Care Financing Review, 8,* 87-100.

Liu, K., Manton, K., & Liu, B. M. (1985). Home care expenses for the disabled elderly. *Health Care Financing Review, 7,* 51-58.

Neu, C. R., & Harrison, S. (1988). *Hospital care before and after the Medicare prospective payment system* (Cooperative Agreement No. R-3590-HCFA). Santa Monica, CA: Rand Corporation.

Ruther, M., & Helbing, C. (1988). Health care financing trends: Use and cost of home health agency services under Medicare. *Health Care Financing Review, 10,* 105-108.

Scanlon, W. J. (1988). A perspective on long term care for the elderly. *Health Care Financing Review* (Annual Suppl.), pp. 7-15.

Scanlon, W. J., & Feder, J. (1984). The long term care market place: An overview. *Healthcare Financial Management, 14,* 18-36.

Selz, M. (1990). Home health-care companies learn painful lesson. *The Wall Street Journal,* p. B2.

Soldo, B. J. (1985). In-home services for the dependent elderly. *Research on Aging, 7,* 281-304.

U.S. General Accounting Office. (1986). *Medicare: Need to strengthen home health care payment controls and address unmet needs* (Report to the chairman, Special Committee on Aging, U.S. Senate; GAO/HRD-87-9). Washington, DC: Author.

U.S. General Accounting Office. (1987). *Medicare: Need to strengthen home health payment controls and address unmet needs* (Report to the chairman, Special Committee on Aging, U.S. Senate, GAO/HRD-87). Washington, DC: Author.

U.S. General Accounting Office. (1989). *In home services for the elderly: Cost sharing expands range of services provided and population served* (Report to the Subcommittee on Labor and Human Relations, U.S. Senate; GAO/HRD-90-19). Washington, DC: Author.

Weissert, W. G., Cready, C. M., & Pawelak, J. (1988). The past and future of home- and community-based long-term care. *The Milbank Quarterly, 66,* 309-389.

THREE

Examining Respite:
Its Promise and Limits

RHONDA J. V. MONTGOMERY

Respite care refers to a wide range of services intended to give temporary relief to families caring for disabled members. This concept of care
developed in the United States as a corollary of the early 1970s
deinstitutionalization movement for developmentally disabled children
and adults. As families assumed the primary responsibility for the developmentally disabled, the need for temporary relief from their caregiving responsibilities created a demand for respite services. The
recognition of the parallel need for relief of family members caring for
frail and disabled elderly in the United States has been very recent, and
formal respite services are not widely available.

Still, respite services continue to be among the most widely advo-
cated forms of support for families assisting impaired elders in their
homes. Both practitioners and researchers have suggested that respite
care can relieve the burden of the caregiving situation and perhaps even
allow families to continue care for elders who would otherwise have
been placed in a nursing home (Brody, 1985; Doty, 1986; Pratt,
Schmall, Wright, & Cleland, 1985; Scharlach & Frenzel, 1986;
Zarit, Todd, & Zarit, 1986). Despite this belief in the benefits of

AUTHOR'S NOTE: Portions of the introduction and background descriptions included
in this chapter are taken directly from three previous publications of the author (Montgomery, 1986, 1988a, & 1988b).

respite, information about respite, particularly the impact of these services on families, is limited, widely scattered, and often difficult to obtain.

Defining Respite

One barrier to increased knowledge of respite and its impact is the lack of a concise definition and uniformity in the services. While there is general consensus that *respite* means "an interval of temporary relief," there is almost no agreement as to the composition of the services that are to provide this relief.

The ambiguity of the concept makes the inclusion of a clear definition essential for any specific discussion or evaluation of respite. While it is unlikely that respite services will ever be uniformly defined, the essential element of any service that is designated as respite is the folowing purpose: *to provide a rest for caregivers.* Beyond this commonality there are many variations.

Respite Models

The three dimensions of *time, place,* and *level of care or tasks* can be used to develop a typology of respite models (Montgomery, 1988a). The most basic dimension is the location or setting in which services are provided (Cohen & Warren, 1985). Three general types of models can be distinguished by the setting. Services can be provided in a client's home (in-home services), in a group or institutional setting (out-of-home services), or in multiple settings (combination program). Out-of-home services include foster homes, adult day-care centers, respite facilities, nursing homes, and hospitals.

Within the three general models there are a number of possible variations depending upon the level of care and the duration and frequency of respite episodes, and programs may vary along a continuum from low to high levels of care. Respite episodes may be for short periods of a few hours to long stays of up to six weeks. Clients may be able to use services as frequently as once or twice a week or as infrequently as once or twice a year.

Institutional Models

The earliest respite programs for the elderly population were established in hospitals in Great Britain (Delargy & Belf, 1957; Packwood, 1980). This institutional model has been replicated in the United States and Canada in acute hospitals, nursing homes, and specialized facilities (Crossman, London, & Barry, 1981; Dunn, MacBeath, & Robertson, 1983; Ellis & Wilson, 1983; Hasselkus & Brown, 1983; Huey, 1983; MacCourt & Southam, 1983; McFarland, Howells, & Dill, 1985). Institutional respite usually takes the form of holiday admissions or intermittent readmissions. Holiday admissions allow the caregiver to vacation while the elder is placed in the institution for a one- or two-week period. Some programs limit respite care to a single two-week admission, while others allow repeated admissions. Intermittent readmissions or floating-bed programs provide for scheduled repeated admissions. Intermittent readmission programs may be for short periods of two or three nights repeated as frequently as every two to three weeks or for longer periods of one or two weeks repeated less frequently. Both nursing homes and hospitals can offer personal care, skilled nursing care, and intermediate care. Some programs are limited in the level of care that can be provided, however (New York State Department of Social Services [NYSDSS], 1985).

OUT-OF-HOME COMMUNITY CARE

Out-of-home respite can also be provided in adult day-care centers, in adult foster homes, and through family cooperatives (Montgomery, 1984; Stone, 1985; Washington State Department of Health and Human Services [WSDSHS], 1986). Usually respite care is offered in adult day-care centers on a regularly scheduled basis providing about five to six hours of care for each visit (Sands & Suzuki, 1983). Adult day-care centers are best able to serve clients who need minimal assistance and often will not enroll clients who are incontinent or who wander (Danaher, Dixon-Bemis, & Pedersen, 1986). Although respite in the form of foster care and family cooperatives is frequently discussed in the literature concerned with the developmentally disabled, these models of respite appear to be less available and less widely used for frail elderly (Hildebrandt, 1983).

IN-HOME CARE

In-home respite care can be provided by a sitter/companion, home-maker, home health aide, or nurse (Isett, Krauss, & Malone, 1984; McFarland, Howells, & Dill, 1985; Wisconsin Department of Health and Social Services [WDHSS], 1982). Some programs provide all of these levels of service while others offer only companion or sitter services. When volunteer respite workers are used, services are usually confined to the companion level of care (Lidoff, 1983; Montgomery & Borgatta, 1985). The duration of respite varies among in-home programs. Some programs limit their services to short periods of 2 to 4 hours while others only provide in-home respite for periods of 24 hours or greater (Nyilis, 1985). Overnight respite for extended periods of several days or a week is far less common. While most programs provide planned respite care that requires advanced scheduling, some programs do offer emergency respite care.

COMPREHENSIVE CARE MODELS

Comprehensive respite programs consist of combinations of the different respite models. Such programs offer multiple levels of care in multiple settings for a variety of time periods. These combined programs are often able to meet the needs of a wide range of clients (Connecticut Department of Health Services [CDHS], 1985; Dixon-Bemis, 1986; WDHSS, 1981; WSDSHS, 1986).

COMPARISONS ACROSS MODELS OF CARE

Despite the numerous documents describing different models of respite, little information is available about the relative merits and problems associated with the different models. No completed study was located that formally evaluated different models. A number of observations and comments have been included in program descriptions. Out-of-home respite care is seen as having the advantage of allowing caregivers to remain in their homes and enjoy privacy and time alone with other family members, which are so often craved (Crossman et al., 1981). The care receiver in turn has the opportunity to meet new people and to be stimulated by new activities. This is an advantage emphasized by respite programs operating in adult day-care centers (Danaher et al., 1986; Ellis, 1986; Sands & Suzuki, 1983). Advocates of out-of-home care also note the benefit of the health screening process that accompanies placement in an institution or in adult day care. (Ellis, 1986). Staff members can make suggestions for improved care and changes in medical routines.

Institutional respite tends to be less flexible than in-home care. Most programs offering institutional respite find it extremely difficult to offer emergency respite due to the cost of setting aside a bed for emergency cases (Foundation for Long Term Care [FLTC], 1983; Scharlach & Frenzel, 1986). Placement in an institution for short periods can also be very disruptive for some patients who suffer from dementia or confusion. Some institutions are not able to care for very confused clients who are inclined to wander (Ellis, 1986). Even clients who are not prone to confusion need time to become oriented to the new environment (FLTC, 1983). Sometimes elders are resistant to institutional respite, fearing that respite is the first step toward permanent placement. There is some indication in the literature that this is not an unrealistic fear (FLTC, 1983; Scharlach & Frenzel, 1986). Although the daily cost of institutional care is usually less than that of in-home services for the same amount of time, the overall costs are higher because stays are usually much longer (Montgomery, 1988b). Clients who are minimally impaired sometimes find placement in an institution too confining (Packwood, 1980). In contrast, Huey (1983) notes that staff frequently complain that respite clients tend to be demanding and want room and maid services. Respite care in a nursing home setting may be preferable to a hospital because the nursing home is often able to provide an environment that is less medical in focus and closer to a home environment (Packwood, 1980).

PREFERENCES

The most frequently requested and used service is in-home respite care provided for short periods, usually by a home health aide (CDHS, 1985; Montgomery & Borgatta, 1987; NYSDSS, 1985; WSDSHS, 1986). Two programs that initially offered respite for a minimum period of 24 hours reported changing their policies to offer respite for shorter periods (CDHS, 1985; WSDSHS, 1986). Programs that offered both in-home and out-of-home services have discovered that in-home services were most often preferred (CDHS, 1985; WSDSHS, 1986). Families tend to find such services most convenient and relatively economical when respite is offered for short periods. The one program that reported a preference for institutional services also indicated that these services were covered by Medicare while the in-home respite services were not (Nyilis, 1985). In-home programs also have the advantage that caregivers do not have to arrange for transportation, and the routine of the elder is not disturbed. When an in-home program offers multiple levels of service, this model can be very flexible. Programs that are limited to companion-level care are, however, unable to serve a large proportion of the target population (Montgomery & Hatch, 1987; NYSDSS, 1985). There is also an indication that some families are uncomfortable with strangers coming into their homes (Danaher et al., 1986; Hildebrandt, 1983).

Delivery of Respite Care

In addition to the dimensions of setting, level of care, and time that have been used to delimit a typology of respite services, other critical characteristics vary among programs and should be considered in the development and study of respite. These characteristics include financing, eligibility criteria, and staffing.

FINANCING

Respite care has been financed through a broad range of public and private mechanisms (Stone, 1985). In Britain and other countries respite care has been fully funded as a part of the national health care system. In the United States respite care has been unevenly funded and, for the most part, offered as a pilot or demonstration program or as part of another ongoing program. The funds for these services have come from Medicare waivers, Medicaid waivers, state funds, private agencies, and fees. Most recently respite benefits were introduced as a benefit of the now repealed Catastrophic Health Care Bill, albeit with very restrictive eligibility criteria. To date there has been as little consistency in the financing of respite as there has been in the services offered.

ELIGIBILITY

Often the eligibility criteria of respite programs are dictated by the financing mechanism. When respite is offered on a fee-for-service basis, few criteria have been established. When services have been offered through publicly funded programs, eligibility is often restricted to low-income persons and/or persons vulnerable to nursing home placement (Meltzer, 1982; Stone, 1985). As in the case of financing, no clear patterns of eligibility have emerged.

STAFFING

The staffing of programs is also related to financing mechanisms and eligibility criteria. When programs are restricted to elders with high levels of disability, the staff must have higher levels of skill. When funding sources are limited, an effort has been made to employ volunteers. As noted above, however, this practice can influence eligibility criteria because volunteer programs cannot offer skilled care. In short, while it is clear that the issues of financing, eligibility, and staffing are interrelated and critical, the literature provides little consistent information about these aspects of respite services.

Service Utilization: Client Profiles

DEMOGRAPHIC CHARACTERISTICS OF ELDERS

The variation in respite models and eligibility criteria and the small number of reports that include data on client characteristics make it difficult to discern a client profile for respite services. A few patterns emerge from the literature, however, that are of interest. First, the elders being served by respite programs are the old old. The average age of the care recipients is consistently reported to be around 80, with about 40% of client populations over the age of 85. Female clients tend to be older and male clients tend to be younger (Burdz & Bond, 1988; FLTC, 1983; Lawton, Brody, & Saperstein, 1989; Montgomery & Borgatta, 1985, 1989; NYSDSS, 1985; Robertson, Griffiths, & Cosin, 1977). Males are overrepresented in the client population in comparison with the sex distribution of this age group in the general population. While there is some variation among programs, about 60% of the clients are female and 40% are male (Burdz & Bond, 1988; CDHS, 1985; Dunn, MacBeath, & Robertson, 1983; FLTC, 1983; Packwood, 1980; WSDSHS, 1986). Most (85%-95%) of these elders live with their caregivers, who are either spouses or adult children (Lawton et al., 1988; Montgomery & Borgatta, 1989). Elders who live alone are more likely to be female and cared for by an adult child, usually a daughter (FLTC, 1983; Montgomery & Borgatta, 1985; Scharlach & Frenzel, 1986).

HEALTH AND FUNCTIONAL STATUS OF ELDERS

Patterns in health status are more difficult to identify due to the large variation in health measures that have been used in the different studies and due to targeting practices. Several investigators report that respite is most frequently used when the elder is mentally impaired or confused (CDHS, 1985; Dunn et al., 1983; WSDSHS, 1986). However, this may be a consequence of the fact that many programs are specifically targeted to persons with Alzheimer's disease or other related disorders. Montgomery and Borgatta (1989) found no differences in respite use associated with level of mental impairment or the presence of Alzheimer's disease. On the other hand Montgomery, Kosloski, and Borgatta (1989) did find that families caring for Alzheimer victims used more adult day-care and transportation services than did families caring for elders with other impairments. The client population also includes a large number of elders who have impaired mobility (Hasselkus & Brown, 1983; Robertson et al., 1977; WSDSHS, 1986). Most elders have multiple impairments that limit their ability to perform both instrumental and daily activities of living (CDHS, 1985; Howells, 1980; Montgomery & Borgatta, 1985; Robertson, 1977; WSDSHS, 1986).

Reports from programs that provided respite in nursing home settings indicated that almost 80% of their clients have functional impairments that would make them eligible for institutional placement. About 40% to 50% of the clients would be eligible for a skilled nursing care facility (Ellis, 1986; FLTC, 1983; Hasselkus & Brown, 1983; Howells, 1980; Nyilis, 1985). Programs that provided multiple levels of in-home services have indicated that the majority of care is provided through home health services with few requests for companion-level care or for LPN or RN services (CDHS, 1985; Montgomery & Borgatta, 1985; NYSDSS, 1985; WSDSHS, 1986). It should be noted that in-home services are usually limited to a few hours; therefore the need for nursing skills is probably more limited than is the case in institutional settings.

CAREGIVER CHARACTERISTICS

The average age of the family members providing care for elders is in the 55-58 range. Generally spouses providing care are in their early seventies and adult children are in their early fifties. The distribution between adult children and spouses varies considerably among programs. There is some indication, however, that children care for older but healthier persons while spouses care for more disabled but younger persons (Montgomery & Borgatta, 1985). Caregivers provide a full range of services to the elder with the majority receiving little assistance from formal service providers (CDHS, 1985; FLTC, 1983; Montgomery & Borgatta, 1985; NYSDSS, 1985).

Outcomes of Respite

SATISFACTION

The most pervasive finding in the literature regarding the impact of respite services is that caregivers like the service and are generally very satisfied with it. Reports of respite evaluation studies have been unanimous in their conclusion that caregivers had high levels of satisfaction with the program and found the programs to be valuable (Burdz & Bond, 1988; FLTC, 1983; Howells, 1980; Lawton et al., 1988; Montgomery & Borgatta, 1985, 1987; NYSDSS, 1985; Packwood, 1980; Scharlach & Frenzel, 1986; WDHSS, 1982). Although it is not unusual for families to be initially apprehensive, with few exceptions caregivers have felt that the respite programs in which they participated satisfactorily met their needs. Among the benefits identified by caregivers were relief from tasks, psychological support, stimulation for the elder, and health assessments of the dependent that led to changes in medical routines. Concerns of the caregivers or dissatisfaction with respite care tended to center on increased confusion and dependency of the elder and disruption of home routines, all of which were sometimes created by the respite service, especially in hospital settings (FLTC, 1983; Packwood, 1980; Robertson et al., 1977). Scharlach and Frenzel (1986) noted that some care recipients did not like the nursing home setting because they did not like being around persons more handicapped than themselves. Studies that queried caregivers about future use of respite indicated the majority would use respite again (Lawton et al., 1988; Montgomery & Borgatta, 1985, 1987; Packwood, 1980).

CAREGIVER BURDEN/WELL-BEING

While there are those who would argue that satisfaction and felt relief are sufficient criteria to support the need for respite (e.g., Lawton et al., 1988), others who are concerned with public policy argue that the benefits of respite must be demonstrated in more substantial ways (Callahan, 1989). Specifically there has been a general expectation that respite care will (or should) result in net savings to the public purse by reducing or delaying the use of more costly forms of care, especially institutional care. Therefore the impacts of most interest to public policymakers and researchers have been the impact of respite care on caregiver burden and/or well-being and the impact on nursing home placement. To date there have been only four controlled design studies completed that look at these critical variables, and this evidence regarding burden and well-being is uneven. Burdz and Brody (1988) assessed the impact of a two-week respite stay in a nursing home for 55 caregivers. Based on interviews conducted with caregivers three weeks after the stay, these researchers found that persons receiving respite care reported significantly fewer memory and behavior problems for the elders regardless of the diagnosis. They did not find significant differences between the treatment and comparison groups in the burden scores. Similarly Lawton and his colleagues (1988) reported no differences between the experimental and control groups in caregiver well-being in their study of 642 caregivers. In a study of volunteer respite care, Montgomery and Borgatta (1985) reported a reduction in objective burden for spouse caregivers. A more recent study (Montgomery & Borgatta, 1989), of 541 caregivers participating in a study of paid respite programs, did not replicate this finding but did reveal a significant difference between the control group and the treatment groups in subjective burden when the sample was restricted to those caregivers assisting elders who continued to reside in the community one year after services were initiated. However, this pattern was not repeated for the data collected 20 months after eligibility for respite services.

INSTITUTIONALIZATION

Findings related to nursing home placement have been even more limited than those related to caregiver burden or well-being. The study of volunteer respite by Montgomery and Borgatta (1985) reported no impact of the respite on nursing home placement. Lawton and his colleagues (1988) found no differences between the experimental and control groups on risk of death for the impaired elder or on risk of institutionalization. They did, however, report a 22-day difference between the two groups in the number of days spent in the community. This finding is difficult to interpret because movement from the community could be due to institutionalization or death. Finally, Montgomery and Borgatta (1987) found no differences between the control group and the treatment groups in nursing home placement. For the subsample of elders who did move to the nursing home, there was, however, a difference between the treatment and control groups in the number of days elders resided in the nursing home. The effect of the treatment differed by the relationship of the caregiver to the elder. In the group of elders cared for by adult children, there appeared to be a delay in nursing home placement. In contrast, among the elders cared for by a spouse, the number of days the elder spent in a nursing home was greater for the treatment group than for the control group (Montgomery, 1988b). Hence the evidence to date is best summarized by Lawton and his colleagues (1988, p. 15), who state that "the conclusion that ordinary respite care is a mild intervention with modest effects seems inescapable."

Certainly the evidence is disappointing if one is using the criterion of monetary savings to measure the success of respite services. Not only has there been a failure to demonstrate a change in service use patterns among caregivers provided respite but there has also been a failure to indisputably document caregiver relief in terms of measured state of stress or well-being. This state of knowledge has led at least one observer to question the appropriateness of and need for respite services, especially if they are to be funded by the public purse (Callahan, 1989). However, this response would seem premature given the limited number of studies completed to date and the myriad research and service delivery issues that remain unaddressed. It is important at this early stage of knowledge accumulation to remember that the limitations in knowledge affect our ability to draw both negative and positive conclusions about the efficacy of respite care.

Research Issues

Given the widespread belief among service providers and policy-makers that respite care is a means of assisting caregivers in their efforts to care for impaired elders, it is imperative that any decisions regarding its efficacy as a support service be based on adequate data. The small number of controlled design studies completed to date should not be considered an adequate base from which definitive conclusions can be drawn about the relative merits of respite care. Rather, these studies should be viewed as sources of guidance for the future research that is necessary to advance our knowledge.

CLARITY AND INTENSITY OF RESPITE SERVICES

One barrier to an adequate test of the impact of respite services consists of the sheer diversity of services that have been considered respite services. It is quite likely that the impact of an institutional respite program will be substantially different than that of an in-home service or that of respite care provided through the informal network. To date, insufficient attention has been given to accurately describing the service intervention and/or differences between services in impact (Lawton et al., 1988; Montgomery & Borgatta, 1989). Future studies need to carefully describe the type of services delivered as well as the intensity of the service so that accurate conclusions can be drawn. It may well be that the impact of respite care will not be uniform for all types of respite services. Furthermore there is evidence that the impact of services may depend upon elder and family characteristics (Lawton et al., 1988; Montgomery & Borgatta, 1989). Attention also needs to be given to other services that families might use that could be alternate forms of respite care. Because alternate forms can include informal as well as formal services, this description can become very complicated.

REPRESENTATION OF SAMPLES

A second consideration for future research must be sampling procedures and sample composition. Previous studies have relied upon clinical and self-selected convenience samples that are not likely to be representative of the larger population of families who could potentially benefit from respite care. Indeed, past studies have tended to include families with higher income and educational levels than the national samples of caregivers (Lawton et al., 1988). Also, minority groups have been underrepresented in all studies of caregivers—a fact that appears to hold true for studies of respite care as well.

While the lack of demographic representation is a concern, a more serious problem for the assessment of respite is the tendency for families to wait until a crisis point to seek and use any type of care support service. This fact can have implications for the accurate assessment of respite services. If families do not use services until a crisis point, the preventive purpose of respite may never be realized. It is possible that the lack of observed impact on families in previous studies is in part due to the lateness of families in seeking help. There may be little potential for delaying or preventing nursing home placement if support services are sought too late in the caregiving career (Montgomery & Borgatta, 1987).

In contrast, if studies include families with very limited needs (e.g., the elder is not very impaired or caregiver stress is very low), then the impact of respite care may not be easily documented. Lawton et al. (1988) suggest that there may be some threshold level of very high need that is required for respite intervention to affect subjective well-being. These two opposing possibilities point to a major issue for future research: factors affecting use.

USE

Apart from the obvious dearth of controlled design studies that are necessary to test the impact of any service intervention, the biggest barrier to the assessment of the impact of respite has been patterns of use. In both the Philadelphia-based study (Lawton et al., 1988) and the Seattle-based study (Montgomery & Borgatta, 1987), investigators reported substantial lack of use of intervention services by persons in the treatment groups. Lawton et al. (1988) reported that only half of per-

sons eligible for the experimental program used these additional resources. Montgomery (1986) reported that 36% of eligible caregivers
used no project services and, on the average, those who did use services
used only 63% of the resources available to them. This pattern has also
been reported by George (1988). This lack of use by eligible caregivers
is an important research issue that must be addressed by future studies.
First, the low-use pattern substantially decreases the likelihood of observing statistically significant differences between treatment groups
and control groups in the respite studies because it substantially decreases the strength of the intervention. This is especially true when
large numbers of persons in the control group are receiving some form
of service from sources other than the program under study that functions as respite, as was the case in the study conducted by Lawton and
his colleagues. In truth the studies to date have been weak tests of the
possible impact of respite and thus illustrate the aptness of Benjamin's
statement (in Chapter 1 of this volume): "The study of service use is
critical to the investigation of service effectiveness."

Future Directions

CONCEPTUAL ISSUES IN USE STUDIES

The patterns of respite use are very important to study not only because lack of use can prevent accurate assessment of impact but also
because patterns of use may provide valuable knowledge and insight
concerning the needs of caregiving families, the appropriate design and
delivery of respite services, and targeting issues. Although little is
known about the correlates of respite use, a few recent studies have
focused specifically on the use of services by caregivers. Additionally
a much larger literature has developed on service use among older persons in general (Krout, 1983a; McCaslin, 1988; Wolinsky, Moseley, &
Coe, 1986), and special attention has been given to home care use as
evidenced by the chapters in this volume. For the most part the work in
this area has been guided by the Andersen-Newman model (1973),
which advances three classes of variables as predictors of service use:
predisposing, enabling, and need. Future investigations of respite care
would do well to build upon this literature to learn more about the predictors of respite use.

DEFINING NEED

Of special interest are variables that define need. In the past numerous variables have been advanced as indicators of need, including functional status, diagnosis, and perceived health status. Yet these more objective measures of need have not accounted for as much variance in service use as measures of perceived or self-reported need. In the study conducted by Caserta, Lund, Wright, and Redburn (1987), which focused on caregivers' participation in Alzheimer support groups, the most common reason given for not using respite was a perceived lack of immediate need.

Perceived need, or the perception that a service is a source of assistance for one's own situation, really entails two judgments. The first is the judgment that, in one's current situation or status, assistance or support of some sort is required. The second is the judgment that a particular service, either a specific program or a generic service such as "respite," will provide that assistance or support. That is, the second element of perceived need is really a judgment as to whether a service will be "useful" in one's situation. Hence "need" as most frequently defined by providers in terms of impairment levels, health status, or stress is not necessarily "need" as perceived by caregivers. McCaslin (1988) notes that self-reported need for a service appears to be expressive of a view that a given program is personally useful rather than indicating actual or intended use. This latter dimension of "perceived need" is closely related to knowledge or awareness of services.

KNOWLEDGE OF SERVICES

To judge a program useful or not useful—therefore needed or unneeded—a caregiver would have to have some "awareness" of the services provided and the way in which they are provided. For example, where is the service delivered? How much will it cost? How well trained are the workers? Is it difficult to arrange for? This knowledge of services does not necessarily have to be accurate for a caregiver to arrive at a judgment of need, but it would seem that accuracy would improve the ability of the caregiver to make a judgment. In the past, while knowledge has consistently been shown to be one of the best predictors of service use of all types, measurements of knowledge have been vague or ambiguous (McCaslin, 1988). Among the elderly, knowledge of a service or a program name, such as "Meals on Wheels," is seldom accompanied by an awareness of what services are actually provided or where such programs can be found (Krout, 1983). Because *knowledge* of a service (or lack of it) is likely to influence an individual's *perception of need* for that service, the two concepts, as most frequently measured in previous research, are not distinct concepts. McCaslin (1988, p. 597) suggests that *need* and *knowledge* are "best understood as representing a general positive orientation to the formal service system which is perceived as a known resource with relevance to the individual's current or future situation."

Hence, despite the fact that self-perceptions in terms of need, service, and knowledge have consistently accounted for a large amount of explained variance in service use, operational measures of these concepts have been too vague to predict usage rates or guide the development of programs that will actually be used by their intended clientele. Information is needed on the relationship between service delivery characteristics and caregivers' perceptions of perceived need and ultimately use or nonuse of services (Krout, 1983a; McCaslin, 1988). In this way findings can be used to identify or modify and target specific service delivery characteristics.

FACTORS INFLUENCING USE

The general literature on home care services as well as the more limited literature on respite care suggest a large number of factors that could potentially affect respite use and require simultaneous investigation. These variables can be grouped under three general headings: (a) demographic and background characteristics, (b) factors that determine the timing of respite use or the point in a caregiving career that the caregiver "perceives need," and (c) aspects of service delivery that are likely to affect respite use.

Demographic and background variables. Although the profile of respite users presented earlier provides a description of users, it does not address the more important question of how representative such samples of "users" are of the total population of potential users. Indeed, there is evidence that users of respite services are a select subpopulation that tends to have higher income and education levels than the larger population of potential users and tends to include high proportions of Whites and low proportions of minority groups (Lawton et al., 1988). Any effort to evaluate the efficacy of a respite program must focus on the total population of caregivers who could benefit from respite care rather than the subpopulation from which most samples have been drawn.

Factors affecting the time that respite is sought and used. As noted above, the perception of need for a service—and ultimately the decision to seek the service—involves a judgment as to whether one's condition or situation requires some form of assistance. The literature suggests several factors that would create a condition of need, including measures of health, levels of assistance, measures of burden, and the availability of alternative sources of help from the formal system and informal support networks. These measures might all be conceived of as factors that determine the "time" that need is recognized in a caregiving situation.

Aspects of service delivery. The least studied variables hypothesized to affect service use are aspects of service delivery and clients' perceptions of the utility of the service. As is true for any product, services that do not appear useful will not be used. The two factors that most affect a client's perception of service utility are the quality and convenience of the service. These two factors are influenced by a number of aspects of the service utility: whether the caregiver is a professional or a volunteer, the amount of training of workers, the extent of advertising and outreach attempts, the cost of respite to the family, the type of setting, the availability of transportation, the flexibility of scheduling, and the reliability and consistency of workers.

Inclusion of these variables in any future investigation will enable the assessment of the program design (as experienced by the lay public) and its influence upon respite use. This direction in research will be very important because program characteristics are much more amenable to change than are individual attitudes, and they could conceivably be designed to minimize resistance to use of respite services.

As the discussion above illustrates, the investigation of use patterns and factors affecting use will not only enhance our ability to judge the merits of respite programs but should have implications for the design and delivery of services.

RETHINKING TARGETING

Closely tied to the investigation of use patterns is the issue of targeting. Because respite has been put forth as one of a constellation of home and community-based services intended to reduce institutionalization, it has usually been targeted to families most vulnerable to nursing home placement, where vulnerability is usually determined by the functional level of the elder. Yet to date there are few data to support the assumption that the most impaired are the most vulnerable. More important, as noted above, this practice, which makes respite available only to those close to or at a crisis point, may actually work against the viability of respite services being the preventive force they are intended to be. The appropriate targeting of services remains a question worthy of serious investigation and will likely rest upon greater investigation of use patterns.

Similarly the ideal or desired forms of respite services will remain unknown until greater knowledge of use patterns is obtained. It is very likely that the flexibility that families need to meet their changing needs will require a continuum of services. Greater knowledge, however, about the relationships between individual and family characteristics and the characteristics of services they use is required to design services that will meet the need of a wide range of caregiving families and continue to meet their needs as their circumstances change.

Conclusion

In summary, like other forms of home care, respite care has been subjected to the "cost-effectiveness trap" (Weissert, 1985). It has been developed primarily under the auspices of small pilot programs and demonstration projects with the expectation that it will reduce costs of long-term care. Due to the lack of consistent financing, respite has not, in reality, been widely available, and its merits have not been adequately assessed. As researchers and policymakers have studied respite, the primary outcomes of interest have been caregiver burden, caregiver well-being, and the reduction of institutionalization.

To date the evidence that such outcomes will be positively affected is gloomy. Yet the number of studies completed is extremely small and they have suffered from some serious limitations, including lack of clear definitions, lack of controlled design studies, and low use. The low use of available services is especially problematic. Without more substantial knowledge about the factors that influence respite use, it is impossible to assess its true merits. At this point there is insufficient evidence to argue for or against respite services, but there is ample evidence to argue for more carefully designed studies of respite use and impact. It is anticipated that such studies will help guide the development and targeting of respite services in the future.

References

Andersen, R., & Newman, J. M. (1973). Societal and individual determinants of medical care utilization in the United States. *The Milbank Memorial Fund Quarterly, 5,* 95-124.

Brody, E. M. (1985). Parent care as a normative family stress. *The Gerontologist, 25*(1), 19-25.

Burdz, M. P., & Bond, J. B. (1988). Effect of respite care on dementia and nondementia patients and their caregivers. *Psychology and Aging, 3,* 38-42.

Callahan, J. J., Jr. (1989). Play it again Sam: There is no impact. *The Gerontologist, 29*(1), 5.

Caserta, M. S., Lund, D. A., Wright, S. D., & Redburn, D. E. (1987). Caregivers to dementia patients: The utilization of community services. *The Gerontologist, 27*(2), 209-214.

Cohen, S., & Warren, R. D. (1985). *Respite care: Principles, programs and policies.* Austin, TX: Pro-Ed.

Connecticut Department of Health Services (CDHS). (1985). *Respite care program* (Report to the Hospital Care Sub-Committee of the Appropriations Committee, General Assembly). Hartford, CT: Author.

Crossman, L., London, C., & Barry, C. (1981). Older women caring for disabled spouses: A model for supportive services. *The Gerontologist, 21*(5), 465-470.

Danaher, D., Dixon-Bemis, J., & Pedersen, S. (1986). The merits of paid and volunteer staff. In R. Montgomery & J. Prothero (Eds.), *Developing respite services for the elderly.* Seattle: University of Washington Press.

Delargy, J., & Belf, M. B. (1957). Six weeks in; six weeks out: A geriatric hospital scheme for rehabilitating the aged and relieving their relatives. *Lancet, 1,* 418-419.

Dixon-Bemis, J. (1986). Respite as a continuum of services: The Arizona approach. In R. Montgomery & J. Prothero (Eds.), *Developing respite services for the elderly.* Seattle: University of Washington Press.

Doty, P. (1986). Family care of the elderly: The role of public policy. *The Milbank Memorial Fund Quarterly, 64*(1), 34-75.

Dunn, R. B., MacBeath, L., & Robertson, D. (1983). Respite admissions and the disabled elderly. *Journal of the American Geriatrics Society, 31,* 613-616.

Ellis, V. (1986). Respite in an institution. In R. Montgomery & J. Prothero (Eds.), *Developing respite services for the elderly.* Seattle: University of Washington Press.

Ellis, V., & Wilson, D. (1983). Respite care in the nursing unit of a veterans hospital. *American Journal of Nursing, 83,* 1433-1434.

Foundation for Long Term Care (FLTC). (1983). *Respite care for the frail elderly: A summary report on institutional respite research and operations manual.* Albany, NY: Center for the Study of Aging.

George, L. K. (1988). *Why won't caregivers use community services? Unexpected findings from a respite care demonstration/evaluation.* Paper presented at the 41st annual meeting of the Gerontological Society of America, San Francisco.

Hasselkus, B. R., & Brown, M. (1983). Respite care for community elderly. *American Journal of Occupational Therapy, 37,* 83-88.

Hildebrandt, E. (1983). Respite care in the home. *American Journal of Nursing, 83,* 1428-1431.

Horowitz, A. (1985). Family caregiving to the frail elderly. In C. Eisdorfer (Ed.), *Annual review of gerontology and geriatrics* (Vol. 5). New York: Springer.

Howells, D. (1980). *Reallocating institutional resources: Respite care as a supplement to family care of the elderly.* Paper presented at the meeting of the Gerontological Society of America, San Diego, CA.

Huey, R. (1983). Respite care in a state owned hospital. *American Journal of Nursing, 83,* 4131-4132.

Isett, R. D., Krauss, C., & Malone, M. (1984). *A study of the Intercommunity Actions, Inc. in-home respite care project.* Unpublished manuscript, Mid-Atlantic Long Term Care Gerontology Center.

Krout, J. A. (1983a). Knowledge and use of services by the elderly: A critical review of the literature. *International Journal of Aging and Human Development, 17*(3), 153-167.

Krout, J. A. (1983b). Utilization of services by the elderly. *Social Service Review, 58,* 281-290.

Lawton, M. P., Brody, E. M., & Saperstein, A. R. (1988). A controlled study of respite service for caregivers of Alzheimer's patients. *The Gerontologist, 29*(1), 8.

Lidoff, L. (1983). *Program innovations in aging: Vol. 7. Respite companion program model.* Washington, DC: National Council on the Aging.

MacCourt, P., & Southam, M. (1983). Respite care provides relief for caregivers. *Dimensions of Health Service, 60,* 18-19.

McCaslin, R. (1988). Reframing research on service use among the elderly: An analysis of recent findings. *The Gerontologist, 28*(5), 592-599.

McFarland, L. G., Howells, D., & Dill, B. (1985). Respite care. *Generations, XI*(3), 46-47.

Meltzer, J. (1982). *Respite care: An emerging family support service.* Washington, DC: Center for the Study of Social Policy.

Montgomery, R. J. (1984). Services for families of the aged: Which ones will work best? *Aging, 347,* 16-21.

Montgomery, R. J. (1986). Introduction. In R. Montgomery & J. Prothero (Eds.), *Developing respite services for the elderly.* Seattle: University of Washington Press.

Montgomery, R. J. (1987). Social service utilization. In G. Maddox (Ed.), *Encyclopedia of aging.* New York: Springer.

Montgomery, R. J. (1988a). Respite services for family caregivers. In M. D. Peterson & D. L. White (Eds.), *Health care for the elderly An information sourcebook* (pp. 139-152). Newbury Park, CA: Sage.

Montgomery, R. J. (1988b, December). Respite care: Lessons from a controlled designed study. *Health Care Financing Review* (pp. 133-138). Baltimore, ML Health Care Financing Administration, U.S. Department of Health and Human Services.

Montgomery, R. J., & Borgatta, E. (1985). *Family support project* (Final report to the Administration on Aging). Seattle: University of Washington, Institute on Aging.

Montgomery, R. J., & Borgatta, E. (1987). *Effects of alternative support strategies* (Final report to the Health Care Financing Administration). Detroit, MI: Wayne State University, Institute of Gerontology.

Montgomery, R. J., & Borgatta, E. F. (1989). Effects of alternative support strategies. *The Gerontologist, 29*(4), 457-464.

Montgomery, R. J., Gonyea, J. G., & Hooyman, N. (1985). Caregiving and the experience of subjective and objective burden. *Family Relations, 34*(1), 19-26.

Montgomery, R. J., & Hatch, L. R. (1987). The feasibility of volunteers and family forming a partnership for caregiving. In T. Brubaker (Ed.), *Family and long-term care.* Newbury Park, CA: Sage.

Montgomery, R. J., Kosloski, K., & Borgatta, E. F. (1989). The influence of cognitive impairment on service use and caregiver response. *Journal of Applied Social Sciences, 13*(1), 142-169.

New York State Department of Society Services (NYSDSS). (1985). *Respite demonstration project: Final report.* Albany, NY: Author.

Nyilis, M. (1985). *Final report: Coordinated respite care in the Capital District.* Albany, NY: Foundation for Long Term Care.

Packwood, T. (1980). Supporting the family: A study of the organization and implications of hospital provision of holiday relief for families caring for dependents at home. *Social Science and Medicine, 14a,* 613-620.

Pratt, C. C., Schmall, V. L., Wright, S., & Cleland, M. (1985). Burden and coping strategies of caregivers to Alzheimer's patients. *Family Relations, 34,* 27-33.

Robertson, D. A., Griffiths, R. A., & Cosin, L. (1977). A community-based continuing care program for elderly disabled: An evaluation of planned intermittent hospital readmission. *Journal of Gerontology, 32,* 334-337.

Sands, D., & Suzuki, T. (1983). Adult day care for Alzheimer's patients and their families. *The Gerontologist, 23,* 21-23.

Scharlach, A., & Frenzel, C. (1986). An evaluation of institutional-based respite. *The Gerontologist, 26*(1), 77-82.

Stone, R. (1985). *Recent development in respite care services for caregivers* (Grant No. 90AP003; prepared for the Administration on Aging). San Francisco: Aging Health Policy Center.

Wan, T. H., & Odell, B. G. (1981). Factors affecting the use of social and health services among the elderly. *Aging and Society, 3,* 240-256.

Washington State Department of Social and Health Services (WSDSHS). (1986). *Respite care demonstration* (Report to the Washington State Legislature). Olympia, WA: Bureau of Aging and Adult Services.

Weissert, W. G. (1985). Home and community-based care: The cost-effectiveness trap. *Generations, 10,* 47-50.

Wisconsin Department of Health and Social Services (WDHSS). (1981). *Division of Community Services respite care projects.* Madison, WI: Bureau of Aging, Division of Community Services.

Wisconsin Department of Health and Social Services (WDHSS). (1982). *Respite care and institutionalization.* Madison, WI: Bureau of Aging, Division of Community Services.

Wolinsky, F. D., Moseley, R. R., & Coe, R. M. (1986). A cohort analysis of the use of health services by elderly Americans. *Journal of Health and Social Behavior, 27,* 209-219.

Wright, R., Creecy, R. F., & Berg, W. E. (1979). The Black elderly and their use of health care services: A causal analysis. *Journal of Gerontological Social Work, 2,* 11-28.

Yankelovitch, Skelley and White, Inc. (1986). *Caregivers of patients with dementia* (Contract report prepared for the Office of Technology Assessment, U.S. Congress). Washington, DC.

Zarit, S. H., Todd, P. A., & Zarit, J. M. (1986). Subjective burden of husbands and wives as caregivers: A longitudinal study. *The Gerontologist, 26*(3), 260-266.

FOUR

Board and Care Homes:
From the Margins to the Mainstream in the 1990s

J. KEVIN ECKERT
STEPHANIE M. LYON

Board and care is defined as a noninstitutional, residential setting that provides a room, meals, up to 24-hour-per-day oversight supervision, and, in some cases, personal care to unrelated adults for a fee. It is frequently viewed as a segment of the Assisted Living Movement. As a nonmedical residential care option, board and care falls within the continuum of care for elderly people who need assistance with some activities because of physical or mental disabilities. Board and care homes, within the scope of this chapter, are community based, small, and have homelike features. However, unlike family homes, board and care homes may be subject to regulation by state or local agencies, particularly when public funds and services are involved. Lawton (1981) classifies board and care homes as "semi-institutional" because they have shared bedrooms and some restrictions on activity.

Board and care homes may be referred to by many names including *domiciliary care homes, adult foster care homes, personal care homes, sheltered housing,* and, more recently, *assisted living.* McCoin (1983, p. 60) and others stress the need for "a unifying concept," common definitions, and terminology for this mode of alternative housing for adults.

Small board and care homes tend to serve marginal populations—"marginal" because they are usually poor, without adequate social supports, and suffering from long-term disabilities including dementias, mental illness, mental retardation, and chronic physical conditions (Eckert & Lyon, 1991; McCoin, 1983; Sherman & Newman, 1988). Demographic trends (McCoy & Conley, 1990; O'Hare, 1985; U.S. Senate Special Committee on Aging, 1988) indicate that there will continue to be a significant portion of the elderly population with limited financial and social resources for care well into the next century. For the less marginal elderly who have resources, options for assisted living are becoming more readily available, provided by a willing private sector economy in response to market demands.

Care for dependent adults in the homes of unrelated individuals can be documented back to the fourteenth century. In Gheel, Belgium, adults with emotional problems were housed in private homes under the auspices of the Catholic Church. The practice was established in Scotland in the mid-nineteenth century and the concept spread to the United States. In 1855 Massachusetts adopted a policy to provide adult foster care to mental patients (McCoin, 1983). Although other states were slow to follow, regulations governing housing of dependent adult populations (deinstitutionalized mentally ill, mentally retarded, physically disabled, dependent elderly) now exist, in various forms, in all states.

In a nationwide study using 1980 data, Mor, Sherwood, and Gutkin (1986) describe the status of residential care homes. They found that such homes range from small, family-run board and care homes (those considered here) to large institutions. Large institutions are generally regulated by state health departments while the smaller homes are regulated, if at all, by a mix of programs administered by various state agencies. For example, in Maryland, residential care programs for homes with up to 15 residents are regulated by separate state agencies for health, human resources, and aging as well as individual jurisdictions within the state (Dobkin, 1989). Each agency sets its own requirements for size, with the minimum size ranging from 1 to 21 residents and the most frequent minimum being 1 or 3 (U.S. General Accounting Office [GAO], 1989). States may also specify what types of services must be provided; a 1985 survey found that food preparation, medication, housekeeping, and laundry were the most frequently required services. The GAO study also found that licensing agencies focus primarily on physical plant and operational aspects of the homes. The study reports that a 1987 industry survey identified about 563,000 board and care beds in 41,000 licensed homes. Generally studies have not included those homes that are not licensed or regulated, because they are difficult to locate and count. However, the Select Committee on Aging, U.S. House of Representatives, estimates that approximately 1 million elderly and disabled adults reside in 68,850 licensed and unlicensed facilities; as many as three times that number are at risk of board and care placement (U.S. House Select Committee on Aging, 1989).

Research on Board and Care

NEED FOR RESEARCH

Most research to date has focused on regulation and reimbursement for services in multistate, national, or single-state studies. Three factors can be identified that have had impact on the perceived need for regulation of semi-institutional housing for older adults. First is the continuing growth of the elderly population, particularly those who are dependent and without social and financial resources. A second factor is concern for potential, and in some cases real, abuse and neglect of elderly residents of such housing. In a report published by the National Citizens Coalition for Nursing Home Reform (n.d.), several problem areas were considered: poor sanitation, lack of social services and recreational activities, inadequate provisions for medical care, inappropriate placements, violation of fire codes resulting in deaths, lack of financial protection, and inadequate diet. Third, changes in policies that affect elderly and disabled populations have created needs and means to meet those needs that had not previously existed.

Since the mid-1960s three policies have affected the marginal elderly population in need of protective housing. First, at the federal level, Supplemental Security Income (SSI), enacted in 1972, provides a minimum income for aged, blind, and disabled persons, allowing those who were formerly without any resources to purchase a minimal level of care. In addition, states may provide supplements to SSI for care of adults in residential care settings. Second, a controversial effect of the prospective payment system under Medicare, according to many who work with the elderly, is the shifting of sicker old people from hospitals to the community, where they may not have adequate resources for care. Third, the discharge of patients from state mental institutions into the community produced a demand for protective housing for those who did not have family or other resources available. Although the policy was established in the early 1950s, it gained momentum with the passage of the Community Mental Health Centers Construction Act, which became law in 1966 (Donahue & Oriole, 1983). In a special issue of *Psychiatric Quarterly,* Donahue and Oriole (1983, p. 83) state that "housing, in particular, is an essential element for a successful return of older patients to the community." These deinstitutionalized people were routed into other institutions, such as nursing homes, or semi-institutional settings, such as regulated or nonregulated board and care homes. Since the 1960s many of them have been "aging in place," in many instances becoming more frail and dependent.

EXAMINATION OF SERVICE AND REGULATORY ISSUES

In response to growing needs and concerns, the Department of Health and Human Services sponsored several research projects that were completed in the early 1980s that examined broad service and regulatory issues related to board and care. Through a contract with the Hebrew Rehabilitation Center for the Aged (HRCA), Reichstein and Bergofsky (1980) reported on a mail and telephone survey of state-administered domiciliary care programs that provided housing for elderly residents in the 50 states and Washington, D.C. Nationwide they found 118 state-administered and regulated programs using 21 different program titles and serving a variety of subpopulations, the largest being 65 and over. Three primary functions offered were case management, regulation, and eligibility determination and income maintenance. An interesting finding of the survey was that more regulation and greater enforcement of regulations was positively correlated with greater availability of beds and lower inspection and monitoring costs.

In 1981 the Department of Social Gerontological Research of the HRCA (Sherwood, Mor, & Gutkin, 1981) published the results of a study of domiciliary care homes in six states with an in-depth analysis of one state program. In addition to descriptive data, programs were compared using measures of cost-effectiveness, quality of life, and quality of care. Some findings indicated a positive relationship between poorer facilities and a greater number of clients with mental problems. Larger facilities that charged higher rates tended to accept clients with greater physical impairments. They found no differences between smaller and larger facilities and the number of linkages to community social service systems, thereby suggesting that these programs and facilities are meeting most of the needs of the residents. Based on clinical judgment they determined that 87% of the residents were adequately placed. In addition, in comparison with the costs of mental institutions and nursing homes—the only other residential alternatives for much of the domiciliary care population—domiciliary care is less costly.

The American Bar Association, in cooperation with the University of California at San Francisco's Aging Health Policy Center, conducted a comprehensive survey of laws and residential programs affecting elderly and disabled adults in all 50 states and the District of Columbia (American Bar Association, 1983). Based on this survey, the project developed model board and care licensing legislation using analyses of over 130 programs.

The Denver Research Institute (Dittmar, Smith, Bell, Jones, & Manzanares, 1983) conducted a survey of facilities in seven states to intensively evaluate board and care homes and the systems that have been developed to manage services to adult residents. Facilities surveyed were limited to those that housed four or more adults. Within such areas as resident characteristics, physical and mental health status, and staffing, the study compared types of facilities. They found that the mentally retarded did well in smaller facilities designed to meet their needs and had more community involvement. The mentally ill and aged poor tended to be found in less differentiated, larger, and more institutional settings. The elderly poor were observed to be in a "no-man's land" within the human services system. Bleakness of surroundings and isolation seemed endemic for this population, thus suggesting a special focus for further research and policy development.

Taken together, these studies provide a base from which to assess the status of regulation and characteristics of regulated board and care homes in the United States. A limitation of these studies, however, is lack of information about homes that are not regulated and house smaller numbers of residents—those homes of most concern to us here. Beyond the effects of regulations, an area for further study is policy research on how regulations are implemented and the effect of regulatory processes and procedures on quality of care and other outcomes.

More recently, in an overview of the 50 states and a more in-depth survey of 7 states, the Center for the Study of Social Policy (1989) looked at the issue of income supplementation for residents of board and care facilities who receive SSI. To contrast reimbursement methods, a study was conducted of 754 facilities and 2,786 residents in Oregon for which adult foster care services are subsidized under a Medicaid waiver (Kane, Illston, Kane, & Nyman, 1989). Each study presents valid arguments for using each of these methods to subsidize care for adult board and care residents. Finding adequate and equitable funding for board and care services for low-income dependent adults should continue to be recognized as an important policy issue. The impact of these policies on residents requires more research.

A survey of facilities and regulations in six states conducted by the U.S. GAO (1989) found that current regulation does not adequately protect residents. A report from the U.S. House Select Committee on Aging (1989) further reinforces negative findings (unsafe, unsanitary conditions and inadequate care of residents) in board and care facilities, both regulated and nonregulated. In response to these reports, the Department of Health and Human Services has contracted with the Research Triangle Institute in North Carolina to examine the effect of regulation on quality of care in board and care homes. The two goals of this study are to (a) analyze the impact of state regulations on quality of care and (b) describe the characteristics of board and care homes, their owner/operators, and their residents.

Results of in-state studies of board and care programs have been published on Pennsylvania (Conservation Company, 1986), New Jersey (Gioglio, 1984), Oregon (Kane et al., 1989), Missouri (Missouri State Senate, 1978), Ohio (Warner & Smith, 1985), and elsewhere. The American Association of Retired Persons (AARP) made a series of recommendations concerning board and care homes based on the status of regulation of board and care homes in Maryland (Dobkin, 1989). The report calls for the establishment of reimbursement and other financing mechanisms to adequately and equitably support board and care services; the clarification of regulations and consolidation of regulatory authority; increased visibility and accountability of board and care homes and related service providers; increased attention to resident needs for appropriate placement and matching care needs with community services; and providing training and technical assistance to both board and care staff and those who serve and regulate the industry.

BOARD AND CARE ENVIRONMENTS

A still limited but growing number of studies have been carried out to examine board and care homes, their operators, and their residents in smaller geographic areas. Sherman and Newman (1988) have reported results of their study of foster care residents in New York state, focusing on concepts of familism and community integration. Research was carried out with samples of homes involved in three state programs that included mentally ill, mentally retarded, and elderly residents. They found that familism, defined by four factors (affection, social interaction, social distance, ritual), was demonstrated in two thirds of the homes in their samples. Integration into the community was predicted by resident characteristics, provider involvement, number of residents in the home, and access to community services. Based on these findings they recommend strengthening the family model, maintaining small home size, and facilitating participation within the community with provider involvement.

Results of a study of 285 residents in 177 small, nonregulated board and care homes in Ohio were reported by Eckert, Namazi, and Kahana (1987) and Namazi, Eckert, Kahana, and Lyon (1989). The research provided descriptive data about the homes, their operators, and their elderly residents. Research questions addressed the effects of environmental, social, and personal characteristics, as well as interactions among these characteristics, on the psychosocial well-being of the residents. Findings indicate that 85% of residents reported high or moderate levels of psychological well-being. Personal feelings of comfort in the social and physical environment, the quality of relationships with other residents, personalization of care by operators, and affordable cost were found to have influenced this outcome. This study is continuing through the collection of longitudinal data, over two years, from operators of 100 homes and through objective health measures of 100 residents of board and care homes in Maryland using both quantitative and qualitative methods. The research will examine factors—including stress and burden, formal and informal support, personal backgrounds of operators, and financial issues—that affect the decisions that the operators make as well as the impact of the movement of residents from one environment to another.

McCoin's book, *Adult Foster Homes: Their Managers and Residents* (1983) qualitatively assesses adult foster care programs in the United

States, past and current. In addition to reviewing current programs, he focuses on issues of residential care as a therapeutic environment for mentally ill, mentally retarded, and disabled adults. McCoin concludes that there is need for more thorough theory building and empirical testing of concepts relevant to adult residential care. He identifies a need for mental health and social service practitioners to give equal priority to the target groups mentioned above. Additionally, he calls for unified national policy covering these environments.

USE OF MEDICATIONS

An area of interest that has captured some attention is the use of medications in board and care homes. Avorn, Dreyer, Connelly, and Soumerai (1989) gained national attention reporting on a study of the use of psychoactive medication and quality of care in board and care homes. This research supports findings in the deinstitutionalization literature (Donahue & Oriole, 1983) that residents do not always receive adequate medical follow-up and treatment once they are returned to the community. Further research is needed on the use of medications in these settings as well as on development of policy to realistically allow appropriate monitoring and administration of medication.

Review of Current Knowledge

McCoin (1983, p. 60) makes the statement: "The literature in the field [adult foster care], while proliferous, is often repetitious, contradictory, not solidly grounded on human behavior and social science theories, and the research methodology employed often makes replications of studies difficult." Additionally, national information is lacking concerning the number and types of board and care homes as well as the number of residents of these homes, their characteristics, types of services, quality of care received, and other data relevant to the provision of board and care services (McCoy & Conley, 1990).

As the above review indicates, there has been significant investigation of the board and care industry in its broadest definition. A summary of findings indicates that there has been, and continues to be, no standardization of regulation at the national level with a proliferation of regulations at the state and local levels that vary widely. These regulations are promulgated by a widely varying mix of programs and agencies. Although some studies have included nonregulated homes, they have been limited. The literature also indicates that, whereas there are programs in place to subsidize this form of alternative housing for low-income adults, availability and amounts also vary widely from state to state and within states. In addition, subsidies are generally not available to facilities or residents in small, nonregulated homes. Resources at both the federal and the state levels for the monitoring of homes and provision of supportive services are also very limited.

Based on those studies that collected resident information, the elderly board and care home population consists of two cohorts: (a) deinstitutionalized mentally ill and mentally retarded adults who may be aging in place and (b) low-income females with physical and/or mental disabilities. These residents are marginal because they differ from the larger population in several important ways: many have never been married and are childless; their income is low; they have little education; and, if they worked at all, it was in low-skill jobs with few benefits.

The literature indicates that, although there continue to be horror stories about abuse and neglect, many residents' needs are adequately met for room, board, and personal care in a satisfying homelike environment (Eckert et al., 1987; Namazi et al., 1989; Sherman & Newman, 1988). This research also indicates that areas of need include adequate financing, casework to facilitate service delivery and to match residents with appropriate homes, and respite for the operators as caregivers.

Policy and Legislation

During the past two decades policymakers have directed their attention to residential care homes, including small family-run homes. However, while problems with resident abuse and neglect and unsafe and unsanitary facilities must be acknowledged, they appear to be the only side of the board and care industry that is discussed in hearings and in the media (U.S. House Select Committee on Aging, 1989; U.S. GAO, 1989). Therefore, this negative image has guided much of the regulatory legislation that has been proposed. It is essential that constructive legislation is proposed to support this option to provide a full range of options along the long-term care continuum.

The Keys Amendment (Section 505[d] of Public Law 94-566), was passed by Congress in October 1976; it became section 1616(e) of the Social Security Act. It requires states to establish, maintain, and enforce standards in institutions or other group living arrangements in which a significant number of SSI recipients reside or are likely to reside. The standards cover such matters as admission policies, safety, sanitation, and protection of civil rights. Whereas the Keys Amendment reinforced the regulatory role of the states, it also established, for the first time, federal recognition of the need for standardization nationwide (Reichstein & Bergofsky, 1980). Reichstein and Bergofsky (1980) also report that 25% of states indicated that the Keys Amendment had had some effect on legislation. However, the only penalty built into the act is to reduce the SSI payment to the resident of a facility that does not meet the state standards. Because this provision clearly punishes the resident, not only by reducing personal income but very likely by resulting in loss of placement in the facility, states have been understandably reluctant to report abuses, thus undermining the effectiveness of the act. Reichstein and Bergofsky (1980) reported that only 2% of states were in compliance with this provision of the act. In addition, the act does not provide financial assistance to the states for enforcement. This places the full burden of financing on the states in an area that is not usually well funded, frequently resulting in spotty or lax monitoring.

On May 3, 1989, shortly before his death, Claude Pepper introduced the National Board and Care Reform Act of 1989 in the House of Representatives. The bill requires that every board and care facility in the country that provides care to two or more recipients of Social Security or SSI meet national minimum standards. State standards for regulation, should this legislation become law, must include residents' rights, admission requirements, adequate staff, physical structure and fire safety, sanitation, proper diet, access to needed health care, and resident activities. States will continue to have latitude in determining specifics in these areas. The bill includes requirements for the states to conduct monitoring and enforcement activities. In addition, it includes two sets of federal grants to improve the quality of care and protection of board and care home residents as well as SSI program improvements and reforms in the representative payee system. [The bill was not enacted by congress. The bill has been resubmitted in the 102nd Congress as the National Board and Care Reform Act of 1991, H.R.2551, by Representative Roybal. The new legislation adds language about physical and chemical restraints and extensive language concerning medications. In addition, a National Commission of Board and Care Facility Quality would be established if H.R.2552, the National Commission on Board and Care Facility Quality Act of 1991, were to be enacted (U.S. House of Representatives, 1991).]

Unlike the Keys Amendment, which was punitive in nature, the Pepper legislation is an opportunity to create a positive regulatory climate with uniform minimum standards. Research can inform the specific standards incorporated into state regulations within the categories defined by the federal legislation. The essential element assuring success or failure of this regulatory effort is appropriate levels of federal and state funding for monitoring of homes, supportive services to operators and residents of the homes, and appropriate subsidization of low-income residents. We agree with Sherman and Newman (1988) that it is important to strike an appropriate balance between protection of residents and preservation of the familylike atmosphere of these smaller board and care homes, so as not to regulate them out of business.

At this time several states are in the process of creating or revising regulations covering board and care homes. As Stone and Newcomer (1986, p. 208) point out:

> Two factors . . . will help to determine the relative success or failure of state strategies [in regulating board and care]. One is that the future of board and care policy depends, in large part, on the level of financial commitment from state and local governments to support the development and coordination of board and care programs. In addition, *the design and monitoring of effective policy requires more complete national and state data documenting client and facility characteristics, changes in board and care regulations and standards, enforcement activities, and utilization patterns.*

Setting the Research Agenda

To inform policymakers at all state levels, more research is needed on small family-run board and care homes. To date, board and care homes and the people who operate and reside in them have been marked by social marginality. The concept of marginality can provide a useful focus for framing research questions.

Board and care is on the margin between the housing system and the health care system. While providing services associated with both systems, it does not fit neatly into the regulatory, organizational, or financing structures of either. For example, we suspect that very limited—if any—high- or low-technology, in-home health services, case management, and respite services are extended to the small board and care home. Board and care facilities that are regulated and receive funding to provide care do so under the auspices of numerous and diverse programs and regulatory authorities (Center for the Study of Social Policy, 1989; Dobkin, 1989).

Board and care environments are also marginal in their place on the continuum from private to public, family to institutional, housing environments. The majority of board and care homes, especially the smaller homes included in the Cleveland and Maryland studies, are private, single-family dwellings, often with minor or no modifications. They are located in a range of urban, suburban, and rural locations representing the socioeconomic spectrum. Clearly they do not fit at either end of the continuum but fall somewhere in between.

Demonstration studies are required that specifically link smaller board and care homes to the home care end of the long-term care continuum rather than the institutional axis. Such an approach could examine various case management models and efficient ways to target clients who would benefit from various levels of case management. Other studies might assess the impact of multidisciplinary, in-home health service supports for the ill elderly residing in board and care homes in reducing nursing home and hospital use. Systematic studies applying health behavior and use models to the board and care setting are required. Benjamin (Chapter 1 in this volume) provides helpful direction by exhorting researchers to (a) remain aware of the inherent complexity of use research, (b) be explicit in defining board and care, (c) direct attention to characterizing the informal and formal care/support systems operating among caregivers and residents, (d) direct attention to describing the dominant models of board and care home use, and (e) examine client transitions in health status or from one setting to another.

Relationships within board and care homes are marginal in that they are neither family bonds nor typical professional/client bonds. Agencies and policies in most states do not recognize quasi-familial relationships that often develop between operators of the small homes and their residents. Thus regulatory agencies perceive the right and obligation to intervene to ensure appropriate care in a way that is deemed inappropriate within the privacy of the family household. Physicians, for example, are hesitant to reveal health information to board and care home operators, yet operators are responsible for aftercare following hospitalization or illness. Many policymakers who propose regulations for board and care facilities adopt an institutional perspective applied to nursing homes and hospitals. We need to discover how the quasi-familial bonds that develop between operators and residents of small board and care homes can be preserved and supported. In addition, what services (respite, high and low tech, in-home services) can be extended to the board and care home environment? And to what extent are formal supports (e.g., professional and paid nonprofessional) versus informal supports (e.g., operator and resident family, friends, and neighbors) used in the board and care context?

As discussed earlier, board and care serves a population that is atypical of the larger elderly population in terms of select characteristics. Many board and care residents are never married or are childless and of low economic status and education. Release following long-term institutionalization often means that they are socially marginal. Kin may be distant or deceased, employment impractical, and social networks of support unavailable. Because clientele of board and care homes include deinstitutionalized mentally ill and disabled individuals, older persons with multiple physical and mental handicaps, and Alzheimer's disease victims (among other groups), marginality of home residents is common. With social marginality comes financial marginality because many residents are recipients of financial support from state and federal government programs. Half of the residents in the Cleveland study paid for their housing and care with Social Security (retirement, disability) checks, while others relied on SSI, private sources, or state financial supplements (Center for the Study of Social Policy, 1989; Eckert et al., 1987).

Several questions need to be addressed: Within specific geographic areas and among specific ethnic groupings, who uses the smaller board and care home? How impaired is the client population? In addition, what actual levels of care are being provided? What is the impact of care on outcomes? How are outcomes defined, and from whose perspective? What are appropriate measures/indicators of outcome? How do we measure quality of life and satisfaction, and from whose perspective?

Operators of small homes are "between two worlds" in defining what they do for their residents. On the one hand, most consider their work primarily a contribution to community service— doing necessary and important work. As revealed in the Cleveland study, only a few appear to think of this as primarily running a business. However, there are clearly elements of "doing business" that operators face daily, such as payment for services, managing costs of providing housing and care, keeping records, and interacting with various local and state agencies that serve specific residents' needs or monitor aspects of the home environment and operations. Few of these are characteristics of familial relationships, yet most operators appear to resist characterizing what they do as operating a business.

What are the personal backgrounds and histories of board and care operators that contribute to their ability to offer care against significant disincentives? Recent evidence (the Maryland study) suggests that those who continue as board and care operators are a highly select group able to withstand the burden of caregiving, to maintain morale, and to resist burn-out. What sorts of training and support programs can assist board and care operators? With proper training and supervision, to what degree can operators substitute for trained professionals? To what extent will this contain costs or affect the quality of care provided?

Nonfamily households, like board and care, frequently lack local neighborhood support. Some homes operate anonymously in their neighborhoods to avoid negative reactions. Resistance is acute in more affluent neighborhoods, where there is fear that board and care homes housing socially marginal clients, such as former mental patients, may adversely affect property values. Questions to address include these: How can community-based fears about board and care be minimized? To what degree has community resistance limited the development of board and care? What are the characteristics of neighborhoods that support board and care?

Public opinion regarding board and care homes is largely negative. Both government and media attention has focused on singularly negative reports of abuses and deficiencies. News reporting and the recently published U.S. House Select Committee on Aging report (1989) make no attempt to balance individual testimony, anecdotal reports, and newspaper articles with systematically obtained information representing the industry. To what extent has public opinion, what there is of it, contributed to the marginality of small unlicensed board and care homes? How do we go about changing these stereotypes?

As an economic venture, small board and care homes are marginal. Given the payment level of residents and the costs associated with their care, some operators are barely deriving money from their efforts, while others fare quite well (Chen, 1990; Eckert et al., 1987). The wide range of payment levels found in Ohio is mirrored in data being collected in Maryland, which has one of the highest supplemental payments available in the country in one limited state program serving mentally disabled and elderly clients (Center for the Study of Social Policy, 1989). The inadequacy of income supports to this client population is felt especially in small homes, where the volume of clientele cannot mask the low incomes (and hence payment rates) of one or more residents. What are the economic aspects of operating both smaller and larger (up to 20-25 residents) homes? What are the costs associated with the acquisition of a home, start-up, and ongoing operations? What level of financing would be required to assure adequate and consistent levels of quality and services, keeping in mind the needs and preferences of residents? What are the benefits and costs of board and care versus other options? For selected subpopulations, do other options, in fact, exist?

Summary

The 1990s will be the watershed decade for board and care. A growing aged population in search of affordable supportive housing will sustain the demand for board and care; however, overzealous regulatory legislation at the federal, state, and local levels may hasten its demise.

The small board and care home performs a balancing act and is extremely vulnerable on several levels. Overly restrictive regulations, which require the operator to hire staff and make substantial renovations to the home to meet institutional-type fire and safety standards, could easily persuade operators to discontinue caring for clients. Low profitability coupled with the costs of maintaining and repairing aging homes present challenges to maintaining and replenishing the existing board and care housing stock. Currently the entire informal and non-regulated board and care industry is reliant on the continued health and willingness of the operators to provide housing and service to their clientele. Given the older age of the operators and potential burn-out from constant supervision of individuals with severe physical and mental impairments, the risks for closure are substantial.

A characteristic of many small board and care homes observed in Cleveland and noted by other authors (Sherman & Newman, 1988) is the familylike or homelike atmosphere available to residents. Factors that constitute homelikeness vary among residents depending on individual background. Factors such as food preferences, personalization of space, and need for privacy may vary on the basis of ethnic and personal history. Therefore persons who develop and implement regulations governing board and care should be sensitive to these factors to assure adequate flexibility for those factors that constitute the distinct social fabric of individual homes.

References

American Bar Association. (1983). *Board and care report: An analysis of state laws and programs serving elderly persons and disabled adults* (Report to the Department of Health and Human Services). Washington, DC: Author.

Avorn, J., Dreyer, P., Connelly, K., & Soumerai, S. B. (1989). Use of psychoactive medication and the quality of care in rest homes. *The New England Journal of Medicine, 320*(4), 227-232.

Center for the Study of Social Policy. (1989). *Completing the long term care continuum: An income supplement strategy.* Washington, DC: Center for the Study of Social Policy.

Chen, A. (1990). The cost of operation in board and care homes. In M. Moon, G. Gaberlavege, & S. J. Newman (Eds.), *Preserving independence, supporting needs: The role of board and care homes* (pp. 61-75). Washington, DC: Public Policy Institute, American Association of Retired Persons.

The Conservation Company. (1986). *A study of the characteristics and condition of personal care home residents in Pennsylvania I* (Prepared for the Pennsylvania Department of Public Welfare, the Pennsylvania Department of Health, and Pennsylvania Department of Aging). Philadelphia: Author.

Dittmar, N. D., Smith, G. P., Bell, J. C., Jones, C. B. C., & Manzanares, D. L. (1983). *Board and care for elderly and mentally disabled populations: Final report* (HEW Contract 100-790117). Denver, CO: University of Denver, Denver Research Institute, Social Systems Research and Evaluation Division.

Dobkin, L. (1989). *The board and care system: A regulatory jungle.* Washington, DC: American Association of Retired Persons.

Donahue, W. T., & Oriole, W. E. (Eds.). (1983). Housing the elderly deinstitutionalized mental patient. *Psychiatric Quarterly, 55*(2/3), 81-224.

Eckert, J. K., & Lyon, S. M. (1991). Regulation of board and care homes: Research to guide policy. *Journal of Aging and Social Policy, 3*(1-2), 147-162.

Eckert, J. K., Namazi, K. H., & Kahana, E. (1987). Unlicensed board and care homes: An extra-familial living arrangement for the elderly. *Journal of Cross-Cultural Gerontology, 2,* 377-393.

Gioglio, G. R. (1984). *Demographic and service characteristics of the rooming home, boarding home and residential health care population in New Jersey.* Trenton: New Jersey Department of Human Services.

Kane, R. A., Illston, L. H., Kane, R. L., & Nyman, J. A. (1989). *Adult foster care in Oregon: Evaluation.* Minneapolis: University of Minnesota, School of Public Health, Division of Health Services Research and Policy.

Lawton, M. P. (1981). Alternative housing. *Journal of Gerontological Social Work, 3,* 61-80.

McCoin, J. M. (1983). *Adult foster homes: Their managers and residents.* New York: Human Sciences Press.

McCoy, J. L., & Conley, R. W. (1990). Surveying board and care homes: Issues and data collection problems. *The Gerontologist, 30,* 147-153.

Missouri State Senate. (1978). *Nursing and boarding home licensing in Missouri.* Jefferson City, MO: Health Care Committee.

Mor, V., Sherwood, S., & Gutkin, C. (1986). A national study of residential care for the aged. *The Gerontologist, 26,* 405-417.

Namazi, K. H., Eckert, J. K., Kahana, E., & Lyon, S. M. (1989). Psychological well-being of elderly board and care home residents. *The Gerontologist, 29,* 511-516.

National Citizens Coalition for Nursing Home Reform. (n.d.). *Boarding home abuse: An outgrowth of the deinstitutionalization process.* Washington, DC: National Citizens Coalition for Nursing Home Reform.

O'Hare, W. P. (1985). Poverty in America: Trends and new patterns. *Population Bulletin, 40*(3), 1-44.

Reichstein, K. J., & Bergofsky, L. (1980). *State regulations governing domiciliary care facilities for adults and the relationship between standards to program characteristics.* Paper prepared for the Hebrew Rehabilitation Center for the Aged, Boston, MA.

Sherman, S. R., & Newman, E. S. (1988). *Foster families for adults.* New York: Columbia University Press.

Sherwood, S., Mor, V., & Gutkin, C. (1981). *Domiciliary care clients and the facilities in which they reside.* (Available from the Department of Social Gerontological Research, Hebrew Rehabilitation Center for the Aged, 1200 Centre Street, Boston, MA 02132)

Stone, R., & Newcomer, R. J. (1986). Board and care housing and the role of state governments. In R. J. Newcomer, M. P. Lawton, & T. O. Byerts (Eds.), *Housing an aging society: Issues, alternatives and policy* (pp. 200-209). New York: Van Nostrand Reinhold.

U.S. General Accounting Office (GAO). (1989). *Board and care: Insufficient assurances that residents' needs are identified and met.* Washington, DC: Government Printing Office.

U.S. House Select Committee on Aging. (1989). *Board and care homes in America: A national tragedy* (No. 101-711). Washington, DC: Government Printing Office.

U.S. House or Representatives. (1991). *The National Board and Care Reform Act (H.R. 2551)*. Washington, D.C.: Government Printing Office.

U.S. Senate Special Committee on Aging. (1988). *Aging America: Trends and projections*. Washington, DC: Government Printing Office.

Warner, E., & Smith, C. (1985). *Adult care facilities: An undeveloped resource for Ohio's elderly*. Cleveland: Northeast Ohio Family Home Care Coalition and the Boarding Home Advocacy Program.

FIVE

A Model of a Comprehensive Care System: Case Management, Assessment, and Quality Assurance

JAMES G. ZIMMER

It has long since become a truism that community-based health and social services for the chronically ill elderly, in fact for people of all ages, are fragmented, uncoordinated, and poorly accessible for many, even as single services. While an ultimate solution might be some form of highly integrated and structured comprehensive national health service, this is unrealistic in the United States in the foreseeable future.

Nonetheless, approaches to improving the situation are conceivable and could be developed at least on a local and regional basis. This was the major motivation behind the national long-term care and channeling demonstrations, along with the usual emphasis on improving efficiency and cost saving. While the results of analysis of these demonstrations were far from uniformly encouraging ("The Evaluation," 1988; Kemper, Applebaum, & Harrigan, 1987; Weissert, 1985; Weissert, Cready, & Pawelak, 1988; Zawadski, 1984), important experience and insights have been gained.

In fact the recent Pepper Commission report, though viewed by many as overly optimistic especially in respect to the realities of financing, demonstrates interest and some sense of commitment at the federal level (Pepper Commission, 1990). This interest reflects a growing desire nationally for the development of universal health insurance, at least for the basic health care needs of all Americans, and for some

115

form of guaranteed support for long-term care when needed. These two elements would facilitate the development of a well-coordinated system that might approach the ideal. However, in the meantime it should be possible to proceed with at least partial improvements within existing structures and financing systems.

The Model

This chapter suggests a conceptual framework or model for integrating and coordinating community services for chronically ill elderly, composed of several assessment and service provision elements that are accessed through a case management mechanism. The objective of such a system is to improve accessibility, evaluation and appropriate placement, and efficient utilization of the various levels and types of community-based health and supportive care services that are discussed in this volume. Virtually all of the elements in the model have been developed individually, at least on a temporary demonstration or experimental basis, in a number of locations but have never been organized and integrated into a truly comprehensive system of care for an entire community. While it is not possible in a chapter of this scope to review thoroughly the work done relating to all the components in the model, some examples of evaluated demonstrations can be given that relate to the various elements. This chapter draws heavily on research conducted over the past few years in Rochester, New York. Unfortunately some of these demonstrations have had limited lifetimes, in spite of evidence for reasonably successful outcomes, largely because of lack of a stable financial basis for continuation after the research grants terminated.

The key elements that are basic to and would ideally need to be incorporated into this proposed model of comprehensive care are as follows:

1. case identification, enrollment, screening, and assessment;
2. case management and advocacy;
3. available primary medical care and referral for appropriate geriatric and chronic disease consultation;
4. available sources of financial support;
5. optimization of informal support systems;

6. available formal support options: home care, day care, respite care, institutional care;
7. effective and practical quality assurance mechanisms; and
8. communitywide coordination—partly centralized and partly decentralized.

A critical element in accomplishing client appraisal and movement through the system is appropriate case management. While there are a number of models of, and approaches to, case management, its first goal is to identify, screen, and target clients for appropriate levels both of case management and of service provision based on client need and preference. Case management also includes follow-up and reassessment when changes in health and care need status occur. Figure 5.1 illustrates the options and flow patterns that could occur in such a system with patients identified at the two usual entry points into long-term care: community residing or in hospital. The primary concept is the channeling of patients toward optimum community-based services as needed or to institutionalization when necessary. The latter of course can be either permanent, if home placement is not possible, or temporary, if rehabilitative, restorative, or respite care is indicated.

The assumption underlying the need for assessment, triage, and reassessment, when indicated, is that there will be a spectrum of patients ranging from those needing only very limited or no attention from case managers, and few or temporary services, to those needing intense management, geriatric and other specialty evaluation, and multiple long-term care services. This kind of a scheme would probably work best, at least in the current environment, in a health maintenance organization type of setting, with an identified population and motivation for efficiency. Clearly the model would need to be as adaptable as possible to the various community and state organizational and fiscal configurations of today and the near future, but clearly system modifications would be necessary to put it in place in any location.

The elements in the model have all been attempted, at least through pilot and demonstration projects, and of course some exist individually on a permanent basis. Following is a brief discussion of three of the elements that appear to be most critical in facilitating the operation of this kind of coordinated system.

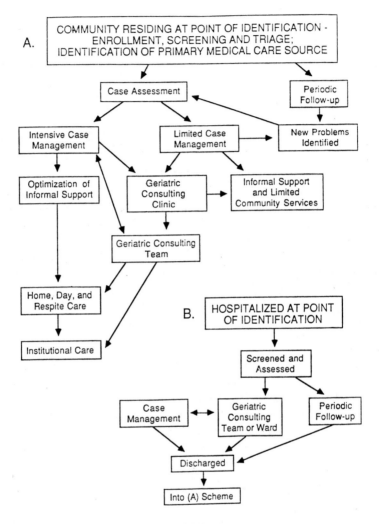

Figure 5.1. Coordination and Integration Schemes

Case Management

A number of models of what is called "case management" have evolved over recent years. Case management as a function has of course existed for much longer and had traditionally been carried out in varying degrees by social case workers, community health and public health nurses, and to some extent primary care physicians. In recent times it has become more formalized, with professionals now being labeled "case managers," and has been emphasized in community-based Medicaid and other long-term care programs, in community mental health programs, and increasingly in managed care and health maintenance organizations.

There has been some argument, especially in the literature on the long-term care and channeling demonstrations, as to the efficacy and cost-effectiveness of the use of formally designated case managers who are used solely or largely for that purpose. The main problem in settling that issue is the lack of studies that isolate formal case management as the only intervention variable (Eggert, Friedman, & Zimmer, 1990). Even in studies that are reasonably well controlled, there have almost always been other concurrent interventions in the treatment groups, including Medicare and Medicaid waivers for additional services as well as direct service provision. Nonetheless case management has become a core function of numerous state and local Medicaid and other long-term care programs (Austin, Low, Roberts, & O'Connor, 1985) and is emphasized as a crucial element in the recent Pepper Commission report (1990). Much has been learned and specified regarding the role, function, and training needs of case managers (Applebaum & Wilson, 1988; *Improving Access for Elders,* 1987). In spite of uncertainty as to resultant cost saving, there is emerging consensus that case management is associated with improved quality and accessibility of care, and possibly quality of life, and thus is probably "cost-effective."

With respect to differing models of case management, there is evidence for the greater efficacy of a neighborhood-based team (nurse, social worker, case aide), with a smaller caseload, as compared with a centralized, single-manager system largely using telephone contact with clients (Eggert, Zimmer, & Friedman, 1987; Eggert, Zimmer, Hall, & Friedman, 1991). Much more in-home contact was possible for the team, allowing for both better assessment and ongoing management of the severely incapacitated subjects, who, by eligibility criteria, would have been cared for at the skilled nursing facility level if institutionalized. The neighborhood team-managed cases used 26% fewer hospital days and 24% less estimated home care costs. Nursing home use, however, was 48% higher, in part due to substitution of nursing home for hospital care. Overall, total estimated costs were 14% lower for the team-managed group. Mortality based on survivorship analysis was slightly lower for the team cases, suggesting that critical health care services were not overly restricted by too rigorous case management. The team also appeared to have a delaying effect on Medicaid "spend-down," with 43% fewer team cases going into Medicaid during the study (Eggert, Friedman, & Zimmer, 1990). Finally, of interest with respect to implications for targeting, the team cases with diagnoses of dementia had the greatest cost savings of any subgroup analyzed. Use of and estimated costs for hospitalization were 69% lower, for home care 47% lower, and for nursing home care about equal, yielding 41% lower total estimated costs for care (Zimmer, Eggert, & Chiverton, 1990).

More research is needed to clarify further the most appropriate case management models for different settings and types of clients and to identify the most efficient ways of targeting patients who will benefit from case management at differing levels of intensity. The current research base is inadequate to answer such important questions as these: Which patients need only information and referral? What can best be accomplished to train patients and informal caregivers to be their own case managers? Who needs case management for only a limited time, and who needs it more intensely and perhaps continuously?

Geriatric Assessment and Consultation

Most medical care for older adults with acute and chronic illnesses is provided by primary care physicians and traditional specialists. However, there is rapidly growing recognition that physicians specializing in geriatric medicine are highly desirable for providing primary care to some kinds of patients, in particular the very old with complex chronic problems. Geriatric specialists, especially in view of their relative scarcity, also are felt to have an important role to play in patient assessment and consultation with primary care physicians, who can then continue to provide care for their patients. Despite the growing research literature on geriatric assessment in recent years, there are still many areas where information is scant or contradictory (Cohen & Feussner, 1989; "NIH Consensus Statement," 1988). The general impression of the efficacy of specialized geriatric assessment has been borne out mainly in the hospital inpatient assessment unit setting and largely as a result of one randomized controlled study (Rubenstein et al., 1984). Some studies of geriatric consultation and assessment teams in hospitals and outpatient clinics have shown trends toward efficacy while others have not (Barker et al., 1985; Becker, McVey, Saltz, Feussner, & Coehn, 1987; Gayton, Wood-Dauphinee, deLorimer, Tonsignant, & Hanley, 1987; Hogan, Fox, Bradley, & Mann, 1987; McVey, Becker, Saltz, Feussner, & Cohen, 1989; Saltz, McVey, Becker, Feussner, & Coehn, 1988; Williams, Hill, Fairbank, & Knox, 1973; Williams, Williams, Zimmer, Hall, & Podgorski, 1987). Additional research is needed to establish their efficacy and to specify what kinds of patients to target for these services and what aspects of the assessments produce particular results. The evidence and the issues are nicely summarized in a recent editorial by Cohen and Feussner (1989), which concludes that assessment alone is not likely to be sufficient without adequate treatment follow-up.

In another randomized, controlled study (Zimmer, Groth-Juncker, & McCusker, 1985), hospitalization and nursing home use was reduced through increased home care of homebound chronically ill elderly patients. The intervention consisted of a physician, geriatric nurse practitioner, and social worker team that was available for home visits at any time. Total health care expenditures were estimated to be 8.6% less for the team patients over the six months of the study. Although this reduction was not significant at the 5% level, family caregiver satisfaction was significantly greater for those receiving the team intervention. The strongest effect of the intervention was on patients who died during the study, for whom average estimated expenditures were 26% lower in the treatment than in the control group, and almost twice as many died at home rather than in a hospital (Zimmer, Groth-Juncker, & McCusker, 1984). These findings have implications for targeting, and of course the intervention constituted not only geriatric assessment but primary care treatment and total patient management. This may support the contention that assessment alone is not sufficient without appropriate follow-up. The team assessed and reassessed its patients and provided medical care as needed through the physician and nurse practitioner and social work services through the social worker. They made referrals to and monitored any other community-based care services needed, such as those discussed elsewhere in this book. They also cared for their patients when hospitalized or admitted to a nursing home.

Quality Assurance

Methods to ensure quality of care in long-term care facilities are in a stage of early development compared with those in place in hospitals (Zimmer, 1989). For home care and other community-based care services, the "state of the art" is even less developed (Applebaum & Phillips, 1990). Problems with the quality of formal health care in the home have been well publicized in recent years. The inspector general's report of 1987 describes problems in the care of Medicare patients including failure to perform many required services and to document activities, poor aide supervision, and failure to meet Medicare requirements for recruitment, hiring, and training of home health aides (Office of the U.S. Inspector General, 1987). An interview survey of state officials, providers, and consumer groups in two states further documented problems with delivery, supervision, and coordination of care; inadequate training and supervision of staff; theft, fraud, alcohol and drug abuse, and absenteeism of personnel; dispensing of medications by inappropriate personnel; and inadequate clinical records (Grant & Harrington, 1989). In the regulatory sphere there is great inconsistency between states (Macro Systems, 1989). Not all states even require licensing of home care agencies: Only 39 did in 1988, and they only tied the standards to Medicare requirements, which are quite limited. In 1988 only five states had authority to impose civil or administrative fines against home health agencies that were found not to be in compliance with regulations (Johnson, 1988). Thus what little regulation of home health agencies has existed in the past seldom has had any "teeth."

Conceptualization of an adequate quality assurance system for health care services delivered in the home is especially problematic, given the separate locus of care for each patient. Added to this are the sheer numbers: There are an estimated 12,000 to 14,000 agencies, certified and noncertified, offering home care services (Applebaum & Phillips, 1990). There is great variation in types of home care agencies, which include (a) licensed, noncertified for Medicare and Medicaid; (b) licensed and certified; (c) nurse registries; (d) employment agencies; (e) temporary personnel agencies; and (f) public contract providers (Harrington & Grant, 1988). Furthermore there has been little research to clarify the role and efficacy of regulatory systems in controlling the quality of home care.

Fortunately we are seeing a significant awakening of concern about ensuring better quality of home care. The Omnibus Budget Reconciliation Act (OBRA) of 1987 (Public Law 100-203) requires assurance of specific patient rights, establishes home health aide training requirements and competency evaluations, and requires unannounced surveys, evaluations of individual clients, stronger enforcement mechanisms, and the use of complaint hot lines and investigations. Many aspects of the quality issues were explored at the National Invitational Conference on Home Care Quality held in 1988. These included accountability, certification and surveying, accreditation, training and supervision of home care workers, empowerment of consumers, and assessment of quality through structure, process, and outcome measures (Office of the Assistant Secretary for Planning and Evaluation, 1988). Over the past two years several books and book chapters have been published that explicitly describe methods, procedures, and forms for doing home care quality assessments (Avillion & Mirgon, 1989; Bulau, 1989; Meisenheimer, 1989; Wagner, 1988; Waltz & Strickland, 1988). In spite of these welcome signs of renewed interest and activity, there is a need for much research to better establish definitions of what constitutes quality of home and other community-based care, how to measure it, and how to assure it.

References

Applebaum, R., & Phillips, P. (1990). Assuring the quality of in-home care: The "other" challenge for long-term care. *The Gerontologist, 30,* 444-450.

Applebaum, R. A., & Wilson, N. L. (1988). Training needs for providing case management for the long-term care client: Lessons from the national channeling demonstration. *The Gerontologist, 28,* 172-176.

Austin, C., Low, J., Roberts, L., & O'Connor, K. (1985). *Case management: A critical review.* Seattle: University of Washington, Pacific Northwest Gerontology Center.

Avillion, A. E., & Mirgon, B. B. (1989). Quality assurance and home health care. In *Quality assurance in rehabilitation nursing: A practical guide.* Rockville, MD: Aspen.

Barker, W. H., Williams, T. F., Zimmer, J. G., Van Buren, C., Vincent, S. J., & Pickrel, S. G. (1985). Geriatric consultation teams in acute hospitals: Impact on back-up of elderly patients. *Journal of the American Geriatrics Society, 33,* 422-428.

Becker, P. M., McVey, L. J., Saltz, C. L., Feussner, J., & Cohen, H. (1987). Hospital-acquired complications in a randomized controlled clinical trial of a geriatric consultation team. *Journal of the American Medical Society, 257,* 2313-2317.

Bulau, J. M. (1989). *Quality assurance policies and procedures for home health care.* Rockville, MD: Aspen.

Cohen, H. J., & Feussner, J. R. (1989). Comprehensive geriatric assessment: Mission not yet accomplished. *Journal of Gerontology: Medical Sciences, 44,* 175-177.

Eggert, G. M., Friedman, B., & Zimmer, J. G. (1990). Models of intensive case management. *Journal of Gerontological Social Work, 15,* 75-101.

Eggert, G. M., Zimmer, J. G., & Friedman, B. (1987). ACCESS neighborhood team model of case management proves more cost effective. *Aging Network News, 4,* 6, 16.

Eggert, G. M., Zimmer, J. G., Hall, W. J., & Friedman, B. (1991). Case management: A randomized controlled study comparing a neighborhood team and a centralized individual model. *Health Services Research, 26,*(4).

The evaluation of the National Long Term Care Demonstration. (1988). [Special issue]. *Health Services Research, 23*(1).

Gayton D., Wood-Dauphinee, S., deLorimer, M., Tonsignant, P., & Hanley, J. (1987). Trial of a geriatric consultation team in an acute care hospital. *Journal of the American Geriatrics Society, 35,* 723-736.

Grant, L. A., & Harrington, C. (1989). Quality of care in licensed and unlicensed home care agencies: A California case study. *Home Health Care Services Quarterly, 10*(2), 115-138.

Harrington, C., & Grant, L. A. (1988). *The delivery, regulation, and politics of home care: A California case study.* San Francisco: Institute for Health and Aging.

Hogan, D. B., Fox, R. A., Bradley, B. W. D., & Mann, O. E. (1987). Effect of a geriatric consultation service on management of patients in an acute care hospital. *Canadian Medical Association Journal, 136,* 713-717.

Improving access for elders: The role of case management—final report. (1987). Seattle: University of Washington, Institute on Aging.

Johnson, S. H. (1988). *Assuring quality of home health care for the elderly: Identifying and developing tools for enforcement* (Report prepared for the AARP/Andrus Foundation). Saint Louis: Saint Louis University, School of Law.

Kemper, P., Applebaum, R., & Harrigan, M. (1987). Community care demonstrations: What have we learned? *Health Care Financing Review, 8,* 87-100.

Macro Systems, Inc. (1989). *Review of state quality assurance programs for home care* (Unpublished report submitted to the U.S. Department of Health and Human Services, Office of the Assistant Secretary for Planning and Evaluation, Washington, DC).

McVey, L. J., Becker, P. M., Saltz, C. C., Feussner, J. R., & Cohen, H. J. (1989). Effect of a geriatric consultation team on functional status of elderly hospitalized patients: A random controlled clinical trial. *Annals of Internal Medicine, 110,* 79-84.

Meisenheimer, C. G. (1989). *Quality assurance for home health care.* Rockville, MD: Aspen.

National Institutes of Health Consensus Development Conference consensus statement: Geriatric assessment methods for clinical decision-making. (1988). *Journal of the American Geriatrics Society, 36,* 342-347.

Office of the Assistant Secretary for Planning and Evaluation. (1988). *National Invitational Conference on Home Care Quality: Issues and accountability.* Washington, DC: U.S. Department of Health and Human Services.

Office of the U.S. Inspector General [Richard P. Kusserow]. (1987). *Home health aide services for medicare patients* (0A101-86-00010). Washington, DC: U.S. Department of Health and Human Services.

Pepper Commission. (1990). *Access to health care and long-term care for all Americans: Recommendations to the Congress.* Washington, DC: Author.

Rubenstein, L. Z., Josephson, K. R., Wieland, G. D., English, P. A., Sayre, J. A., & Kane, R. L. (1984). Effectiveness of a geriatric evaluation unit: A randomized clinical trail. *The New England Journal of Medicine, 311,* 1664-1670.

Saltz, C. C., McVey, L. I., Becker, R. M., Feussner, J. R., & Cohen, H. J. (1988). Impact of a geriatric consultation team on discharge placement and repeat hospitalization. *The Gerontologist, 28,* 344-350.

Wagner, D. (1988). *Managing for quality in home health care.* Rockville, MD: Aspen.

Waltz, C., & Strickland, O. (1988). *Measurement of nursing outcomes* (2 vols.). New York: Springer.

Weissert, W. G. (1985). Seven reasons why it is so difficult to make community-based long-term care cost-effective. *Health Services Research, 20,* 423-433.

Weissert, W., Cready, C. M., & Pawelak, J. (1988). The past and future of home-and community-based long-term care. *The Milbank Quarterly, 66,* 309-388.

Williams, M. E., Williams, T. F., Zimmer, J. G., Hall, W. J., & Podgorski, C. A. (1987). How does the team approach to outpatient geriatric evaluation compare with traditional care: A report of a randomized controlled trial. *Journal of the American Geriatrics Society, 35,* 1071-1078.

Williams, T. F., Hill, J., Fairbank, M., & Knox, K. (1973). Appropriate placement of the chronically ill and aged: A successful approach by evaluation. *Journal of the American Medical Association, 226,* 1332-1335.

Zawadski, R. T. (Ed.). (1984). *Community-based systems of long term care.* New York: Haworth.

Zimmer, J. G. (1989). Quality assurance. In P. R. Katz & E. Calkins (Eds.), *Principles and practice of nursing home care.* New York: Springer.

Zimmer, J. G., Eggert, G. M., & Chiverton, P. (1990). Individual versus team case management in optimizing community care for chronically ill patients with dementia. *Journal of Aging and Health, 2,* 357-372.

Zimmer, J. G., Groth-Juncker, A., & McCusker, J. (1984). Effects of a physician-led home care team on terminal care. *Journal of the American Geriatrics Society, 32,* 288-292.

Zimmer, J. G., Groth-Juncker, A., & McCusker, J. (1985). A randomized controlled study of a home health care team. *American Journal of Public Health, 75,* 134-141.

SIX

Home and Community-Based
Mental Health Services for the Elderly

MARY S. HARPER

The mental health needs of older people are often overlooked. Yet the noninstitutionalized elderly person suffers disproportionately from emotional, social, behavioral, and mental disorders. Psychopathology increases with age. Most notably functional disorders such as depression and paranoia, organic brain disease, and even suicide are more common in old age (Kruse & Jones, 1990, Wasylenki, 1982). In spite of the higher prevalence of mental health disorders in old age, the home and community-based mental health services for the elderly are basically inadequate, fragmented, unaffordable, and seldom used. Needed services are often underused because older people and their health care providers do not differentiate comorbid psychiatric conditions that are treatable from those that are untreatable. In addition problems of poor access are often combined with an unwillingness to seek care for "stigmatized" mental health conditions.

As a result, the general health sector functions as the "de facto" mental health service system for the elderly (Schurman, Kramer, & Mitchell, 1985). National studies such as the 1980 Medical Care and Utilization and Expenditure survey indicate that psychiatrists and psychologists see relatively few older people in their practices (Bonham, 1983).

AUTHOR'S NOTE: This chapter was written by a government employee as part of official duties; therefore the material is in the public domain and may be copied or reproduced without permission.

Yet older people make millions of visits to nonpsychiatric physicians for mental health services, psychotropic drug prescriptions, and couseling/psychotherapy (Regier, Goldgerg, & Taube, 1978; Schurman et al., 1985). Recent analysis of data from the Epidemiological Catchment Area Program (ECA), however, does not corroborate this finding; George, Blazer, and Winfield-Laird (1988) found that the rates of older persons with mental illness seeing a general medical provider for mental health reasons across the four ECA sites are only around 1.5 times higher than for such diagnosed persons using outpatient mental health services.

Extent of Mental Disorders in Old Age

The ECA program supported by the National Institute of Mental Health (NIMH) during the early 1980s was a population-based study conducted in five communities (New Haven, Baltimore, St. Louis, Durham, and Los Angeles) that added samples of elderly persons in three of the communities to enable estimates of mental illness in the older person. The overall estimate of mental illness for one-month prevalence rates was 12.3% in the elderly population, with the most frequently occurring conditions being anxiety disorders (5.5%), severe cognitive impairment (4.9% total with 2.9% for ages 65-74, 6.8% for ages 75-84, and 15.8% for ages 85 and over), phobias (4.8%), and affective disorder (2.5%). A more conservative (8.7%) estimate of mental illness in the elderly could be obtained by eliminating phobias, given concerns about how effectively this category was assessed by the Diagnostic Interview Schedule (DIS; Thompson et al., 1988). Even so only 1.5% of mental health expenditures go to the elderly living in the community, and only 6% of community mental health centers' patients are elderly (Light, Lebowitz, & Bailey, 1986). Hence evidence demonstrates that the elderly are greatly underserved in the area of mental health services (Talbott, 1985).

Research findings also indicate that the incidence of mental illness among the elderly is higher than that for the under-65 population. The likelihood of psychosis—the most serious form of mental disorder—increases significantly after age 65 and even more so beyond age 75. In fact it is more than twice as common in the over-75 age groups as in the 25- to 34-year-old group (Butler & Lewis, 1977). In addition the incidence of transient but significant symptoms of depression (as distinct from depressive illness) is significant in persons aged 65 and older; based upon psychiatrists' diagnosis, prevalence rates for depressive disorders in older community residents are in the range of 10%. In a study of poststroke patients, investigators noted that depression or dysrhythmia occured in 30% to 50% of stroke patients in the acute poststroke period (Moss & Benhorn, 1990; Van Gorp & Cummings, 1989). Certain illnesses, including hepatitis, cirrhosis of the liver, digitalis toxicity, and postviral infection, present with depression, and depression may occur in an elderly person who is taking diuril for hypertension or may occur as a result of a low serum potassium. In addition cerebrovascular disease in the elderly may result in mood disturbances. Finally, 86% of the elderly have chronic health problems that often result in psychological stress, and approximately 50% of the physically handicapped elderly also have psychiatric disabilities severe enough to warrant assistance (Brody & Ruff, 1986).

Shapiro, Skinner, and German (1986) estimated that 7.8% of the elderly in the community are in need of mental health services, and recent studies have revealed that psychiatric disorders are common among elderly residents of urban public housing (Roca, Storer, Robbins, Tlasek, & Rabins, 1990). Although the rates of mental disorders in nursing homes are higher than in the community, by virtue of the sheer numbers of older people in the community, there is a great need for attention to the community-based elderly who are mentally ill. Most surveys of the mental health needs of the elderly exclude many sites such as day-care centers, respite programs, home care services, and acute medical units, indicating that final figures may be higher.

The attitudes of the elderly and family members, adequacy of assessment and diagnosis, scope of insurance coverage or other funds, providers' experiences with the mental health system, access to transportation, and stigma all influence the delivery of mental health services to the elderly. According to Burns and Taube (1988) only about 37% of the elderly in actual need of mental treatment receive it. Moreover only about a third of the elderly in need receive help from the mental health sector. Older persons receiving most of their mental health treatment from nonpsychiatrist physicians are four times as likely to be prescribed a psychotropic drug than to receive a psychosocial intervention such as counseling or psychotherapy.

Home and community-based mental health services for the elderly include a broad array of health care, rehabilative, and social services provided by several disciplines, including adult day care, nutrition sites, outpatient clinics, and respite and hospice programs. In addition the availability of mental health services does not mean access to quality services. Services are greatly influenced by a variety of factors, including whether they are provided by for-profit agencies or nonprofit agencies; whether the source of payment is Medicare, Medicaid, the Older American Act, private insurance, or some other source; and whether they are regulated by quality assurance programs, state or federal regulations, and licensure (Harrington & Grant, 1990). Evaluation of one study concluded that the psychiatric needs of the elderly at a clinic for the impaired elderly had not been adequately addressed, particularly in the use of outpatient settings, and that the potential role of the family in caring for such patients had not been sufficiently supported (Reifler & Eisdorfer, 1980).

Why Home Visit and Home Care

Familiarity with the elderly person's home environment can help the clinician to fully assess the effect of the illness, disability, and psychological and family interactions of daily living. Rational decision making on the provision of specific services or intervention into family pathology requires knowledge and understanding of the context of the patient's illness. Factors in the home environment may cause dependency as much as factors in the patient. While in the home the clinician can observe life-styles in terms of nutrition, smoking, medication compliance, home safety and cleanliness, hidden illnesses, and problems such as incontinence, sleep disorders, depression, and behavioral disturbances. After assessing the needs of the elderly person in his or her home, the physician or nurse can best identify the type of worker and type of supervision the patient requires (Ham, 1986).

HOME CARE

Home care is the centerpiece of the health care delivery system, because most research studies have demonstrated that the elderly prefer home care to other types of care (Keenan, 1989; Maraldo, 1989).

Indeed all care starts at home and with the family. Home care has expanded rapidly during the last few years. For example, between 1977 and 1986 the federal government's bill for home care under the Medicare program rose from $100 million to $2 billion. It is further anticipated that home care costs will reach $18 bilion in the 1990s (Monk & Cox, 1989). Part of a continuum of care for the mentally ill elderly and other elderly people, home care is supplemented and/or complemented by other modalities such as hospitals. The continuum of home and community-based mental health services for the elderly include (a) community mental health centers; (b) nurse-managed neighborhood clinics; (c) day-care centers for supervision and maintenance; (d) emergency services for crisis interventions, behavioral management, or medical intervention; (e) outpatient treatment, including case management, psychotherapy, drug management, and support groups; (f) evaluation for detection, diagnosis, and referral; (g) partial hospitalization for treatment of symptoms, crisis intervention, and stabilization, (h) respite care to give relief to caregivers; (i) group homes or personal care homes to assist with activities of daily living and coping; (j) hospice care for the terminally ill; (k) nursing homes; and (l) board and care homes.

A written care plan that is frequently updated should be kept for each patient. The patient and family or significant other(s) must be involved in the development, implementation, and evaluation of outcomes of the plan. Psychosocial assessment taken in home and community-based mental health programs for the care plan must include the following domains: Family relations as perceived by the patient and the family as well as access to problem-solving resources in the family and community must be examined. Signs of abuse or neglect and caregiver tendencies to foster autonomy and independence are likewise important to check. Family "spirit," social support, and environmental characteristics should be included as all affect the elderly person's ability to cope. The elderly person's attention span and memory, physical functioning, need for specific medical or rehabilitative therapies and devices, compliance with health care plan, attitude toward health, self-care deficits, and sleep patterns should be observed.

In addition, the care provider must be able to function in specific areas, such as observing and assessing the patient, assisting in prevention of excessive dependency, advocating compliance with the medication regime, and encouraging use of community mental health resources.

Most elderly are not diagnosed for the major mental disorders (Myers et al., 1984) but present emotional, social, behavioral, and mental disorders that are often associated with physical illness. These behavioral manifestations in the elderly present the greatest challenges to informal caregivers, members of the family, and paraprofessionals, frequently giving rise to institutionalization and use of restraints (physical and chemical). Although 30% of home health care is provided by home health aides (HHAs; Office of the Inspector General, 1987), there was no federal mandatory training for the HHA until the Omnibus Budget Reconciliation Act of 1987. Only about 20 states require training, which is of various lengths. One of the reasons for turnover for aides, nurses, and many others who work with the elderly is the problem of lack of training in dealing with behavior management (Harper, 1988). HHAs report that over half of their elderly patients have behavioral and mental disorders, and the behavioral disorders increase with age (Harper, 1989). Older persons with behavioral, emotional, and mental disorders are heavy users of care and difficult to care for (Wan, 1987). Likewise adult family member caregivers frequently do not have the knowledge, resources, or skills necessary to care for a severely depressed elderly individual or an "acting-out" elderly person with dementia (Nelson, 1990).

INTERDISCIPLINARY MENTAL HEALTH TEAM

There are examples of programs aimed at overcoming these problems with the elderly's use of mental health services. For example, the Visiting Nurses Service (VNS) of New York provides comprehensive mental health services for six hospitals. The service was formed after hospital staff noted increasing numbers of patients with complex diagnoses that is, comorbidity compounded by multiple social and emotional problems, which make discharge planning and arrangement for home care increasingly difficult. The team, including a psychiatrist, a psychiatric nurse, a psychiatric social worker, and a social work assistant, forms the only home health agency of its kind in New York City that is able to assess and diagnose a patient in the hospital and give a written opinion about whether or not home care is appropriate. Services include outreach/screening, assessment, diagnosis, crisis intervention, short-term counseling, formulation and implementation of treatment plans, linkage with mental health and social service providers, and follow-up (Holt, 1989).

COMMUNITY HOME HEALTH CARE

Similarly the Community Home Health Care Program (CHHCP), composed of psychosocial/community health nurses, social workers/occupational therapists, and a consulting psychiatrist, makes visits related to in-home mental health services. These services include assessment, treatment, case management, social services, referral to an independent living center, individual and family therapy, medication administration and management, training for independent living skills, and nursing home consultation. During the period in which the CHHCP was studied, conditions treated included confusion, disorientation, memory impairment, dementia, anxiety, depression, paranoia, and marked personality changes (Kruse & Wood, 1989).

COMMUNITY PSYCHIATRIC NURSING TEAMS

In Great Britain over 200 Community Psychiatric Nursing Teams help expand mental health services to the elderly. Based on clinical assessment, the nurses establish diagnoses, prescribe appropriate drugs and dosages and conduct individual and group psychotherapy. They coordinate services with the general practitioner physician, who frequently has a caseload of 2,300 patients (Grau, 1986).

Summary

Nearly 2 million elderly persons in the community require mental health services. Psychopathology increases with age, and comorbidity is very common among the elderly, who often manifest their pathology in atypical manners. Several medical conditions also manifest themselves as emotional, behavioral, and mental disorders. The primary providers of mental health services to the elderly are primary care physicians, but home and community-based mental health services are a part of the continuum of care. In home and community mental health programs, the patient, family, and significant others should be involved in planning, implementing, and evaluating a care plan.

The primary provider of home care to the elderly is the family. In fact the elderly generally underutilize formal mental health services in the community. Several research home health programs, however, have demonstrated their effectiveness in preventing institutionalization and enhancing the quality of life for the elderly in the community. More research is needed pertaining to the quality and outcomes of mental health services delivered in home and community-based programs.

References

Bonham, G. S. (1983). *Procedures and questionnaires of the National Medical Care Utilization and Expenditure Survey* (Series A, Methodological Report No. 1, DHHS Pub. No. ADM 83-2001, National Center for Health Statistics, Public Health Service). Washington, DC: Government Printing Office.

Brody, S. J., & Ruff, G. E. (1986). *Aging and rehabilitation: Advances in the state of the art.* New York: Springer.

Burns, B. J., & Taube, C. A. (1988, October 18-20). *Mental health services for the elderly in the general health sector.* Presented at the national conference on access and financing for neuropsychiatric care for the elderly, Brown University, Providence, RI.

Butler, R. N., & Lewis, N. J. (1977). *Aging and mental health: Positive psychosocial approaches* (2nd ed.). St. Louis, MO: C. V. Mosby.

George, L. K., Blazer, D. G., & Winfield-Laird, I. (1988). Psychiatric disorders and mental health services: Use in later life evidence from the epidemiological catchment area program. In J. Brody & G. Maddox (Eds.), *Epidemiology and aging* (pp. 189-219). New York: Springer.

Grau, L. (1986). Britain's Community Psychiatric Nursing Team. *Geriatric Nursing, 6*(2), 143-147.

Ham, R. J. (1986). Getting the most out of a home visit. *Canadian Family Physician, 32*(12), 2677-2683.

Harper, M. S. (1988). *Behavioral, social and mental health aspects of home care for older Americans.* New York: Haworth.

Harper, M. S. (1989). Providing mental health services in the homes of the elder: A public policy perspective. *Caring, 8*(6), 5-9, 52-53.

Harrington, D., & Grant, L. A. (1990). The delivery, regulation and politics of home care: A California case study. *The Gerontologist, 30*(4), 451-461.

Holt, S. W. (1989). Securing the future through innovations: New dimensions in home health care. *Caring, 8*(6), 35-41.

Keenan, M. P. (1989). *Changing needs for long term care: A chartbook* (Public Policy Institute Publication N. WI 4269[189], D13535). Washington, DC: AARP.

Kruse, E. A., & Jones, G. (1990). Development of a comprehensive suicide protocol in a home health care and social service agency. *Journal of Home health Care Practice, 3*(2), 47-56.

Kruse, E. A., & Wood, M. (1989). Delivering mental health services in the home. *Caring, 8*(6), 20-34.

Light, E., Lebowitz, B. D., & Bailey, F. (1986). Community mental health centers (CMHC) and elderly services: An analysis of direct and indirect services and service delivery sites. *Community Mental Health Journal, 22*(4), 294-302.

Maraldo, P. J. (1989). Home care should be the heart of a nursing-sponsored national health plan. *Nursing and Health Care, 10*(6), 301-304.

Monk, A., & Cox, C. (1989). International innovations in home care. *Aging International, 12,* 11-23.

Moss, A. J., & Benhorn, J. (1990). Prognosis and management after a first myocardial infarction. *The New England Journal of Medicine, 322*(11), 743-753.

Myers, J. K., Weissman, M. M., Tischler, G. L., Holzer, C. E., Leaf, P. J., Orvaschel, H., Anthony, J. C., Boyd, J. H., Burke, J. D., Kramer, M., & Stoltzman, R. (1984). Six month prevalence of psychiatric disorders in three communities. *Archives of General Psychiatry, 4*(10), 959-967.

Nelson, M. K. (1990). Care of the mentally ill older person in the home. In M. O. Hogstel (Ed.), *Geropsychiatric nursing* (pp. 283-302). St Louis, MO: C. V. Mosby.

Office of the Inspector General [Richard P. Kusserow]. (1987). *Home health aide services for medicare patients* (0A101-86-00010). Washington, DC: U.S. Department of Health and Human Services.

Reifler, B. V., & Eisdorfer, C. (1980). A clinic for the impaired elderly and their families. *American Journal of Psychiatry, 137*(11), 1399-1403.

Roca, R. P., Storer, D. J., Robbins, B. M., Tlasek, M. E., & Rabins, P. V. (1990). Psychogeriatric assessment and treatment in urban public housing. *Hospital and Community Psychiatry, 41*(8), 916-920.

Rogier, D. A., Goldberg, I. D., & Taube, C. A. (1978). The de facto U.S. mental health services system. *Archives of General Psychiatry, 35*(2), 685-693.

Schurman, R. A., Kramer, P. D., & Mitchell, J. B. (1985). The hidden mental health network. *Archives of General Psychiatry, 42*(2), 89-94.

Shapiro, S., Skinner, E. A., & German, P. S. (1986). Needs and demands for mental health services in an urban community: An exploration based on household interviews. In J. Barrett & R. M. Rose (Eds.), *Mental disorders in the community: Progress and challenge.* New York: Guilford.

Talbott, J. A. (1985, February 9). *Clinical and policy issues.* Presented at the conference on meeting the needs of the aged mentally ill, New York Academy of Medicine.

Taube, C. A., Burns, B. J., & Kessler, L. (1984). Patients of psychiatrists or psychologists. *American Psychologist, 39*(2), 1433-1447.

Thompson, J. W., Burns, B. J., Bartko, J., Boyd, J. H., & Taube, C. A. (1988). The use of ambulatory services by persons with and without phobias. *Medical Care, 26*(2), 183-198.

Van Gorp, W. G., & Cummings, J. L. (1989). Assessment of mood, affect and personality. In E. J. Pirozzolo (Ed.), *New developments in neuropsychological evaluation* (pp. 441-459). Philadelphia: W. B. Saunders.

Wan, T. T. (1987). Functionally disabled elderly: Health status, social support and use of health services. *Research on Aging, 9*(2), 61-78.

Wasylenki, D. (1982). The psychogeriatric problem. *Canada's Mental Health, 30*(3), 16-19.

APPENDIX A

Annotated Bibliography

MERYL B. RAPPAPORT
A. E. BENJAMIN

This bibliography is intended to be a resource for scholars and policymakers with interests in in-home health and supportive services for older persons. It is selective with respect to topical focus, time period, and type of publication reviewed. Topics covered include home care, board and care, respite, and case management for older persons—the primary themes of chapters originally included in this volume. The temporal focus of our literature search was material published since 1985, although some widely cited earlier items also are included. Finally, inclusion was limited to (a) empirical studies that meet widely accepted scientific standards and (b) nonempirical papers that provide original perspectives on or syntheses of existing research. Generally very small empirical studies and items from minor journals and professional association sources were excluded. Annotations are intended to convey the method of the research and content of the publication. They are primarily descriptive and do not explicitly judge the quality of the research and presentation. However, an attempt was made to limit inclusion in this review to publications that have contributed to scholarship in the field.

Applebaum, R. A., & Wilson, N. L. (1988). Training needs for providing case management for the long-term care client: Lessons from the national channeling demonstration. *The Gerontologist, 28*(2), 172-176.

This article summarizes key areas for training of long-term care case managers based on the experience of the national channeling demonstration. Case managers were social workers and nurses who faced special challenges in working with elderly clients over an extended period of time; clients had high morbidity and mortality. Three areas for orientation and ongoing training are identified: (a) population-specific training on understanding clients, (b) analysis of the service environment, and (c) techniques of case management. Also important are ongoing supervision and support of case managers. The article demonstrates that little research has been done on how to increase efficacy and training needs of case managers and suggests that the growth of case management in long-term care would argue for more training. A recommended caseload size of 45-75 was used in channeling, but practical experience was that more than 55-60 cases was extremely difficult to staff and supervise adequately. Key factors identified as crucial to the success of a case management program are the ratio of case managers to clients, supervision, administrative requirements, and ongoing support of case managers. Social workers and nurses were identified as being as mutually important as case managers. Specific training needs are identified for each type of case manager, and the role of professional training programs is noted in developing case management skills.

Avorn, J., Dreyer, P., Connelly, K., & Soumerai, S. (1989). Use of psychoactive medication and the quality of care in rest homes. *New England Journal of Medicine, 320*(4), 227-232.

This report, on the results of a survey of use of psychoactive medications among deinstitutionalized psychiatric patients residing in rest homes, provides an overview of rest homes, the nature of their residents, the lack of information on patterns of medication use within the facilities, and licensure and quality issues. In a random sample of 55 rest homes in Massachusetts, at least one psychoactive medication was being taken by 55% of the residents; 39% of the residents were receiving antipsychotics and, of these, 18% were receiving two or more such drugs. In most cases the prescriptions had been written in the remote past and were automatically refilled. Typically drugs were administered orally by staff members, usually daily. A follow-up study examined 837 residents in 44 rest homes who had especially high levels of antipsychotic drug use. About half the residents had no evidence of physician participation in decisions about their mental health during the study year. Statistics on residential location prior to the rest home are provided as well as a summary of medication use and clinical measures for these patients. Widespread cognitive impairment was found, but the causal relation of such impairment to medication use could not be determined. Also 6% of residents evidenced tardive dyskinesia, probably the result of medication side effects. An assessment of staff competence revealed a low level of comprehension of the purpose and side effects of commonly used psychoactive drugs. The authors conclude that, while there is a very high level of psychoactive medication use in these facilities, as well as a high proportion of deinstitutionalized residents, the staff of these rest homes have limited knowledge concerning practical patient care issues. The findings suggest that some rest homes may require more vigorous regulatory monitoring than they have historically received, and recommendations are offered.

Barker, W. H., Williams, T. F., Zimmer, J. G., Van Buren, C., Vincent, S. J., & Pickrel, S. G. (1985). Geriatric consultation teams in acute hospitals: Impact on back-up of elderly patients. *Journal of the American Geriatrics Society, 33*(6), 422-428.

This article reports the outcomes of a study evaluating the effectiveness of geriatric consultation teams in acute hospitals. The teams were developed to help alleviate problems of discharge backup for older patients. Established to promote greater attention to restoration of patient function and comprehensive discharge planning, geriatric consultation teams operating in six Monroe County, New York, hospitals were evaluated over a six-month period in 1982. Of 4,326 newly hospitalized patients aged 70 and over who were briefly screened by a member of the consultation team, 366 (8.5%) judged to be at risk of requiring prolonged hospital stays received geriatric consultations. Consultation included a full listing of diagnoses, treatments, and nursing and social problems from the patient's charts, supplemented by information from nurses, social workers, and medical personnel caring for the patient and from the interview with and examination of the patient. A summary of findings and recommendations were entered in the patient's chart and team follow-up over the next several weeks monitored the degree of implementation of the plan. The principal objective of the project was to reduce the number of elderly backed up in the community's acute hospital beds. In addition the project aimed to document barriers in the hospitals to maintaining or restoring functioning and timely discharge and to improve the skills of staff members caring for elderly patients. Results of the study showed that the mean monthly census of elderly patients backed up in the hospital declined 21%, a reversal of previous rises that could not be explained by any other identifiable factors. The impact was on length of stay on backup status rather than rate of entry to that status. This outcome is attributed to a variety of social, rehabilitative, and medical interventions. A variety of patient care issues, hospital systems obstacles, and financial/legal issues were identified as contributing to patient backup. Geriatric consultation was found to be a successful intervention in acute hospitals, and applications to other settings are positively discussed.

Bass, D. M., & Noelker, L. S. (1987). The influence of family caregivers on elder's use of in-home services: An expanded conceptual framework. *Journal of Health and Social Behavior, 28*, 184-196.

This article uses an expanded version of the Andersen model including predisposing, enabling, and need characteristics of both the primary family caregiver and the elderly care recipient. In addition the role of secondary kin caregivers in the provision of care to the elder is represented by family-related enabling characteristics. The study examined the influence of characteristics of the primary and secondary family caregivers on the elders' use of aide and in-home nursing services. Family-related enabling factors, such as household income, were found to be the most important predictors of the amounts of services used by elders. Caregiver need characteristics (such as activity restrictions due to caregiving, perceived change in health, and caregiving burden) accounted for significant variation in whether or not services were used.

Becker, G., & Kaufman, S. (1988). Old age, rehabilitation, and research: A review of the issues. *The Gerontologist, 28*(4), 459-468.

This article reviews the literature on the relationship among old age, rehabilitation, and related research, identifying the roles culture, the health care system, and physical, functional, and psychosocial factors play in rehabilitation. Problems in the optimization of rehabilitation, and implications for quality of life and well-being of the elderly rehabilitation patient, are noted. The literature shows that rehabilitation, while beneficial for elders, does not consistently recognize and target the needs of this population in an appropriate way. Alternative research directions suggested include a new focus on how rehabilitation can be adapted to better meet the needs of older people and how the transition from the hospital to the home can be eased, yielding more cost-effective results.

Beland, F. (1987). Living arrangement preferences among elderly people. *The Gerontologist, 27*(6), 797-803.

Canadian elderly living either with a spouse only or alone were more likely than those who lived with a child, relative, or friend to prefer to move into an alternate setting such as a nursing home or senior housing. Analyses of associations between preferred living arrangements and the wishes, as well as requests, for an alternate setting revealed limited evidence to support the hypothesis that residing with others is a substitute for an alternate setting.

Beland, F. (1987). Identifying profiles of service requirements in a non-institutionalized elderly population. *Journal of Chronic Disease, 40*(1), 51-64.

This article reports the results of a cluster analysis done on housing environments of the elderly. Data were gathered on a noninstitutionalized population in Quebec, Canada, that identified 12 living arrangement groups. A cluster analysis of the service requirements performed for each of these groups identified similarities across them. Four different service requirement profiles were identified. (a) The first profile includes elderly with service requirements common to middle-aged adults in the community. This group constituted about 50% of the sample. (b) Of the elderly studied, 9% needed all of the services presented in the study. They lived in residential arrangements that provided the most supportive social and physical environments to meet their level of service needs. (c) Heavy housework was the only service need required by one third of the sample. (d) Another 6% of the elderly sample did not have access to the help they needed with many activities of daily living. Implications are that service requirements should be more significant in planning processes than illness, handicaps, and/or functional disabilities; needs assessments of individuals should always consider the resources and service requirements available.

Benjamin, A. E. (1986). Determinants of state variations in home health utilization and expenditures under Medicare. *Medical Care, 24*(6), 535-547.

Although Medicare is a federal program, use of and expenditures for home care vary widely across the states. This article presents theory and data in an effort to illuminate the reasons these variations exist. Use of Medicare home health services by state in 1982 was analyzed using regression equations, and user and expenditure data were found to vary considerably. Nearly three fourths of the variation in home health use ($R^2 = 0.72$) is explained by seven state characteristics. About three fifths of the variation in expenditures ($R^2 = 0.61$) is accounted for by six state factors. Of most explanatory importance are home health agency (HHA) supply, need levels, presence of alternative sources of care, sources of referrals, and state resources. HHA supply, case-mix severity, costs of inputs, and the availability of alternatives emerge as important in understanding variations in average expenditures per user across states. Supply factors play a consistently strong role in explaining both use and expenditures. The results suggest the need to give more analytic attention to the impact of the market share of proprietary HHAs in explaining expenditure variations and the effects of total supply on use and spending.

Benjamin, A. E. (1987). *Trends and issues in reimbursement for home health care* (unpublished).

This paper discusses the rapid growth in use and expenditures for home health care, which has generated pressure to moderate the costs of care as well as confusion about how to do so. Discussion of reimbursement sources and thorough, concise description of the history of the growth of each are useful. The author argues that Medicare, as the most visible and largest payer for home health services, has set the standard for home health reimbursement by other insurers. Federal approaches to cost containment have relied on administrative approaches rather than comprehensive reform. The author suggests that this policy approach has generated consternation among providers and potential hardships for current and future users of home health care.

Benjamin, A. E., Feigenbaum, L., Newcomer, R. J., & Fox, P. J. (1989). *Medicare Posthospital Study: Final report.* (Available from the Institute for Health and Aging, UCSF, 210 Filbert Street, Suite 500, San Francisco, CA 94133-3203)

This report summarizes the results of an 18-month study of posthospital home health care and skilled nursing facility (SNF) use; the study was funded by the Commonwealth Fund's Commission on Elderly People Living Alone. The study surveyed 540 subjects with and without Medicare. Analysis of the characteristics of experimental and comparison groups indicate that Medicare posthospital services seem to be provided to those most in need of care following hospitalization, although age, gender, ethnicity, and informal caregiving do not differentiate between those who receive or do not receive Medicare home health services. Both functional status and medical severity are strongly related to home health referral; other things being equal, those living alone are more likely to receive Medicare home health care. The experience of recently hospitalized elderly who receive Medicare home health services shows important changes and continuing problems in the posthospital period. About one third of the sample improved, and about 50% of home health users showed no change in overall rating of medical status during the home care period. The majority of users experienced an improvement in ADLs during the home health period, but the vast majority of study participants (85.6%) were left with functional and/or medically related tasks that required continuing attention at discharge from home care. One third of the sample continued to have medical tasks to complete at Medicare home health discharge, a fact seen as problematic because of the skilled nature of some of these tasks. Of the 52% of the study participants who used non-Medicare reimbursable services during the Medicare home health care period, five sixths received personal care or homemaker-chore services. Multiple care needs remained six months after hospitalization. Rehospitalization was required for 27.8% of the home health care recipients and for 21.6% of the comparison group. Of the entire study group, 60% had used personal care or chore services since hospitalization, and those with greater functional impairment and more severe disabilities were more likely to receive such services; 17% of the home health group and 16.5% of the comparison group died during the study period—a statistically significant difference. The area of greatest service need continues to be personal care attendant/homemaker chore services. While substantial numbers of both the home health (55.8%) and the comparison (42.9%) groups need such services, the difference between the two is statistically significant. Data from this study indicate that both medical and functional status (controlling for the other) influence the interaction of medical and functional problems. Medicare policy persists in attempting to isolate the medically relevant aspects of care by limiting eligibility for and range and duration of services provided. Data suggest that functional status is associated with expensive reinstitutionalization. As a result Medicare's medical orientation, which excludes "custodial services" appropriate to the chronic care needs of recently hospitalized elderly, may appear to save public funds but in fact be more costly overall. The authors advocate more public investment in formal care at home during the posthospital period. Medicare is seen to be only partially responsive to the acute and chronic service needs of the elderly.

Benjamin, A. E., & Newcomer, R. J. (1986). Board and care housing: An analysis of state differences. *Research on Aging, 8*(3), 388-406.

Using 1983 survey data, a regression analysis of board and care bed supply in 50 states and the District of Columbia was conducted to explain variance in bed supply. Through telephone interviews with representatives of 92 state agencies responsible for licensing, regulating, and monitoring board and care homes in the states, data on the total number of facilities and beds and the populations using them were collected. Supplemental data were also gathered from relevant documents. Using regression analysis, about 65% of the variability in total beds across states in 1983 can be accounted for by SSI policy, board and care regulation, Medicaid nursing home rates, and the percentage of elderly in the state. The authors suggest that appropriate policy analysis should recognize that there is considerable interconnectedness across service areas, that income programs are important determinants of supply (and use), that providers across services compete for overlapping populations, and that service substitution is part of the fabric of long-term care policy.

Bergner, M., Hudson, L. D., Conrad, D. A., Patmont, C. M., McDonald, G. J., Perrin, E. B., & Gilson, B. S. (1988). The cost and efficacy of home care for patients with chronic lung disease. *Medical Care, 26*(6), 566-579.

In a randomized controlled trial designed to assess the cost and efficacy of sustained home care for patients with chronic lung disease, 301 patients were studied. Subjects were assigned at random to one of three groups: respiratory home care (RHC) provided by respiratory home care nurses, standard home care (SHC) provided by regular home care nurses, or office care (OC) provided only in the office with no home care component. At the end of one year of study, no difference in survival, pulmonary function, or everyday functioning among the three groups was found. The health care costs for patients in the RHC group averaged $9,768; for those in the SHC group, $8,058; and for those in the OC group, $5,051. The authors conclude that these results suggest the current policy of limited coverage of home nursing services by Medicare and other third-party payers may be appropriate. It is also suggested that a longer-term study of two to five years would aid in understanding whether the increased care provided by home care nurses results in improved outcomes over time.

Berk, M. L., & Bernstein, A. (1985). Use of home health services: Some findings from the National Expenditure Survey. *Home Health Care Services Quarterly, 6*(1), 13-23.

National estimates of the use and sources of payment for home health care services for different demographic groups are presented in this article. Findings from data from the 1977-1978 National Medical Care Expenditure Survey (NMCES) suggest that health status and age are strongly associated with home health care use, and the vast majority of home health care services are delivered based on these factors. A large number of younger, relatively healthy people also use home health care services, although their use is generally nonintensive—often requiring only one visit. About 57% of all users are under age 65. More than a third of all elderly users had more than 15 visits compared with only 7.9% for nonelderly users. Most persons who had a home health visit did not have a hospitalization, although hospitalization during the year was strongly associated with having a home health visit. Private insurance is seldom mentioned as a source of payment for home health care. A table showing sources of payment for home health visits is included and is broken into age categories of 0-64 years and 65 and older.

Branch, L. G., Friedman, D. J., Cohen, M. A., Smith, N., & Socholitzky, E. (1988). Impoverishing the elderly: A case study of the financial risk of spend-down among Massachusetts elderly people. *The Gerontologist, 28*(5), 648-652.

This study reports risk of impoverishment as the result of long-term care costs for elders aged 66 and older and for those aged 75 and above. A large number of elders are at risk of impoverishment, based on these findings. Of married couples aged 75 or older, 25% would be impoverished in 13 weeks and 57% would be within one year of nursing home placement. Of elders aged 75 and living alone, 46% would become impoverished within 13 weeks of placement in a skilled nursing facility. Comparable rates of impoverishment were found for those 66 and older. The analysis factored in the costs of skilled nursing home placement or home care for a spouse with Alzheimer's disease. The data highlight a substantial problem of potential impoverishment as the result of long-term care for older Americans. Policy approaches to develop long-term care insurance are suggested.

Branch, L. G., Horowitz, A., & Carr, C. (1989). The implications for everyday life of incident self-reported visual decline among people over age 65 living in the community. *The Gerontologist, 29*(3), 359-365.

Community-resident elders over age 65 with self-reported vision loss were studied to assess the impact of visual decline on daily activities. Vision impairment is the second most prevalent physical impairment among those 65 and older, and the number of those affected is growing. Compared with elders reporting excellent or good vision, those with visual decline were older but were not different in terms of any other demographic characteristic, use of formal supports or health services, or activities of daily living/functioning. When age and gender were controlled, visual loss was significantly correlated with a variety of unmet instrumental daily needs such as food preparation, housekeeping, and grocery shopping. Physical and emotional status reported by elders with vision impairment also reflected greater decrements than in those without vision problems. A pattern of extensive unmet need among older people who report vision decline emerges; despite their large numbers and reports of struggles with daily life activities, visually impaired elders are not more likely to receive formal social services or to use health or mental health services than other elders. Policy and care for elders and other visually impaired persons is frequently dichotomized, leading to systems with inappropriate orientations to the problems of elders with visual impairment. The authors suggest that the problem of underserved visually impaired elders as a subgroup of the nation's elderly can best be addressed by a coordinated effort and improved communication between the system serving the blind and the system serving the aging. Future research directions are suggested.

Branch, L. G., & Jette, A. M. (1983). Elders' use of informal long-term care assistance. *The Gerontologist, 23*(1), 51-56.

This article summarizes a descriptive study of the use of informal long-term care assistance by community-resident elders aged 71-97 in Massachusetts (*n* = 825). The informal support network is defined as the relatives or significant others with whom the elder has close contact. Both informal and formal support systems are potential sources of long-term care assistance for this population. This study found that only a minority of elders use assistance with basic activities of daily living (ADLs), but 82% of the sample use assistance to perform instrumental ADLs, although these services typically are not provided by existing public support programs. There are gender-based differences in service use. Availability of children is a powerful predictor of women's use of informal support in basic ADLs but has only a minor impact on women's use of informal LTC support. Men are much more influenced than women by degree of disability and living situation. Elders who live alone appear to be less likely than those who live with others to use informal help in instrumental ADLs. They are considered to be prime candidates for formal assistance in such areas. Most elders who use long-term care assistance rely solely on the informal support network in both instrumental (86%) and basic (50%) ADLs. The key predictor of the amount of informal assistance elders use is increasing physical disability. Living situation is the only informal support network characteristic consistently related to use of informal services. The authors point to regional differences between their findings and those of another study of Cleveland elders. They suggest that regional differences should be further explored and, if replicable, that they should form the basis for differential policy planning. The results of this study suggest either that the composition of elders' network of friends and relatives does not play much of a role in their use of informal LTC support or that additional information is necessary to better understand their role.

Branch, L. G., Wetle, T. T., Scherr, P. A., Cook, N. R., Evans, D. A., Hebert, L. E., Masland, E. N., Keough, M. E., & Taylor, J. O. (1988). A prospective study of incident comprehensive medical home care use among the elderly. *AJPH, 78*(3), 255-259.

This two-year study examined a defined community population to determine the predictors of medical home care use. With a sample of 3,706, the study found that those aged 85 or older used medical home care approximately 12 times as much as those aged 65 to 74. Five multivariate predictors of home care use were identified: (a) functional dependency in at least one ADL, (b) dependency in Rosow-Breslau functional health areas, (c) homebound status, (d) mental status, and (e) social isolation. While the dominance of indicators of frailty in physical and cognitive function are consistent with predictors of long-term care clients who enter nursing homes, rates of home care use in this study were no different for those living alone and those living with others. A follow-up study is planned to further differentiate home care use for community dwellers and for those who subsequently enter nursing homes.

Braun, K. L., & Rose, C. L. (1987). Family perceptions of geriatric foster family and nursing home care. *Family Relations, 36*(3), 321-327.

This study compared the attitudes of 62 matched pairs of relatives and patients in geriatric foster homes and nursing homes concerning the care they receive in those facilities. Families with positive attitudes were overrepresented in the sample. Nursing home patients had significantly less positive preplacement attitudes than did foster family patients. Statistics on patient traits and patient and family preplacement attitudes are provided; data on differences among respondents of different races are included. At six months following placement, relatives of foster home patients more often reported that the patient liked the activities, had special friendships, had enough privacy, and had improved during the first six months of placement. Types and frequency of patient complaints to relatives were similar for both placement settings. Using a logistic regression analysis, positive patient and family attitudes preplacement were found to be significant predictors of perceived patient improvement. Actual patient improvement in anxiety correlated significantly with five independent variables but, using ordinary least squares regression, only foster home placement was significant; decreased patient anxiety correlated with a patient's positive preplacement attitude. A series of preadmission counseling sessions provided by case managers is thought to facilitate more positive patient attitudes toward placement. Actual improvement in mobility and ADL did not correlate with any of the independent study variables, contrary to research that links patient preadmission attitudes to objective health outcomes. Results suggest that previously institutionalized patients may be more willing to try foster care. Implications for family intervention and counseling include maintenance of small caseloads for family interventionists to allow more time for patient and family counseling and community education. Because the study suggests that foster care alleviates patient anxiety more than institutional care does, the authors encourage the expansion of foster care for frail elders.

Burdz, M. P., Eaton, W. O., & Bond, J. B. (1988). The effect of respite care on dementia and nondementia patients and their caregivers. *Psychology and Aging, 3*(1), 38-42.

A pretest/posttest design was used to assess the impact of a nursing home-based respite program on the physical and cognitive functioning of patients with dementia and those without dementia. Of 74 caregivers initially interviewed, 55 were reinterviewed five weeks later and constitute the longitudinal sample. Assessment included the Memory and Behavior Problems Checklist and the Burden Interview as well as an ADL assistance measure. Burden and problems variables were significantly intercorrelated at pretest and posttest. Using MANOVA (multivariate analysis of variance) to test burden and problems as dependent variables, nondementia caregivers were found to report both lower levels of burden and lower levels of problems than caregivers of dementia patients. Contrary to expectations, interaction between treatment (respite or wait list), diagnosis (dementia or nondementia), and occasion (pretreatment, posttreatment) was not found. Posttreatment perceptions of respite care found that 81% of caregivers felt the respite program was very beneficial. Yet 68% reported their own situation was unchanged and 45% felt the patient's situation was unchanged, and 71% felt that their relationship with the patient remained unchanged following respite. Diagnosis was significantly associated with perceived change in the quality of the relationship between the patient and caregiver; a diagnosis of dementia was associated with a worsening relationship. Regardless of diagnosis, respite patients showed significant improvement in their reported problems as compared with their waiting-list counterparts.

Capitman, J. A., Arling, G., & Bowling, C. (1987). Public and private costs of long-term care for nursing home pre-admission screening program participants. *The Gerontologist, 27*(6), 780-787.

This study examined the differences between nursing home applicants participating in the Virginia Nursing Home Pre-Admission Screening Program who were either placed in nursing homes or diverted to community care. Applicants who were diverted to community care were less dependent and had greater informal supports than those admitted. Public and private payments for nursing home care were higher than for community care. Public payments for community care were consistently lower than for institutional care even when controlling for differences in nursing resource requirements. These findings suggest that community-based long-term care can be offered at lower monthly public and private costs than nursing home care, at least in the context of a preadmission screening program and Medicaid 2176 waiver-supported personal care services. However, had family members and friends not volunteered their labor, community care costs might have equaled or exceeded institutional long-term care costs.

Caserta, M. S., Lund, D. A., Wright, S. D., & Redburn, D. E. (1987). Caregivers to dementia patients: The utilization of community services. *The Gerontologist, 27*(2), 209-213.

Self-report questionnaires were returned by 597 caregivers of community-residing dementia patients in 16 states to determine their use of supportive services. Despite the limitations of the nonprobability sample used and the 48% response rate, the study collected information from a group of caregivers providing care in a number of different ways. Respite-oriented services were perceived as most needed and were used the most. Of the 43% who knew of available services, more than half used respite-type services. Those stating they were not ready to use services reported significantly less burden and more social support and tended to be spouses caring for less impaired younger patients. However, those caregivers who did not use services for other reasons were similar to those who did. General conclusions drawn from the findings are that significant need exists for respite-oriented services; awareness and access are moderate and do not always lead to service use; and caregivers should be educated in finding ways to facilitate their entry into the system so that their needs will be met.

Cohen, M. A., Tell, E. J., Greenberg, J. N., & Wallack, S. S. (1987). The financial capacity of the elderly to insure for long-term care. *The Gerontologist, 27*(4), 494-502.

This article presents an analysis of the financial capacity of the elderly to purchase any of four long-term care plans emerging as choices: social/health maintenance organizations (S/HMO), long-term care insurance, Life Care at Home, and continuing care retirement communities. A description of each model of care is provided, together with estimates of the income of the elderly from various sources. Assets and estimated expenditures are included in the assessment of affordability of long-term care insurance models. Estimates of affordability are presented in terms of the percentage of discretionary resources the elderly, single and married, would have to spend to purchase each type of long-term care. The greatest proportion of elderly could afford to enroll in the S/HMO. Between 50% and 80% of all elderly could afford to purchase one of these plans depending on the amount of discretionary income they would be willing to spend. The willingness of the elderly to "dissave" by spending assets will determine the market for these long-term care options.

Commonwealth Fund. (1989). *Help at home: Long-term care assistance for impaired elderly people.* (Available from the Commonwealth Fund Commission, 624 North Broadway, Room 492, Baltimore, MD)

This report describes the population of severely impaired elderly living in the community and outlines a strategy to provide financing for long-term care assistance. The extent of severe physical impairment, advanced age, poverty, dependency, living arrangements, health status, and insurance are succinctly described for this frail and vulnerable population. Current sources of home care services are summarized, including informal caregivers and the toll of caregiving, paid home care services, and current sources of home care financing. Charts and tables useful for visual presentations illustrate key facts. Formal care use patterns are examined to identify gaps in services and financing. The report proposes that a supplementary home care benefit be added to Medicare to finance home care and adult day-care services for the 1.6 million elderly who are severely impaired. Recommendations for Medicaid program changes and private insurance coverage expansion are proposed as companions to this measure.

Coughlin, T. A., & Liu, K. (1989). Health care costs of older persons with cognitive impairments. *The Gerontologist, 29*(2), 173-182.

This article analyzes a cognitively impaired subpopulation of the 1981-1982 National Long-Term Care Channeling Demonstration Project to examine the health care costs associated with their home and institutional care. Key findings are that the mean annual cost per capita for home and institutional care for this population was $18,500, as compared with $16,650 for elders who are cognitively intact. Few differences were found in health service use by cognitively impaired versus intact elders, except that the cognitively impaired used nursing homes at twice the rate. Informal costs of care were not included in the analysis. A pre- and postnursing home admission analysis indicated an annual cost of $11,700, whereas the cost of nursing home care for this population was $22,300. Care arrangements for the cognitively impaired in the community also differed by degree of impairment. Overall the severely cognitively impaired used more personal care services but the minimally impaired used more housekeeping services, perhaps reflecting differences in the functional status or living arrangements of the two groups. Cost and use patterns for hospital, nursing home, physician, and ancillary medical services for groups with different levels of cognitive impairment are presented.

Coward, R. T., & Cutler, S. J. (1989). Informal and formal health care systems for the rural elderly. *HSR: Health Services Research, 23*(6), 785-806.

This article summarizes the current state of knowledge about health services for the rural elderly and identifies areas needing further research. Three areas are the focus of discussion: informal/family caregiving, community-based services, and residential/institutional care.

Davidson, G., Moscovice, I., & McCaffrey, D. (1989). Allocative efficiency of
   case managers for the elderly. *HSR: Health Services Research, 24*(4), 534-
   554.

This study assessed the efficacy of case managers' allocating home and community-
based services. Case managers are used in a preadmission screening program that links
nursing home applicants either to nursing home placement or to alternative care in the
community. In a one-year follow-up period after assessment, outcomes were examined
for client placement, health and functional status, informal support, and use of health and
social services for clients in rural and urban counties participating in the Minnesota Pre-
Admission Screening/Alternative Care Grants program. Case managers were found to be
allocating services in a reasonably efficient manner, based on analysis of the relationship
between variation in the level of support of home and community-based services and the
length of time elderly clients remained in the community. As the first empirical analysis
of case managers' efficiency working within a mandatory preadmission screening program, these results initially suggest that case managers can be the individuals in the
health and social service delivery system who are responsible for targeting services to the
community-based elderly.

Dietrich, A., Nelson, E. C., Kirk, J. W., Zubkoff, M., & O'Connor, G. T. (1988).
   Do primary physicians actually manage their patients' fee-for-service
   care? *Journal of the American Medical Association, 259*(21), 3145-3149.

This study found that a substantial portion of patient care was managed—either provided or coordinated—by the patient's primary physician. Over a one-year period, 211
subjects were followed to determine the extent of their primary physicians' roles in managing the patients' care. Criteria for a primary physician's role in management were met
by 75% of 1,379 ambulatory visits to physicians, 33% of 786 visits to nonphysician health
care providers, 81% of 26 nonemergency hospitalizations, and 78% of 2,769 prescriptions. Although not participating in a formal managed care system, primary physicians in
these settings appear to function as case managers.

Donovan, R. (1989). Work stress and job satisfaction: A study of home care
   workers in New York City. *Home Health Care Services Quarterly, 10*(1/2),
   97-114.

This study of New York City home care workers reports sources of work stress and job
satisfaction, working conditions in the home care industry, supervisory support, and wage
and compensation issues. The study suggests several factors likely to influence job satisfaction among home care workers: personally rewarding work that workers perceive requires skill, autonomy, and self-paced work load. Job satisfaction is negatively affected
by low wages, few or no benefits, job insecurity, and psychological stress associated with
the nature of the care and environment in which home care aides work. Cost controls for
the home care budget are achieved through minimizing labor. It is argued that significant
reforms are needed in the current system to eliminate some of the worst features of the
secondary labor market (low wages, minimal benefits, job insecurity). Home care work-

ers, who are predominantly women, single heads of households, minorities, and new immigrants, in effect are forced to subsidize the cost of home health care. Unionization of home care workers is growing in New York City. Policy recommendations are that the system of employment should be restructured to value the paraprofessional home care worker.

Dunn, R. B., MacBeath, L., & Robertson, D. (1983). Respite admissions and the disabled elderly. *Journal of the American Geriatrics Society, 31*, 613-616.

This is a retrospective, descriptive study documenting the use of respite admissions combined with day hospital attendance to maintain disabled elderly in the community who might otherwise have entered an institution. The study was conducted at a hospital in Canada. Although limited by the small sample size of 28 patients over three years, the study provides a profile of inpatient respite users and their family caregivers. In all, 93% of the patients attended the geriatric day hospital and received a respite admission at a mean of every 10.8 months. At the end of the study half of the patients had entered long-term care facilities, and more than a third were still living at home. This option of respite admissions combined with geriatric day hospital attendance is seen as a viable one that should be expanded.

Eggert, G. M., & Friedman, B. (1988). The need for special interventions for multiple hospital admission patients. *Health Care Financing Review* (Annual Suppl.), pp. 57-67.

This article reviews a broad range of research literature on high use of and multiple admissions to acute hospitals by elderly people and studies interventions that have demonstrated reduced hospital use. Cost-effectiveness impacts and interventions aimed both at older community-dwelling and at nursing home residents are examined. It is proposed that interventions should be developed specifically to reduce acute hospital use by the small proportion of elderly who experience chronic patterns of acute hospital use. Demonstration studies that include elements that could assist the development of a program for high users are proposed, and nursing home patients are identified as a subgroup for whom unique interventions are needed to reduce high acute hospital use. Directions for research and needed information are discussed.

Ehrlich, P. (1986). Hotels, rooming houses, shared housing, and other housing options for the marginal elderly. In R. J. Newcomer, M. P. Lawton, & T. O. Byerts (Eds.), *Housing an aging society: Issues, alternatives and policy* (pp. 189-199). New York: Van Nostrand Reinhold.

This chapter addresses community housing options for the *marginal elderly,* defined as those living on the fringe of community life and presenting poverty, atypical life-styles, and/or frailty in terms of physical or mental disorders. Planners and providers must understand the importance of creating policy that preserves housing alternatives for this population and respect their life-styles by preserving diverse housing stock. The author states that this goal should stop being the social workers' problem and become the social planners' problem. Descriptions of SRO housing (hotels and rooming houses), modular housing/granny flats, shared (group) housing, and foster homes define each housing type and present relevant research findings on the applicability of the each setting to marginal elderly. Benefits and drawbacks of each setting for this population are also presented. The chapter concludes with an update on housing legislation affecting these categories of residence. The author states that the needed housing stock for these alternatives already exists. She advocates more flexible definitions of ideas about family constellations and housing-unit needs and continued efforts to promote legislation that supports housing alternatives for the marginal elderly.

Feussner, J. R., & Cohen, H. J. (1989). Comprehensive geriatric assessment: Mission not yet accomplished. *Journal of Gerontology: Medical Sciences, 44*(6), M175-M177.

This editorial challenges the consensus in the literature that comprehensive geriatric assessment is justified and questions whether the "technology" of assessment is the appropriate focus for geriatrics. The authors examine why "consensus" has come about, pointing out that diverse research findings and the tendency to emphasize positive outcomes concerning the efficacy of comprehensive geriatric assessment undermine the consensus position. It is suggested that comprehensive geriatric assessment research should be viewed objectively and critically and that continued outcome-oriented research on this topic is appropriate.

Furstenberg, A., & Mezey, M. D. (1987). Differences in outcome between black and white elderly hip fracture patients. *Journal of Chronic Disease, 40*(10), 931-938.

A retrospective review of the medical records of 119 community-residing subjects aged 60 and older was conducted to investigate the differences between black and white patients' outcomes following hip fracture and at hospital discharge. Blacks were significantly more likely than whites to have a high total number of diagnoses, mental impairment, low admission hemoglobin, and urinary incontinence following surgery. Blacks spent considerably more days in the hospital than whites and at discharge were more likely to be nonambulatory and to return to the community rather than to rehabilitation or nursing home settings, despite greater disability. Statistical analysis indicates that the great amount of illness blacks experience is a significant predictor of these differences in outcomes; additionally, delays in surgery, nonsurgical treatment, and race also significantly contribute to these outcomes. Blacks were referred to in-home rehabilitation and/or supportive home services to a much greater extent than whites: "Thus the larger burden of mental and physical impairment of black patients falls on in-home community services and/or on family members."

Gornick, M., & Hall, M. J. (1988). Trends in Medicare use of post-hospital care. *Health Care Financing Review* (Annual Suppl.), pp. 27-38.

Trends in Medicare use of posthospital care (skilled nursing facilities, home health, and inpatient rehabilitation services) are summarized in this article. Data on coverage, supply of services, use, patient types, geographic variation, and differences in posthospital care use are presented. An overview of two major studies (Abt and Rand) examining the availability of care and other issues related to posthospital care is provided. A discussion as well as suggestions for future research directions indicate that additional studies will focus on the availability and adequacy of posthospital care and the course and outcomes of Medicare- and non-Medicare-covered postacute care received in the home, in skilled nursing facilities, and in inpatient hospital rehabilitation facilities.

Grant, L. A., & Harrington, C. H. (1989). Quality of care in licensed and unlicensed home care agencies: A California case study. *Home Health Care Services Quarterly, 10*(1/2), 115-138.

This descriptive study examines issues of quality of care among California home care agencies, both licensed and unlicensed. Statistical and qualitative primary and secondary data from state and federal sources and 56 key informant interviews were the sources of data for analysis. Findings on quality of care are presented in sections on licensed and unlicensed home care providers. Although definitions of quality differ, many shortcomings in quality are reported for both licensure statuses. One indicator of quality used to assess licensed agencies was number of violations of federal and state regulations found by state agency surveyors. The most common types of deficiencies are discussed. Discussion on other quality problem areas for licensed agencies that were examined includes complaints against agencies and qualitative analysis of those records, coordination of care, supervision and scope of practice issues, personnel policies, and contractual issues. For unlicensed home care agencies, the authors report that data were often subjective and anecdotal because systematic evaluation of such services has not occurred within the state. Commonly cited problems include absenteeism and tardiness of providers, theft and fraud, high staff turnover, inadequate training or poor competence, false advertising, and potential for abuse. Similar types of problems were identified in both types of agencies. Unlicensed home care agencies were regarded by some respondents as a potentially more serious threat to home care clients, although this objectively remains an unresolved issue. The authors conclude that licensure does not assure that the quality of services will be adequate. They also raise concerns about the processes used for identifying problems and assuring quality.

Greene, V. L. (1983). Substitution between formal and informally provided care for the impaired elderly in the community. *Medical Care, 21*(6), 609-619.

Causal modeling techniques were used to assess the extent to which formally provided comprehensive community care tends to substitute for informal care provided by family and friends to community-dwelling impaired elders. After controlling for selective targeting and other intervening factors, the model finds a substantial tendency for informal care to be replaced by formal care. The major variable predicting both informal and formal support levels appears to be unmet need. Although the model suggests that in some cases the provision of formal support may lead to a decline in total support as informal caregivers relinquish care to formal providers, an alternate interpretation is offered. It is suggested that informal caregivers may tend to specialize the support they provide, concentrating their effort in the areas in which formally provided services are not offered. Disentangling specialization and substitution effects is not possible without time-series, true experimental data. The author suggests that these findings should be seen as preliminary and that they be used to guide further, unequivocal research.

Greene, V. L. (1987). Nursing home admission risk and the cost-effectiveness of community-based long-term care: A framework for analysis. *HSR: Health Services Research, 22*(5), 655-669.

This article presents a decision analytic technique to investigate the relationship of prior risk of nursing home entry—among applicants for community-based long-term care (CB/LTC) services—to cost-effective admission decisions. Analysis of the evaluation criteria that commonly have been cited in the major CB/LTC demonstrations shows that the necessary minimum level of prior risk is well above that typical of those actually enrolled. Increasing the rigor and accuracy of enrollment screening is shown to be unlikely to produce much practical effect as a remedy. The author suggests that the benefits of CB/LTC may be defined more broadly, which may allow it to become cost-effective for the enrollment of lower-risk applicants.

Harrington, C. H., & Grant, L. A. (1988). *The delivery, regulation, and politics of home care: A California case study.* (Available from the Institute for Health and Aging, UCSF, Room N631, San Francisco, CA 94143)

This paper describes five basic ways that home care services are regulated and delivered in California. A sixth type of formal home service, that delivered by unlicensed, unregulated agencies and providers, is also discussed. Although many would like to see reform in the current delivery and regulatory system used for home care, the politics of change at the state level are complex. Using data gathered from interviews with key informants and from documents, the paper presents the views of different interest groups on the issues of delivery and regulation—the positions of professional and trade organizations, unions, consumer groups, legislators, and referral agencies are represented. A table provides a useful comparison of structural characteristics of six different types of home care and related service providers in California.

Harrington, C., & Newcomer, R. J. (in press). The financial performance of the Social Health Maintenance Organization Demonstration. *Health Care Financing Review.*

The financial performance of the Social Health Maintenance Organization (S/HMO) Demonstration projects during the first four years of operation is examined in this article. Designed to control costs while expanding long-term care services, the S/HMOs experienced start-up costs significantly higher than expected. During the fourth year of the demonstration, when the projects were at full financial risk, only two of the projects were able to achieve a financial gain. The article analyzes the reasons for initial losses of the S/HMOs, examining risk arrangements, enrollment problems, the competitive market, benefits and eligibility, premiums and service use, and expenditure patterns. The discussion considers the overall effects these financial outcomes may have on the future of S/HMOs.

Hedrick, S. C., & Inui, T. S. (1986). The effectiveness and cost of home care: An information synthesis. *HSR: Health Services Research, 20*(6), 851-879.

This review article synthesizes the results of 12 studies of home care that used experimental or quasi-experimental designs to examine patient outcomes. Methodological soundness is weighed into the analysis. Targeted to chronically ill populations, the 12 home care studies appeared to have no impact on nursing home placement, mortality, or patient functioning. In some of the studies ambulatory care use increased as much as 40% and home care services either had no effect on hospitalization or increased the average length of stay in the hospital. Cost of care outcomes showed either no impact or an increase of 15% in cost. The authors advocate for studies that are better designed to test the effects of different types of home care—more explicitly targeted to different patient populations—and that are outcome-oriented to assess quality of life, quality of care, and family finances as well as the other patient outcomes assessed in the studies.

Hughes, S. L. (1985). Apples and oranges? A review of evaluations of community-based long-term care. *HSR: Health Services Research, 20*(4), 461-488.

This summary of the literature on community-based long-term care evaluation studies uses a theoretical framework to analyze the studies and to try to integrate often contradictory study findings. Thirteen studies are grouped into three models of care tested: evaluations of traditional "skilled" home care programs, evaluations of expanded home care programs, and evaluations of channeling demonstrations. The plausibility of causal inferences drawn from each study is emphasized through consideration of internal validity and external/construct validity. Integration of findings across studies is somewhat hampered by differing study methodologies and heterogeneous study samples. It is suggested that, because the range of possible combinations of community-based long-term care is large, efforts must be made to specify discrete models of care. Review of the studies indicates that expanded or "sociomedical" long-term home care services should be targeted to frail elderly whose ADL limitations are the result of chronic disease and place them at risk of long-term care institutionalization. Three areas for further information are delineated: (a) the determinants of nursing home admission and length of stay by subgroups of users, (b) the appropriateness or likelihood of other community-based care service outcomes for specific client groups receiving specific treatments that may range from restorative to maintenance or palliative in purpose, and (c) the types, levels, use patterns, and cost of home care services that genuinely substitute for and/or prevent specific types of institutional admissions and stays.

Hughes, S. L. (1989). Home and community care of the elderly: System resources and constraints. In J. A. Barondess, D. E. Rogers, & K. N. Lohr (Eds.), *Care of the elderly patient: Policy issues and research opportunities* (pp. 55-61). Washington, DC: Institute of Medicine, National Academy Press.

The author identifies five issues that shape the resources and constraints of home and community care for the elderly: (a) financing, (b) availability of services, (c) reimbursement for community care, (d) availability of low-tech community services, and (e) availability of work force for community care. Key points are that, because services follow dollars, growth in home care has been large. However, there is a drift from traditional providers of home care as new hospital-based, proprietary, voluntary, and not-for-profits accounted for 57% of all home health providers. This suggests great progress in the supply of Medicare home health care as a particular type of community care. Nonskilled care needs may continue to grow, particularly if nursing homes preferentially admit patients needing highly skilled care and the current supply of nursing home beds remains constant. This scenario suggests the potential for a growing number of community elderly with low-tech, long-term supportive service needs. The availability of such low-tech services may not be increasing as rapidly as demand, although more information on availability, staffing, and costs for these services is needed. Staffing shortages in community-based care are not well documented; however, the nursing shortage combined with the trend of community-based programs to use BSNs to case-manage patients suggests that there may be a serious labor constraint for community-based care in the future. The author notes that, in community care, formal providers are secondary to informal caregivers, who provide about 70% of care received by sick elderly in the community. Coupled with the trend for women to be in the labor force, this suggests an appropriate policy response to provide long-term home care, respite, and day-care services that buttress informal caregivers.

Hughes, S. L. (1989). A new challenge: Assuring the quality of social services. *Generations, 13*(1), 26-29.

This article offers a conceptual approach to the state of the art of quality assurance for a variety of different social services that sustain elderly in the community. In this model the bulk of social services provided are in-home and community services, which form the base of a community social services triangle; institutional discharge planning forms the apex of this triangle. Case management is viewed as a key mechanism to facilitate access and monitor use/quality of services based on attributes of structure, process, and outcome of care in addition to access. Degree of client vulnerability is seen as a variable that should guide the amount and methods of formal monitoring of the quality of social services for the elderly.

Hughes, S. L., Conrad, K. L., Manheim, L. M., & Edelman, P. L. (1988). Impact of long-term home care on mortality, functional status, and unmet needs. *HSR: Health Services Research, 23*(2), 269-294.

This is a report of a four-year evaluation of a long-term home care program in Chicago. Outcomes assessed included mortality, comprehensive functional status, and perceived unmet needs of frail elderly clientele. The study used a nonrandom, nonequivalent control group design with pretest and posttest at baseline, 9 months, and 48 months. The goal of the study was to examine the effectiveness of long-term, continuous home care versus fragmented, episodic care. The treatment group ($n = 151$) and comparison group ($n = 156$) were consecutively accepted and interviewed with the OARS Multidimensional Functional Assessment Questionnaire at 0, 9, and 48 months after acceptance to care. No between-group differences in mortality rates were attributable to treatment, based on multivariate analysis. Major findings were that the treatment group experienced a reduction in unmet needs at 9 months and better cognitive functioning. At 48 months longer-range beneficial effects of treatment on cognitive status were observed. The authors concluded that long-term home care provided quality of life benefits to clients at 9 and 48 months and no effect on mortality. However, because only 18% of clients were still alive and receiving community care at four years, it is suggested that four-year findings be interpreted cautiously.

Hughes, S. L., Cummings, J., Weaver, F., Manheim, L. M., Conrad, K. J., & Nash, K. (1989). *A randomized trial of V.A. home care for severely disabled veterans* (unpublished).

This study compares two groups of severely disabled patients (two impairments on the Katz Index of ADL) and their caregivers who participated in a randomized pretest-multiple posttest trial in which they were referred either to the Veterans Administration (VA) Hospital Based Home Care (HBHC) program or traditional VA care (control condition). Findings on patient outcomes indicate no significant group differences in ADL functioning or cognitive status as a result of HBHC treatment at 1 or 6 months in either model. While no significant group difference in patient morale was found at 1 or 6 months, at 1 month a significant beneficial effect of treatment was seen in both models for satisfaction with care; this was not sustained at 6 months. These findings on functional status suggest that HBHC care was at least as effective as traditional health care alternatives. At baseline caregivers of HBHC were significantly less satisfied with care than controls. This finding was reversed at 1- and 6-month posttests. This suggests that something in the process of HBHC distinguishes it from customary alternatives. One difference is that 100% of the HBHC sample received at least one HBHC visit, but only 73% of the severely disabled controls received any home care services. Also controls without health insurance were significantly less likely to receive home care services than those with insurance. HBHC patients received services for a significantly longer period of time, and care was more accessible, continuous, and comprehensive than customary alternative care programs. The cost was as follows: The HBHC group used a significantly greater number of intermediate care bed days than controls and used fewer VA outpatient visits and non-VA ambulatory care services. Total mean costs for the HBHC group were about $490 higher than for the control group, but these costs were offset by lower costs for other services. The net mean costs in the HBHC group, taking intermediate care days and out-patient care use into account, were $520 lower per person. If VA costs only are examined, HBHC treatment appears to be more costly but, when non-VA hospital and private sector Medicare home care costs are included, HBHC becomes 10% less costly. This is a sub-stantial savings, although not statistically significant. The HBHC intervention also as-sisted veterans to access needed home care services. These findings suggest that the VA HBHC should be expanded to meet the needs of these patients.

Hughes, S. L., Manheim, L. M., Edelman, P. L., & Conrad, K. J. (1987). Impact of long-term home care on hospital and nursing home use and cost. *HSR: Health Services Research, 22*(1), 19-47.

This article summarizes data from the Five Hospital Program in Chicago, contrasting hospital and nursing home use and cost for a long-term home care group and a control group. The study reports that the long-term home care group had a significantly lower risk of permanent admission to sheltered and intermediate-level nursing home care; how-ever, the treatment group had no difference in risk of permanent skilled nursing facility admission. Cost analysis shows savings in low-intensity nursing home days, obscured by total costs of care that were 25% higher for the treatment group receiving long-term in-home services. Higher costs were accompanied by significant quality of life benefits.

Institute for Health and Aging, University of California, San Francisco. (1990). *Long-term care public policy agenda for California.* (Available from the Institute for Health and Aging, UCSF, Room N-531, San Francisco, 94143-0646)

This background paper explores the current system of long-term care financing and needs for long-term care in California. A comprehensive discussion of trends, definitions, needs, and expenditures for long-term care in different groups is followed by a detailed analysis of specific elements of a long-term care program, service options and available benefits, eligibility options, delivery system options, and consideration of alternate forms of use control and quality care measures. Costs and financing options and sources com-plete the first part of the document. Part II summarizes the points made at a long-term care public policy conference that sought to build consensus on long-term care policy options in California.

Janicki, M. P., Otis, J. P., Puccio, P. S., Rettig, J. H., & Jacobson, J. W. (1985). Service needs among older developmentally disabled persons. In M. P. Janicki & H. M. Wisniewski (Eds.), *Aging and developmental disabilities* (pp. 289-304). Baltimore, MD: Paul H. Brookes.

This chapter summarizes the similarities and differences in service needs between older developmentally disabled (DD) and non-developmentally disabled persons. The main differences lie in the structure and manner of service delivery, with onset of need for services earlier in the life span for some DD. Special needs particular to older DD include changing relationships and availability of older parents or other caregiving relatives with age, increased need for long-term supportive services to support community living, and assistance with gaining access to needed services within the generic aging services network. The authors identify a need for additional professionals with training in both aging and the needs of DD persons.

Jones, E. W., Densen, P. M., & Brown, S. D. (1989). Posthospital needs of elderly people at home: Findings from an eight-month follow-up study. *HSR: Health Services Research, 24*(5), 643-664.

A study of elderly patients (*n* = 737) discharged from hospitals to their homes in a suburban area in the Midwest found that 60% were assessed as needing help with personal care or housekeeping but only 19% were referred by the hospital to community service agencies. A large proportion of help with housekeeping and personal care was provided by relatives in the period immediately following hospital discharge. This proportion of informal care had decreased and the proportion of paid help had increased at eight months following discharge. Limitations in functioning in activities of daily living were associated with the use of help at the time of discharge. In all, 64% of patients reported no discussion with hospital personnel concerning the way they would manage at home, and many patients were not aware of community services. Implications for the long-term care system are the need for improved communication to facilitate continuing care of hospitalized elderly, comprehensive functional assessment with consistency of definitions and terms among community agencies, and increased community attention to elderly returning home from the hospital.

Kane, N. M. (1989). The home care crisis of the nineties. *The Gerontologist, 29*(1), 24-31.

While demand is increasing, the supply of paid custodial home care of acceptable quality is threatened by the financial condition of providers, which is increasingly vulnerable to reimbursement shifts and economic trends. The article analyzes the trends of publicly owned for-profit providers of home care and provides a good overview of the home care market. A decline in profitability of custodial care is attributed to restrictive public payments and private insurance coverage as well as the limited financial resources of individuals who could pay privately. Social implications for caregivers, patients, home care workers, and companies are discussed, and recommendations for adjusting the business environment are made, emphasizing the role of employers in offering expanded elder care benefits.

Kane, R. A. (1988). The noblest experiment of them all: Learning from the national channeling evaluation. *HSR: Health Services Research, 23*(1), 189-198.

This article identifies some problems of internal validity in the channeling evaluation, then concentrates on the practical meaning of the results more than on the methodological issues. The following questions are raised: (a) Was channeling mounted as intended, and, if so, was it theoretically likely to have its intended effect? The author points to problems with a minimal operational definition of case management and lack of ability to measure and capture the intensity of case management provided and thus its impact. She also identifies the lack of well-being and life satisfaction measures as gaps in long-term care research. (b) If channeling were implemented nationwide, would effects mirror the demonstration? The author points to the nongeneralizability of the demonstration projects because of their "unique case," one-time qualities. She states that ongoing programs are retooled and improve over time—practices not possible in a demonstration project. She shows that channeling underscores the need for a new paradigm to guide long-term care policymaking. It is suggested that a shift in focus to improving quality of nursing home and community care would be more fruitful than a search for cost-effective alternatives to nursing homes—dominant research themes for the past 20 years. Several interesting points are raised about cost-effectiveness and how it is defined. She advocates reformulation of public policies to design a system of long-term care that satisfies consumer preferences and protects them from catastrophic long-term care expenses while promoting an acceptable quality, equitable access, and defensible costs; it is suggested that this should be a priority over targeting patients bound for nursing homes.

Kane, R. A., & Kane, R. L. (1987). *Long-term care: Principles, programs and policies.* New York: Springer.

This book provides a comprehensive examination of long-term care. Beginning with a conceptual framework and definitions of long-term care, Part I introduces evidence about the need for care, and the current state of long-term care, and discusses related issues of quality, access, and cost. Part II presents evidence about the effectiveness of long-term care gleaned from over 215 studies and demonstration reports primarily from the United States in the past 10 years. Chapters on the efficacy of long-term care, home care, and day care; other community long-term care services; nursing homes; the relationship between long-term care and acute care; and systems of long-term care organize research findings in these areas. The strengths and deficiencies of these forms of care are presented based on the research evidence. Well-organized tables summarizing characteristics of research studies conducted on related topics are provided. The concluding section of the book offers a synthesis of the evidence and outlines the next steps needed to improve long-term care. The orientation of the book is humanistic. It uses a minimal amount of jargon and is a thorough, valuable compendium of research on long-term care to date.

Kaplan, M. P., & O'Connor, P. M. (1987). The effect of Medicare on access to hospice care: Patterns of eligibility requiring the availability of a primary care person. *American Journal of Hospice Care, 4*(6), 34-42.

This study surveyed hospice program directors nationwide (88% response rate) to ascertain the impact of Health Care Financing Administration (HCFA) reimbursement criteria requiring the availability of a primary care person (PCP). Findings show that, although Medicare and non-Medicare facilities had a similar requirement rate for PCPs to admit patients to hospice, this requirement increased twice as often in the Medicare facilities from 1980 to 1985 (this period coincided with the congressionally mandated national study to assess hospice care for Medicare reimbursement, which required participating hospices to designate PCPs for their patients). The study results suggest that, for Medicare facilities, federal regulations may have had an effect on access to hospice care by encouraging admission policy decisions that discriminate against persons who have no available PCP.

Kemper, P. (1988). The evaluation of the National Long-Term Care Demonstration: 10. Overview of the findings. *HSR: Health Services Research, 23*(1), 161-174.

This article summarizes the major findings of the National Long-Term Care Demonstration, a project that sought to substitute community care for nursing home care by expanding community services and providing comprehensive case management. The population studied was very frail but not at high risk of nursing home placement as intended. Total costs of the project were increased for the treatment group because the costs of additional case management and community services provided were not offset by reductions in the cost of nursing home use. Expanded formal community care did not cause a substantial decline in informal caregiving. Benefits reported for channeling clients, families, and care-providing friends were increased services, reduced unmet needs, increased confidence in the receipt of care and satisfaction with arrangements for it, and increased satisfaction with life. The author concludes by advocating that expansion of case management and community services must be justified for the benefits to clients and their caregivers rather than on the basis of cost savings.

Kemper, P., Applebaum, R., & Harrigan, M. (1987). Community care demonstrations: What have we learned? *Health Care Financing Review, 8*(4), 87-100.

This is a review article based on analysis of community care demonstrations funded through waivers from the 1970s to 1984. The demonstrations shared the objective of substituting community care for nursing home care whenever it was appropriate. This was expected to reduce long-term care costs and to improve the quality of life of clients. Case management and expanded offerings of community services were the key program elements of the demonstrations. After reviewing these demonstrations, the authors conclude that expanding community services beyond what already exists is likely to increase costs. Small reductions in nursing home use were more than offset by the increased costs of providing services to those who would have remained at home even without the expanded services. Beneficial effects found are that community services appear to make people better off and do not cause substantial reductions in family caregiving. Policymakers are urged to move beyond questions of cost-effectiveness to address quality of life, access, delivery, and value issues for community care.

Kennedy, L., Neidlinger, S., & Scroggins, K. (1987). Effective comprehensive discharge planning for hospitalized elderly. *The Gerontologist, 27*(5), 577-580.

This study reports the effectiveness of a comprehensive discharge planning protocol that was implemented in a double-blind study at one hospital by a gerontological clinical nurse specialist. Eighty hospitalized patients aged 75 and older participated. The treatment group experienced an average of 2 days reduced length of stay, and the average time between discharge and readmission was increased by 11 days. Functional status measures showed that placement at two and four weeks postdischarge was deemed appropriate for over 87% of the patients in both groups.

Kramer, R. M., Shaughnessy, P. W., & Pettigrew, M. L. (1985). Cost-effectiveness implications based on a comparison of nursing home and home health case mix. *HSR: Health Services Research, 20*(4), 387-405.

Comparisons of case-mix differences between nursing home and home health patients, and between Medicare patients in both settings, were conducted using random samples of data collected in 1982 and 1983. In general, patients receiving home health care were younger, less functionally disabled, and had shorter lengths of stay than nursing home patients. Home health patients more frequently had problems requiring skilled nursing services, and nursing home patients had a greater prevalence of long-term care problems requiring personal care. Medicare home health patients were much less likely than nursing home patients to be dependent in activities of daily living; there was no difference in adequacy of social supports for the two groups. In terms of long-term care problems, Medicare home health and nursing home patients were relatively similar, and differences in medical problems were less pronounced than between all nursing home and all home health patients. From a policy perspective the Medicare skilled nursing facility is predicted to continue to provide the treatment of choice for posthospital care patients who require a combination of highly skilled care and functional assistance. Home health care is viewed as more viable for patients without severe disabilities or major functional problems; home health care may offer a cost-effective substitute for acute hospitalization at the end of the hospital stay.

Kulys, R., & Davis, M. A. (1987, Spring). Nurses and social workers: Rivals in the provision of social services? *Health and Social Work,* pp. 101-112.

This article reports on the growing recognition in various disciplines of nurses' competence to perform a number of roles/tasks previously the domain of social workers. The authors raise the possibility that this may have bottom-line consequences for social workers as nurses try to increase their professionalism and have early access to medical patients. What is not dealt with is how the nursing shortage may affect this. One of the key reasons for that shortage is the extension of nurse roles, thereby increasing demand for nurses. This substantiates some of the extension. The article suggests some research that social workers should do to compare the efficacy of social work versus nursing in certain roles.

Lane, D., Uyeno, D., Stark, A., Gutman, G., & McCashin, B. (1987). Forecasting client transitions in British Columbia's long-term care program. *HSR: Health Services Research, 22*(5), 671-706.

This article presents a theoretical model that predicts transitions of clients within the long-term care system. An application of Markov chain analysis, which has been developed, tested, and applied to 9,483 clients in British Columbia's Long-Term Care Program (LTC) during 1978 to 1983, is presented as a model for annual transitions of clients through various home and facility placements. The model gives accurate forecasts of the progress of groups of clients from state to state in the long-term care system from the time of admission until death. The majority of the article is devoted to explaining the procedure for the model and its validation and then applying it to forecasting tasks. Various subsets of the available data are analyzed, and differences among annual cohorts are explained. The best model separates male and female groups for analysis of transition behavior. The model is reported to be valuable for decision makers charged with short-term planning of service requirements and longer-term facilities planning decisions.

LaPlante, M. P. (1989). *Disability in basic life activities across the life span.* San Francisco: University of California, Institute for Health and Aging, Disability Statistics Program.

The data presented are estimated from the 1979 and 1980 Home Care Supplement to the National Health Interview Survey (NHIS), which is sampled from the civilian noninstitutionalized population. Detailed tables present a variety of data by age group, gender, types of need, and health condition. Discussion includes estimates of those receiving assistance in basic physical activities (going outside, walking, bathing, transferring, maintaining continence, eating, dressing), numbers and rates of assistance in selected instrumental activities of daily living, and correlates of assistance needs.

Laudicinia, S. S., & Burwell, B. (1988). A profile of Medicaid home and community-based waivers, 1985: Findings of a national study. *Journal of Health Politics, Policy and Law, 13*(3), 525-546.

The findings of a national survey of Medicaid home and community-based care waiver programs (Section 2176 of the Omnibus Budget Reconciliation Act of 1981) are presented. The article is divided into two sections: one focusing on the profile of waiver programs serving the aged and physically disabled, the other focusing on the mentally retarded. A useful background section describes the 2176 program. Findings are reported on the ways states have cited their waiver authority, how people at risk of institutionalization have been targeted, programs' service use and expenditure levels, and established quality assurance systems. Preliminary findings on the cost-effectiveness of the waivers are presented.

Lawton, M. P., Brody, E. M., & Saperstein, A. R. (1989). A controlled study of respite service for caregivers of Alzheimer's patients. *The Gerontologist, 29*(1), 8-16.

After identifying and interviewing a pool of 642 caregivers of Alzheimer's patients living in the community, subjects were randomly assigned to formal respite care or to a control group. The experimental group received respite care at their request in one of several forms: nursing home respite, day care, or in-home care. Families receiving respite care maintained their impaired relative significantly longer in the community over a period of 12 months. Respite also produced very high caregiver satisfaction, although it did not relieve caregivers' burden or improve their mental health. Respite improved quality of life for caregivers. While further research on the effects of greater intensity of respite remains to be done, "the conclusion that ordinary respite care is a mild intervention with modest effects seem inescapable." However, caregivers show discriminating judgment in their use of the services and thus its continuation can be justified, with the knowledge that principles of consumer demand will most likely regulate the use of and payment for such services.

Lemke, S., & Moos, R. H. (1980). Assessing the institutional policies of sheltered care settings. *Journal of Gerontology, 35*(1), 96-107.

The article describes the development of the Policy and Program Information Form (POLIF), a tool that measures the policies and services of sheltered care settings. As one part of the Multiphasic Environmental Assessment Program (MEAP), the initial form of the POLIF was constructed by drawing from observations and interviews at 93 facilities as well as from a search of the literature. Psychometric characteristics of the facilities reported here show those that provide a higher level of care tend to provide residents with less choice and control. Larger facilities tend to be more selective, to offer more health services and social activities, and to have formal means for transmitting expectations and involving residents in decision making. Uses of the tool are discussed, and sample profiles to illustrate the utility of the instrument for comparing facilities are provided.

Lewis, M. A., Cretin, S., & Kane, R. L. (1985). The natural history of nursing home patients. *The Gerontologist, 25*(4), 382-388.

This article reports the results of a random sample of 197 persons in 24 nursing homes who were followed for a minimum of two years following nursing home discharge. Four patient classification groups were developed based on immediate outcome, use of health care facilities after discharge, and patient status after two years. Findings show that care of nursing home patients is a dynamic process: 37% died in the nursing homes, 54% transferred frequently between hospitals and nursing homes, and just over 9% were discharged to their homes and received no further institutional care during the period of follow-up. The authors point out that reimbursement policies foster a "ping-pong" shuttle of patients between hospitals and nursing homes because there are no incentives for nursing homes to provide episodic acute care services for patients; DRGs are predicted to exacerbate this pattern. Better linkages between the acute and long-term care sectors and improved knowledge about the natural history of nursing home patients are urged for the formulation of new approaches to this problem.

Liebig, P. S. (1988). The use of high technology for health care at home: Issues and implications. *Medical Instrumentation, 22*(5), 222-225.

This article raises some issues concerning the transfer of high technology from the hospital to the home setting. The growth of high technology in health care at home is traced and characterized. The majority of caregivers are older women who may be hesitant to use high technology. Savings may be shifting from hospitals and insurers to individuals. The home may become an in-home hospital. Concerns about the adequacy of training and supervision of paid family caregivers are raised, and the stresses associated with such care are identified as unresearched issues. Ethical issues accompany this change in health care delivery. The author suggests it is time to examine whether the ability to provide high-tech care at home should be a compelling reason for doing so.

Linsk, N. L., Osterbusch, S. E., Simon-Rusinowitz, L., & Keigher, S. M. (1988, Summer). Community agency support of family caregiving. *Health and Social Work*, pp. 209-218.

A self-report survey of community-based home care agencies in Illinois identified the services they currently provide and would provide if resources were available to support family caregiving. More than a third of the responding organizations provided a variety of family support services including information and referral, support groups and training, counseling, and hiring family members as caregivers. Respite was the least favored service to offer if resources became available. Of the small agencies responsible for implementing home services, 56% either currently hire family members or would do so if adequate resources were available. Agencies that did not hire family members to provide home care expressed concern about management and supervision problems. Administrators expressed diverse attitudes toward support of family caregivers who provide home care. Family payments would be allowed, encouraged, and used as incentives by some and discouraged, hidden, or prohibited by others. The authors suggest that state programs should address issues of family involvement and convey a clear policy to service providers.

Liu, K., Manton, K. G., & Liu, B. M. (1985). Home care expenses for the disabled elderly. *Health Care Financing Review, 7*(2), 51-58.

This article summarizes descriptive statistics on noninstitutionalized older Americans with limitations in activities of daily living (ADL) and in instrumental activities of daily living (IADL). The data are drawn from the 1982 Long-Term Care Survey. This article focuses on out-of-pocket expenses for home-based care to assist with ADL and IADL limitations. Amounts of private payments expended relative to the characteristics of the disabled home-based elderly are described. Notable differences in expenditures are linked to available income, level of limitation, and a number of other personal characteristics of out-of-pocket payers. This article identifies a gap in knowledge about private expenses for home-based care. This dearth of information on the private cost of long-term care may partially constrain public policy deliberations on home-based care as a potentially cost-effective alternative to nursing home care. The authors suggest that public policies that aim to divert the disabled elderly from nursing homes must assess the levels of private payments that are incurred to maintain the high-risk disabled elderly in the community so that estimates will be made on the amount of possible public assistance that may be required if private resources are not available.

Macken, C. L. (1986). A profile of functionally impaired elderly persons living in the community. *Health Care Financing Review, 7*(4), 33-49.

This article reports data from the 1982 Long-Term Care Survey, which was designed to develop a better understanding of the number and circumstances of functionally impaired elderly persons living in the community. In 1982 there were approximately 5 million functionally impaired elderly living in the community. The data show that functionally impaired persons in the community are older, are more often female, have lower incomes, and include a larger proportion of black people than the general elderly population. Baseline data on the types of functional impairments and their prevalence, sources of assistance, and types of limitation are also provided. A series of descriptive tables provide an overview of the physical and cognitive limitations of community-dwelling functionally impaired elderly.

Manson, S. M. (1989). Long-term care in American Indian communities: Issues for planning and research. *The Gerontologist, 29*(1), 38-44.

This article summarizes various current approaches to providing long-term care for the Native American elderly population. The most innovative of these efforts have been initiated at the local, tribal level. Services differ in availability and from one tribe and locale to another, and include tribally run nursing homes, congregate care, in-home services, home health care, meals on wheels, senior centers, and some respite functions. Overall, planning and research related to long-term care for this population are judged to be behind state-of-the-art services. A variety of research and planning questions are raised. The policies of the Indian Health Services reflect an active resistance to developing services especially for older tribal members. Changes in policy formulation, coordination, and leadership will be needed to address the demographically driven expansion of long-term care needs for older Native Americans.

McCusker, J., & Stoddard, A. M. (1987). Effects of an expanding home care program for the terminally ill. *Medical Care, 25*(5), 373-385.

A quasi-experimental time-series design was used to compare home care and hospital use data for terminally ill people under the age of 65. Data on cancer deaths from a seven-year period were compiled from a regional tumor registry and compared with Blue Cross enrollment and claims files: 46% of the decedents had used home care services, and a subgroup of high-intensity users was identified. The hypothesis that an expanded program of home care for the terminally ill would reduce hospital use and costs of care during the last month of life was generally supported. A trend of greater cost savings among home care users than among nonusers was observed when more intensive home hospice services were offered. Savings among users were the result of reduced hospital days and reduction in the mean daily cost of hospitalization. Significantly less variability in costs was found for home care users than for nonusers. A discussion of factors involved in careful hospice research design is also informative.

McVey, L. J., Becker, P. M., Saltz, C. C., Feussner, J. R., & Cohen, H. J. (1989). Effect of a geriatric consultation team on functional status of elderly hospitalized patients. *Annals of Internal Medicine, 110*(1), 79-84.

This article reports the evaluation of a geriatric consultation team designed to affect functional status of hospitalized elderly: 88 study group patients received multidimensional assessments by an interdisciplinary geriatric consultation team, and 90 patients in the control group received care as usual. Results of the team evaluation of the intervention group included problem identification and recommendations but no active interventions. Initially comparable, the two groups showed different outcomes. The major outcome variable was independence in the activities of daily living (ADL). Upon admission 39% of the total study population was functionally independent, 27% required assistance with one to three ADLs, 22% required assistance with four to six ADLs, and 12% were completely dependent. In the intervention group 34% improved and 28% declined, while in the control group 26% improved and 36% declined. These results were not statistically significant although they reflect a trend toward greater improvement in the intervention group. The authors conclude that the geriatric consultation team was unable to alter the degree of functional decline; teams may have to offer direct preventive or restorative services in addition to advice to promote patient improvements.

Montgomery, R. J. V. (1988). Respite care: Lessons from a controlled design study. *Health Care Financing Review* (Annual Suppl.), pp. 133-138.

This article describes a study of 541 family units caring for at least one impaired elder and their use of respite services. Families were randomly assigned to one of five treatment programs or to the control group. This article compares those who received no services with those who were eligible either for respite or for all project services. Families in treatment groups could purchase various types of respite on a fee-for-service basis under a Medicare waiver that allowed them $882 per year in services. The majority of families chose in-home respite services in frequent periods of three hours' duration. On average families spent only 63% of their allotted funds and almost one third of the 189 families eligible for respite services did not use any. Respite services appeared to have different outcomes for elders whose caregivers were adult children versus those whose caregivers were spouses. When spouses were the primary caregivers, respite services appeared to encourage nursing home placement, while respite seemed to delay nursing home placement for elders whose caregivers were adult children. All treatment groups indicated high satisfaction with respite services. Expressed preferences for additional community services were for chore services (41.4%) and home health services (37.7%). Feelings of burden were not alleviated over an extended period of time.

Moos, R. H., & Igra, A. (1980). Determinants of the social environments of sheltered care settings. *Journal of Health and Social Behavior, 21*(1), 88-98.

This article is based on a conceptual framework stipulating that the interrelationships among architectural and physical, policy and program, and resident and staff factors influence the type of social environment and social climate that emerges in sheltered care settings. A model of the determinants of the social environment of sheltered care settings is presented as a guide (a) to assess the association between the type of facility and seven dimensions of the social environment; (b) to determine the relation between these seven social climate dimensions and physical and architectural, policy and program, and resident and staff characteristics; and (c) to estimate the variation in the social environment that can be explained by the model and identify the unique and shared influences attributable to each of the four sets of environmental variables. A survey of 90 congregate living facilities for the elderly using the Multiphasic Environmental Assessment Procedure (MEAP) was conducted. The findings support the general idea that the type of facility as well as physical and architectural, policy and program, and resident and staff characteristics are important in influencing the social climate of the setting. Nuances of the findings are discussed.

Moos, R. H., & Lemke, S. (1980). Assessing the physical and architectural features of sheltered care settings. *Journal of Gerontology, 35*(4), 571-583.

This article reports on the development of the Physical and Architectural Features (PAF) Checklist, which measures the physical resources of sheltered care settings; it is one part of the Multiphasic Environmental Assessment Procedure (MEAP). Nine conceptually unified and empirically derived dimensions make up the PAF, which was constructed through data analysis from 93 licensed skilled nursing facilities, residential care facilities, and apartment facilities. The instrument measures physical amenities, social-recreational aids, prosthetic aids, orientational aids, safety features, architectural choice, space availability, staff facilities, and community accessibility. Cost is not related to any PAF dimension, but nonprofit facilities score higher on several dimensions than do proprietary facilities. Characteristics of sheltered care settings identified in developing the PAF include larger facilities being more likely to provide barrier-free environments, more flexible physical settings, and more staff facilities. Observers find facilities with more physical resources to be attractive, and residents find them to be pleasant. Facilities with richer physical resources tend to be more selective, provide more privacy, allow residents more influence and choice, and have clearer, more flexible policies. The PAF is a tool that may be used to compare sheltered care settings for the elderly and to assist staff in changing a setting and monitoring the impact of their efforts.

Mor, V., Sherwood, S., & Gutkin, C. (1986). A national study of residential care for the aged. *The Gerontologist, 26*(4), 405-417.

This is a comprehensive summary of a 50-state national survey of programs providing residential care to the elderly. Data were collected both from home operators and from residents to gather information on the characteristics of the facility and the residents' functioning and prior residential mobility and medical/psychiatric history. The researchers draw a distinction between small, family-operated homes and institutionally oriented homes, which tend to be larger. Differences in patient characteristics are categorized by type of residential care home: health department regulated and integrated programs. The latter are seen to be more institutional than those regulated by integrated social service departments. Elderly residents reported high satisfaction with homes. Issues of availability and appropriateness of different types of residential care beds and the potential impact of increased regulation on family-operated homes are identified as important for policy consideration.

Morris, J. N., Gutkin, C. E., Ruchlin, H. S., & Sherwood, S. (1987). Housing and case-managed home care programs and subsequent institutional utilization. *The Gerontologist, 27*(6), 788-796.

This article reports on an analysis of four kinds of community-based housing and case-managed home care programs and their relationship to subsequent institutional use. Using a nonrandom design the study compared four institutional risk subgroups (high, some, low, very low) using Inst-Risk classifications across the housing settings without focusing on any selected types of elderly. The sample reflected both types of elderly normally found within the five housing/service arrangements as well as types of individuals served by general community-based programs targeted at elderly people. The findings concerning institutional placement supported a limited benefit from providing case-management services in congregate and elderly housing settings. The benefit is primarily limited to those in the high Inst-Risk category and suggests that high-risk elderly will do well when placed in age-segregated housing with service oversight and support. The findings suggest that ongoing provision of case-managed services to elderly persons at large, with the exception of those in the high institutional risk category, can be called into question when the major purpose of such services is to reduce institutional use. The authors suggest that these findings should prompt a reexamination of the utility of ongoing provision of case-managed services to elderly persons at large when the major purpose of these services is to reduce institutional use. Quality of life and other outcomes may justify the continued use and/or expansion of case-managed home care.

Moxley, D. P., & Buzas, L. (1989). Perceptions of case management services for elderly people. *Health and Social Work, 14*(3), 196-203.

To determine their perceptions of these services, this study surveyed referral agents who had referred clients to a community social service agency providing case management services. The majority of the respondents (n = 137) viewed the program as effective in addressing basic social support needs of elderly people and as ineffective in addressing more complex physical and mental health problems. Case management staff were perceived to be generally qualified, but the program was viewed as understaffed and not building adequate awareness of its availability. Correlates of the program's perceived effectiveness were perceptions of the adequacy of staffing and the commitment of staff to serving elderly people. The authors suggest that the latter finding points to the need to better define the differential capacities and uses of social service technicians and baccalaureate- and graduate-trained social workers as case managers.

Namazi, K. H., Eckert, J. K., Kahana, E., & Lyon, S. M. (1989). Psychological well-being of elderly board and care home residents. *The Gerontologist, 29*(4), 511-516.

Data were collected in five counties in Ohio to examine the effect of several social and physical environmental features of small unregulated board and care homes on the psychological well-being of elderly residents. Operators ($n = 177$) were interviewed using a questionnaire focusing on characteristics of the environment and the people providing the service. Residents ($n = 285$) were interviewed to assess cognitive function and subjective measures of physical and mental well-being. The article reports demographics for operators and residents as well as resident characteristics. As expected there were moderate relationships among measures in all four components of well-being examined. Social aspects of the environments, such as peer relationships, had a more significant impact on residents' psychological well-being than aspects of the physical environment. The most critical variables influencing the psychological well-being of residents were those related to their perceptions of physical health and comfort with the board and care home environment. The authors point out that, while some regulation of currently unregulated homes may be beneficial for client protection, the goals of protecting the client and overregulation should be balanced to protect the essence of the familylike climate, which is unique to small board and care homes.

National Center for Health Statistics, & Feller, B. A. (1983). *Americans needing help to function at home* (Advance Data from Vital and Health Statistics, No. 92, DHHS Pub. No. [PHS]83-1250). Hyattsville, MD: U.S. Public Health Service.

This report presents selected data from the Home Care Supplement to the 1979 National Health Interview Survey (NHIS). It includes estimates of the numbers of noninstitutionalized people of all ages who need help in the community, the types of help they need, and their ages and sex. Activities reported include basic physical activities, home management, number of bedbound, those with bowel or urinary trouble, adults needing the help of another person, and those receiving nursing or medical care. A technical notes addendum discusses the sources and limitation of data and definitions of terms for the NHIS.

Netting, F. E., & Williams, F. G. (1989). Establishing interfaces between community- and hospital-based service systems for the elderly. *Health and Social Work, 14*(2), 134-139.

This article explores the interrelationships and issues surrounding the interface of hospitals and community-based care agencies in serving the elderly. The increase in hospital-based services for older people requires shifts in linkages and understanding of missions between agencies, particularly those traditionally part of the community aging services network. The authors based part of their discussion on their experience with seven hospitals in Arizona and New Mexico that had developed case management programs of different kinds. Discussion included the relationships the hospitals forged with community-based case management agencies. Implementation of these programs illustrated the need for models of service integration, and examples of the adaptations these hospitals made to provide more comprehensive service delivery and coordination are provided. It is suggested that social workers in acute and long-term care settings need to understand all aspects of the service delivery system to ensure that elderly clients receive appropriate levels and continuity of care in a complex and constantly changing system.

Neu, C. R., Harrison, S. C., & Heilbrunn, J. Z. (1989). *Medicare patients and post-acute care: Who goes where?* Santa Monica, CA: Rand Corporation.

This study seeks to describe patterns of Medicare hospital and postacute care use and to document which Medicare patients receive or do not receive postacute care. Identifying factors associated with variations in use and assessment of the effect of receiving or not receiving postacute care are presented. The sample is composed of a 20% random sample of Medicare hospital discharges in 1985 (over 2 million cases) and targets five DRG groups (stroke, COPD, heart failure and shock, major joint procedures, and hip and femur procedures); these DRGs account for 41.8% of SNF charges, 22.2% of postacute home health care, and 53.1% of postacute rehabilitation charges for which Medicare pays. Policy implications of the findings are that (a) the Medicare postacute benefit does not provide equal access to postacute care for all Medicare beneficiaries. Those discharged from low-income-heavy hospitals were less likely to use SNFs and more likely to use home health care. (b) The second diagnosis recorded during hospitalization is important in determining whether the patient will use postacute care in a particular setting. The secondary diagnosis was found to influence discharge location. (c) Findings suggest that policies about reimbursement and access to one kind of care should be made with the understanding that these policies affect use of other kinds of care.

Newcomer, R. J., Harrington, C., & Friedlob, A. (in press). Social health maintenance organizations: Assessing the initial experience. *HSR: Health Services Research.*

This article describes the status of the Social/Health Maintenance Organization (S/HMO) Demonstration across the four sites in the first 36 months of operation. Four policy areas are discussed: (a) Have the S/HMO demonstration sites enrolled a broad cross section of the elderly, including Medicare beneficiaries eligible for Medicaid and persons "at risk" of institutionalization? Difficulties in meeting enrollment targets are reported, and reasons for this are analyzed. (b) How aware were Medicare beneficiaries of the S/HMO alternative to traditional fee-for-service Medicare and TEFRA risk-based prepaid health plans? Why did Medicare beneficiaries choose to join an S/HMO? Levels of awareness varied between communities, depending upon general exposure to the concept of HMOs. S/HMO enrollees most often reported finding out about the demonstration through mass marketing campaigns and joined to get more benefits. (c) Have the S/HMOs been successful in organizing and managing acute health and chronic care services? Demonstrations either developed the capacity to provide chronic care services within preexisting HMOs or transformed long-term care providers into prepaid acute care health plans that also continued providing chronic care service benefits. The latter organizations had some problems in providing acute and ambulatory services for their members. All four sites successfully integrated delivery of chronic care services to Medicare beneficiaries within a prepaid health care environment. (d) What has been the financial performance of S/HMOs? The sites had varied success in several dimensions of their operation. The start-up period was not profitable, with all sites reporting substantial losses in the first 36 months of operation. Reasons differed among sites and included service use, administrative costs, and risk-sharing arrangements. Discussion of the findings offer the reminder that the first three years' results do not necessarily foretell the ultimate success or failure of a demonstration. Several conclusions about the status and future of the S/HMO model are offered.

Newman, E. S., & Sherman, S. R. (1979). Foster-family care for the elderly: Surrogate family or mini-institution? *Journal of Aging and Human Development, 10*(2), 165-176.

This article reports the results of a study that examined the extent of the integration of elderly clients into family life in adult foster care homes. Four dimensions were used to assess families: affection, social interaction, performance of ritual, and minimization of social distance. Overall findings on these dimensions indicate that family integration and participation do occur in foster family homes for adults and that, in the majority of cases, the homes could be termed "surrogate families."

Noelker, L. S., & Bass, D. M. (1989). Home care for elderly persons: Linkages between formal and informal caregivers. *Journal of Gerontology: Social Sciences, 44*(2), S63-S70.

This study investigates how personal care and home health services are used in relation to assistance from primary kin caregivers. Chronically impaired and frail elderly were studied to assess their use of kin caregivers and formal service providers to meet their personal and home health care needs. A typology was developed based on task sharing or segregation between kin caregivers and service providers, and four types of informal-formal linkages around these tasks were identified: kin independence, formal service specialization, dual specialization, and supplementation. Findings regarding predictors of the types showed that caregiver and care recipient need variables were most significant in differentiating among them, although caregiver gender also had some discriminatory power.

Office of the Inspector General [Richard P. Kusserow]. (1987). *Home health aide services for Medicare patients* (0A101-86-00010). Washington, DC: U.S. Department of Health and Human Services.

This is a report on an inspection initiated to assess the strengths and weaknesses of existing Medicare standards for home health aide services. Background information on coverage, reimbursement, scope of practice, certification, and definitions pertaining to the use of home health aides in Medicare-certified home health agencies is provided. In-site visits were made to seven states throughout the country; quantitative and qualitative data were collected. Data sources included interviews with key state personnel in licensing and surveying, home health agency and vendor administrative personnel, supervisory visiting nurses, home health aides, Medicare patients, physicians, and other informants. Home visits were made with 44 aides to 62 Medicare patients, and a sample of medical records from each agency were analyzed. Major findings are that (a) Medicare patients' needs for key home health aide services are not being met, (b) standards are not provided, and (c) problems are noted with agency practices in employing aides. Specific points are addressed concerning each of these findings. Five major recommendations are made to the Health Care Financing Administration (HCFA) to address these concerns, including modification of training and instruction programs for state survey agencies, assuring completion of state survey home visits, development of stronger requirements for home health aide training and supervision, revision of the definitions of services allowed to be provided by home health aides, and revision of instructions to fiscal intermediaries regarding Home Health Agency Coverage Compliance Review. Full comments from the HCFA are included as an appendix to the report.

Oktay, J. S., & Volland, P. J. (1987). Foster home care for the frail elderly as an alternative to nursing home care: An experimental evaluation. *AJPH, 77*(12), 1505-1510.

This study randomly assigned 112 elderly hospital patients to either a nursing home or a specially trained foster care home. Foster caregivers were carefully trained and supervised. The researchers interviewed patients and caregivers every three months for a year following placement. Community-based foster caregivers were typically middle-aged black women, married, living with husband and children. Different outcomes were noted for the two placement dispositions. Nursing home patients reported higher life satisfaction and participated in more recreational and social activities. Foster care patients had better nursing outcomes, were more likely to maintain or improve their mental status scores and activities of daily living status, and more frequently got out of the house than the nursing home patients. Foster care was 17% less expensive than nursing home care while it provided 24-hour supervision and daily personal care. The quality of care was judged to be comparable to a nursing home. Foster care was especially attractive to blacks, both as patients and caregivers, as compared with the low rate of nursing home use in the black population generally. Community foster care may offer a viable option to nursing home care for a segment of the population.

Persky, T., Taylor, A., & Simson, S. (1989). The network trilogy project: Linking aging, mental health and health agencies. *Gerontology and Geriatrics Education, 9*(3), 79-88.

This article reports the experiences of aging, mental health, and health agencies in Philadelphia, which formed a partnership to improve, expand, and integrate service delivery for the elderly in need of mental health care. Nationally the estimated need for this care is 18% to 25%, but there is minimal use of private and public services by this population. The Philadelphia trilogy developed a training model to overcome the organizational isolation of agencies serving mutual clients with interrelated problems. The article describes the interagency training experience and the receptivity of the participants and discusses the issues that must be addressed to improve care coordination for these types of clients.

Petchers, M. K., & Milligan, S. E. (1987). Social networks and social support among black urban elderly: A health care resource. *Social Work in Health Care, 12*(4), 103-117.

A community survey of poor, black urban elderly in Cleveland assessed the size, interaction, availability, and adequacy of support and roles of network members: 98% of all respondents had daily or weekly contact with them. A high degree of social connectedness was found with other relatives and friends. In assessing the availability of help and unmet need, only 20% of elderly had been in need of help as a result of illness in the past year; of these, two thirds received help from a family member, 28.6% from a friend, and about 5% reported help from a professional. Ratings of preferred sources of help during an emergency showed that 67.9% of the sample would call on their families, 31.9% would ask a friend, and only 1% would seek professional help. Only 6.8% of the sample indicated they had no source of support in case of an emergency. Thus the study found differential use of support network members for emergency and nonemergency situations. Advice-seeking behavior would more often be directed to friends (49.5%), in comparison with 31.1% who would call on a friend in an emergency or in sickness (28.6%). This finding is consistent with other research, which shows that kinship relationships are more obligatory than the voluntary nature of friendships. As with other populations community assistance was more likely to be needed by the older members of the sample; those aged 80-96 indicated need for assistance with one ADL, on average. Assessment of need for assistance with instrumental activities found that 10.2% needed housekeeping, 11.1% needed grocery shopping, and 2.8% needed cooking assistance. Findings on help-giving behaviors indicate that more than two thirds of elders had not rendered assistance to others in the past month.

Phillips, B. R., Kemper, P., & Applebaum, R. A. (1988). The evaluations of the National Long Term Care Demonstration: 4. Case management under channeling. *HSR: Health Services Research, 23*(1), 67-81.

This article considers the nature of case management under channeling, describes the levels of participation of clients, and compares receipt of channeling's comprehensive case management by the treatment group with receipt of comprehensive case management from other sources by the control group. The success of the demonstration in delivering comprehensive case management was dependent on two things: whether case management functions were in fact implemented as designed and whether most of the treatment group received them. Under both models of channeling (comprehensive case management and direct service expansion), case management was implemented largely as intended. Between 10% and 20% of control group members received case management services comparable to those provided by channeling; this was particularly the case for the financial control model. The channeling demonstration was therefore not a test of case management compared with no case management; instead it compared channeling case management with the existing community care system that already was providing comprehensive case management through existing community agencies to some of the population eligible for channeling. Key conclusions of the analysis are that both models of channeling substantially increased the receipt of comprehensive case management; assessment and care planning were completed and direct services initiated for approximately 80% of clients in each model. A second conclusion is that, despite the large increase in receipt of comprehensive case management by treatment group members as a consequence of channeling, some of the control group received case management approaching or equaling that of channeling. The demonstration thus was not a pure test of the addition of channeling's case management to a system with only service-centered case management. A third conclusion is that the incremental increase in comprehensive case management provided by channeling over the existing system was somewhat greater under basic model case management than under the financial control model.

Phillips, E. K., MacMillan-Scattergood, D., Fisher, M. E., & Baglioni, A. J. (1988). Public home health: Settling in after DRGs? *New England Journal of Medicine, 6*(1), 31-35.

This article reports the results of a study of referrals to the public health department in a city in a rural county. Initially after the implementation of DRGs, the public health agency saw increased acute care, short-term patients as the hospital discharged patients sooner than they had before DRGs. After some months several home health agencies opened that served the same geographic areas in which the public agency had been the sole provider. Post-DRG results over 30 months reflect (a) a decrease in the number of referrals to public home health, (b) increasing length of home care, (c) decreased frequency of visits, and (d) increased use of rehabilitative services in addition to nursing. This picture suggests that, in the 7 to 18 months post-DRG, the health department seemed to be managing patients with chronic care needs, which raises the question of whether nonpublic home health agencies are providing the reimbursable care. The shift in case mix has implications for funding of public health services, which are partially dependent on revenues generated by public health home visits; for issues of access to care for patients with chronic needs that are nonreimbursable; and for longer-term policy questions concerning the role of public home health departments, their work force, and their resources.

Rice, D. P. (1989). Health and long-term care for the aged. *American Economics Review, 79*(2), 343-348.

This article offers a succinct and comprehensive overview of key statistics and issues of health and long-term care of the aged. Issues examined are changing demographics and socioeconomic characteristics of the elderly, health status of the elderly and their medical care use, long-term care (including nursing home care costs and financial access issues) as well as community-based care, long-term care policy issues and dilemmas (rationing, generational equity, long-term care coverage, and financing), and economists' contributions and research opportunities in these areas.

Rowe, J. H. (1985). Health care of the elderly. *New England Journal of Medicine, 312*(13), 827-835.

This article discusses the special considerations important to proper physiological, psychosociological, and pathological evaluation of elderly patients. Current controversies in the field and recent progress in managing several common clinical problems of the aged are also discussed. Illness behavior in the elderly is notable in terms of its underreporting of illness, presence of multiple diseases, and atypical or altered presentation of diseases. Assessment should be functionally oriented, and functional impact of specific diagnoses should be evaluated. Complications in obtaining an accurate medical and medication history are noted, and measures of mental status are suggested. The importance of assessing social and economic status is recognized as key given that the health care of the elderly is influenced by their social support systems. Geriatric assessment units are a controversial clinical approach to assessment. The article also provides summaries of important diseases of the elderly: dementia, urinary incontinence, osteoporosis, and need for coronary artery bypass surgery.

Rubenstein, L. Z., Josephson, K. R., Wieland, D., English, P. A., Sayre, J. A., & Kane, R. L. (1984). Effectiveness of a geriatric evaluation unit: A randomized clinical trial. *New England Journal of Medicine, 311*, 1664-1670.

Elderly inpatients at a Veterans Administration (VA) hospital who were at risk of nursing home placement were randomly assigned either to a geriatric evaluation unit (GEU; $n = 63$) or to a control group that received treatment as usual ($n = 60$). Patients in the GEU receive workups in the first week from an interdisciplinary team, which develops a specific treatment plan. Indicated therapeutic and short-term rehabilitative care is provided in the unit. Community placement is a major goal, and the combined assessment, rehabilitation, and respite care process results in an average length of stay of 43 days. At one-year follow-up, patients who had been assigned to the GEU had much lower mortality than the controls (23.8% versus 48.3%). Their rate of initial discharge placement in a nursing home was also much lower (12.7% versus 30.0%), and GEU patients were less likely to have spent any time in a nursing home during the follow-up period (26.9% versus 46.7%). Unit patients had slightly lower direct costs for institutional care than controls, and, when adjusted to reflect differences in survival, the mean institutional care costs per year survived were much lower for the unit patient ($22,596 versus $27,826). Significantly more GEU patients than controls showed improvement in basic functional status and in ability to perform instrumental activities of daily living. Morale scores improved for many more GEU patients than for controls (42.4% versus 24.1%), and mental status scores also increased for the GEU patients. The beneficial result of the GEU appears to reflect the cumulative effects of a more thorough diagnostic process, more appropriate therapy, and intensive rehabilitation coupled with follow-up care provided by an outpatient geriatric clinic. The expenditure of additional resources at the more intensive end of the hospital stay may recoup later benefits and may be regarded as an investment strategy within the VA setting. Under DRGs neither the hospital nor Medicare has a financial incentive to bear these costs. Extrapolating to national hospital discharges, the authors estimate that a GEU program could reduce nursing home admissions by about 200,000 annually.

Ruther, M., & Helbing, C. (1988). Use and cost of home health agency services under Medicare. *Health Care Financing Review, 10*(1), 105-108.

Data from 1986 and trend data from 1974 to 1986 on the use and cost of home health agency services provided to disabled and aged Medicare beneficiaries are presented in this article. While home health agency reimbursements constitute only 3.6% of all Medicare expenditures (1986), expenditures on home health agency services have grown more rapidly than overall Medicare expenditures—growth averaged 24% per year during 1974 to 1986. Analysis shows that enrollees 85 years of age and older, women, and the aged (as opposed to the disabled) were all significantly more likely to receive home health agency services. The 10 leading primary diagnoses of home health agency recipients are presented, as is an analysis of home health agency charges and visits over the review period.

Scanlon, W. J. (1988). A perspective on long-term care for the elderly. *Health Care Financing Review* (Annual Suppl.), pp. 7-15.

This overview article discusses the factors and principal policy issues affecting the provision of long-term care to the elderly and points out research needs related to this discussion. The author presents concerns about the current long-term care system including access to care, efficient production of care, where care is provided and by whom, quality, and distribution of the burden. Significant social and economic trends are identified that will affect the future of long-term care. The author urges that more robust strategies for dealing with the future demand for long-term care be developed and highlights equity of distribution of the burden as a key aspect for consideration in policy development.

Scharlach, A., & Frenzel, C. (1986). An evaluation of institution-based respite care. *The Gerontologist, 26*(1), 77-82.

This article reports the results of a study of 99 caregivers of patients who used an inpatient respite service provided in a Veterans Administration nursing home. Reasons for using the service included emotional rest (81%) and physical rest (77%) as well as ability to perform other activities in the free time gained while the relative used respite care services. A total of 72% of caregivers perceived that their health had improved as a result of using the respite services. Respite care patients did not seem to experience relocation trauma; the majority displayed no change from previous levels of physical and mental functioning; and some improved, according to their caregivers. Of the caregivers, 94% reported that using the program affected their relationships with the care recipient. Only 38% indicated that using the service fostered difficulties, primarily because the patient displayed fears of being abandoned, and 56% reported improved relationships, primarily as the result of decreased caregiver resentment. Effects of respite use on the ability to maintain the caregiving role were largely positive, with 64% of the caregivers reporting that continued caregiving was much easier, and 20% reporting that caregiving was somewhat easier as a result of the knowledge that the service was available. Contrary to expectation, reported likelihood of institutionalization increased nearly as often as it decreased, reflecting the use of respite services as a transition from home to institution for some families. Families reported that exposure to a nursing home setting on a temporary basis had shown them that some nursing homes were better managed than they had thought and that the homes were able to provide beneficial services that some caregivers were unable to offer themselves. The majority of caregivers (70%) reported very high satisfaction with the respite services, and only 18% stated they were either somewhat or very dissatisfied. The authors outline areas for further investigation of respite, including methodological and outcome issues.

Seltzer, M. M., Ivry, J., & Litchfield, L. C. (1987). Family members as case managers: Partnership between the formal and informal support networks. *The Gerontologist, 27*(6), 722-728.

This study compared the case management tasks performed by family members for elderly relatives with those performed by a control group. Family members of 81 elderly (mean age 83) received an experimental intervention of case management training. At intake there were no differences between family members in the treatment and control groups. The family members were related to the elderly as children (57%), siblings (10%), spouses (6%), other relatives (21%), or friends (6%); the average age was 62. Most of them had frequent in-person or telephone contact with their elderly relatives prior to joining the study; case management was not a new function for them, with an average of six tasks per month reported prior to participating in the study. Both groups received the usual services provided by the agency, including counseling, crisis intervention, and concrete services. The experimental group also received family-centered training through individual contact between master's level social workers and family members. The training program consisted of four components to develop the family member's skill at performing at least one new case management task. The experimental group performed significantly more case management tasks than did the control group following the intervention. Ten variables, analyzed by multiple regression, explained 39% of the variance in the number of case management tasks performed by family members. The two largest predictors were mental status of the elder and whether the family member was in the experimental or control group. Fully half of the explained variance in the number of case management tasks performed by elderly clients on their own behalf was accounted for by the age of the elderly person, with younger clients found to perform more case management tasks. Experimental group family members performed twice as many case management tasks as their counterparts in the control group, demonstrating that the training intervention substantially boosted the level of family performance of case management.

Seltzer, M. M., Krauss, M. W., Litchfield, L. C., & Modlish, N. J. K. (1989). Utilization of aging network services by elderly persons with mental retardation. *The Gerontologist, 29*(2), 234-238.

This study examined the use of aging network services by mentally retarded older adults. Of eight types of community-based services (373 programs) surveyed, it was found that 52% had served mentally retarded elderly in 1987. For adult day health and adult foster care programs, more than 10% of the clientele was from the population of mentally retarded elderly. The article describes the characteristics that differentiate the programs that provide services to this population. It is suggested that the well-developed networks of services for mentally retarded and for the aged in Massachusetts may be contributing to the integration of services for older mentally retarded adults. Policy implications are discussed.

Shapiro, E., & Tate, R. (1988). Who is really at risk of institutionalization? *The Gerontologist, 28*(2), 237-245.

Using multiple logistic regression models, the authors identify the probability of institutionalization in the short and long term for elders with various high-risk characteristics. The authors advocate clustering high-risk traits to increase prediction ability rather than using individual screening predictors. After analyzing 28 variables in the regression model to predict institutionalization in 2.5- and 7-year periods, the authors identify several clusters that indicate especially high risk for institutionalization. This is suggested as an alternative method for discharge planners to use in targeting patients with whom to intervene.

Soldo, B. J. (1985). In-home services for the dependent elderly: Determinants of current use and implications for future demand. *Research on Aging, 7*(2), 281-304.

An analysis of the Home Care Supplement to the 1979 National Health Interview Survey (NHIS) was conducted to determine whether economic status of the family mediates the relationship between the level of home care needed and the probability of formal service receipt. The probability of formal service use was found to respond directly to the severity of care needs and indirectly to the availability of informal care providers. The probability that formal service would be used was only trivially affected by the annual income of the caregiving household. The analysis suggests that frail elderly—and their informal caregivers when present—overcome financial barriers to secure some outside home care services when frail elders have extreme needs to be met.

Soldo, B. J., & Manton, K. G. (1985). Health status and service needs of the oldest old: Current patterns and future trends. *The Milbank Memorial Fund Quarterly, 63*(2), 286-319.

This article reviews methods and theoretical alternatives to assessing the health status and service needs of persons 85 years and older to predict future trends. Statistics on predicted demand for different types of long-term care services are presented. The authors argue that the same factors that are likely to transform the needs profile of future older populations (such as cohort differentiation and succession) may also combine with system changes to alter the demand for specific kinds of health care services, particularly the mix of long-term care services required by the population. The article develops a baseline understanding of the interrelationships among age, health care needs, and patterns of health service use. The factors that mediate these relationships currently are identified, and there is discussion of the ways the process of cohort flow may alter the distributions of these factors over time. The discussion of service need, use, and age points to the complex network of relationships between these factors and the difficulty of using them for long-range planning projections. The rapid growth of the older population in general and the oldest old in particular is expected to affect the nursing home sector most heavily. Several strategies are discussed for projecting the health care needs and service use patterns of the oldest old, a group that disproportionately consumes national health care expenditures and most types of health care services. Aggregate data typically gathered on service demand obscure the concentrated service demand of the most disabled in any age group. Those with manifest disability make the most intensive use of health care services and have a "cost-multiplier" effect. Therefore identifying characteristics of intensive service users among the oldest old and probable changes in their number over time may be more productive methods for policymaking and planning. The article then describes several strategies to assess health care needs of the oldest old. The authors advocate using a model that explicitly recognizes the relation of chronic degenerative disease to the need for health services as the basis for forecasting. A second strategy for accomplishing population-based need assessment would reflect a multidimensional functional understanding of health and the need for specific personal or supportive care services. Because targeting limited health care resources to those most in need is increasingly important, the authors suggest that identification of groups that manifest internal consistency in terms of both need and service use be developed to accurately model targeting. A summary of such a model previously developed by the authors is presented and discussed. The article reviews efforts to pinpoint precisely where along the need continuum transitions to different levels of care occur. The authors discuss a model of predicting service substitution, highlighting implications for demand for informal caregiving. Because the dynamics of health status and life expectancy changes have particular significance for the organization of long-term care reimbursement systems, the authors call for careful coordination of reimbursement policies across service types and for reimbursement policies that take into account the imperatives of health status change.

Stark, A. J., & Gutman, G. M. (1986). Client transfers in long-term care: Five years' experience. *AJPH, 76*(11), 1312-1316.

This study examined the outcomes of 1,653 clients admitted to a long-term care program in British Columbia, Canada, and followed them for a 5-year period. Information on facility, level of care changes, discharges, and deaths is reported. Of the 1,241 clients initially admitted to care at home, 34.3% were still in the program; of these 11.7% were in facilities, 6.7% were at home at a higher level of care, and 14.5% were unchanged. Of the remaining clients 26.8% had been discharged and 38.9% had died. Outcomes for a comparison group of clients initially admitted to care in facilities were similar. After 5 years 28.4% were still in the program and 39.3% had died. The study found few moves from facilities to home care (2.4%). Although the mean age of the study population was 74.7, after 5 years one third of the clients were still in the program and 14.5% were unchanged in place and level of care at admission to care in the home; there were similar findings for those admitted to care in facilities.

Steinhauer, M. B. (1982). Geriatric foster care: A prototype design and implementation issues. *The Gerontologist, 22*(3), 293-300.

This article outlines a prototype for geriatric foster care—the use of family residences
to care for unrelated elders in a comparatively nonrestrictive setting. The article provides
a historical overview of geriatric foster care and describes the current focus of adult foster
care development. Licensure, reimbursement methods, attitudes of service agency administrators, visibility of private residential placement, and different models of care operating in different states are presented as current issues in the field. A chart summarizes
notable characteristics of adult foster care services in 11 states. Emerging trends in geriatric foster care that affect the development of a model are also described; these include
growing legitimacy of the service, housing as a component in community-based service
delivery models, quality controls through PSROs, welfare program images, expansion of
the category of care providers to include relatives, and interest in exchanging and sharing
both theoretical and experiential information on geriatric foster care. The author presents
an operational prototype, which posits that programmatic use of private family residences
for the care of nonrelated elderly persons can provide an important living environment
alternative and may serve as an option to long-term institutional placement while providing additional support to community-dwelling elderly. The dimensions of the four-part
prototype include the dual-level operation structure composed of state office and local
projects, the potential clients, and the reimbursement for services. An additional segment
explores the indicators of success by which the prototype may be evaluated. Appraisals
based on administrative feasibility and client impact are explored. The article concludes
with a discussion of implementation issues for further policy resolution.

Stone, R. (1986). *Aging in the eighties, age 65 years and over—use of community services: Preliminary data from the Supplement on Aging to the National Health Interview Survey: United States, January-June, 1985*
(Advance Data from Vital and Health Statistics, No. 124; pp. 1-6). Washington, DC: U.S. Public Health Service.

This document provides estimates of numbers of people 65 years of age and over who
are using community services. Data were collected from approximately 21,000 interviews completed during the first six months of 1984 as part of the National Health Interview Survey Supplement on Aging. Use data are reported for community-based services
such as senior citizen centers and senior center meals, adult day care, and special transportation for the elderly as well as for in-home services such as homemaker services,
home health aides, visiting nurses, home-delivered meals, and telephone call check services. About 22% of the elderly used community services during the period under study.
The most frequently used community service was the senior center, with over 15% of the
sample reporting use within the 12 months before the interview. In-home services were
used by a much smaller proportion of the elderly. Approximately 1%, about 376,00 persons, used homemaker services and 3%, approximately 775,000 persons, received care
from visiting nurses. About 2% of the elderly, approximately 425,000 persons, received
care from home health aides. Almost four fifths of those aged 65 and over used no
community services during the study period. Of those who used services, 3 million
elderly (11%) used only one service and 2 million (7%) used two community services.

Approximately 3% reported using three or more services. Service use by gender and age, by living arrangement and limitation of activity, and by number of services used is presented.

Stone, R., Cafferata, G. L., & Sangl, J. (1987). Caregivers of the frail elderly: A national profile. *The Gerontologist, 27*(5), 616-626.

This article reports data from the 1982 National Long-Term Care Survey and Informal Caregivers Survey, which profiles informal caregivers of noninstitutionalized frail elderly. An encapsulated caregiver literature review provides a quick overview of key dimensions of caregiver research to date. Study findings summarize the characteristics of care recipients in terms of age, marital status, gender, living arrangements, family income, perceived health status, and functional level. The profile of caregivers includes their gender, relationship to the elder, type of care provided, age, racial background, living arrangements, family income, marital status, and health status. The descriptive profile of caregivers confirmed previous research findings that informal caregivers are predominantly female, many are over the age of 65, and a minority use formal services. Of the overall caregiver population, 80% provided unpaid assistance seven days a week, and the majority of caregivers had done so for one to four years; 20% had done so for five or more years. Evidence of competing demands on caregivers was found, with 21% reporting child care responsibilities, 20% reporting conflict with other work, and 9% indicating that they had quit their jobs. These data may be used by policymakers to examine the implications of various policy options.

Stone, R., & Newcomer, R. J. (1986). Board-and-care housing and the role of state governments. In R. J. Newcomer, M. P. Lawton, & T. O. Byerts (Eds.), *Housing an aging society: Issues, alternatives and policy* (pp. 200-209). New York: Van Nostrand Reinhold.

This chapter examines the effects of state governments in the diverse board and care "industry." Background on major regulatory, administrative, and financing policies that affect the operation of board and care facilities is provided, and appropriate research findings are referenced in this discussion. Definitions of *board and care* are provided. A segment on barriers to effective regulation and oversight addresses the issues of lack of funding and personnel, weak statutory and enforcement authority, an encumbered legal process, an inadequate data base to facilitate regulation and oversight, fragmentation of government agency responsibilities, inadequate knowledge and skills among regulatory officials and operators, and inadequate reimbursement policies. Recognizing the various obstacles to regulation and enforcement, several states have begun to explore nonregulatory alternatives to expanding the supply and availability of facilities and ensuring safety and quality of care. Examples of these efforts are discussed and include coordination among agencies, consultation/technical assistance, financial incentives, establishment of complaint offices, external participation in inspection and monitoring, and integration of board and care with the continuum of care. The authors conclude that reformulation of approaches to financing and regulating this industry are needed to ensure availability, accessibility, and quality of care.

Tell, E. J., Cohen, M. A., Larson, M. J., & Batten, H. L. (1987). Assessing the elderly's preferences for lifecare retirement options. *The Gerontologist, 27*(4), 503-509.

Individuals on the waiting list at two suburban continuing care retirement communities (CCRCs) were surveyed on their preferences for life care housing. Reasons cited for joining a CCRC were primarily to afford access to services to maintain independence and to assure access to medical and nursing home services and avoid burdening family members. Two thirds of the respondents indicated that protection against the costs of long-term care is a very important part of their decision to join a CCRC. Their major concern about joining a CCRC was related to the ability to keep up with fee increases after they joined. Stability in the monthly fee charges was more important to respondents than the actual cost of entry and monthly fees. About half of the respondents expressed interest in life care at home (LCAH), a new long-term care option that provides benefits similar to a CCRC at less cost to the elderly who prefer to remain in their own homes. Those joining CCRCs primarily for social rather than health and financial reasons were less likely to be interested in LCAH. Those most likely to be interested in LCAH were concerned about community living, life-style changes in a CCRC, and its costs.

Tennstedt, S. L., McKinlay, J. B., & Sullivan, L. M. (1989). Informal care for frail elders: The role of secondary caregivers. *The Gerontologist, 29*(5), 677-683.

This article identifies the relationships of secondary caregivers to frail elders, describing the types and amounts of assistance they provide as well as frail elders' use of formal services relative to the help they received from informal caregivers. Secondary caregivers are found to provide much less help than primary caregivers in areas that supplement rather than complement the assistance the latter provide. Secondary caregivers provide a variety of types of assistance and are usually family members—often the spouse and children of the primary caregiver. Friends are more likely to be secondary rather than primary caregivers. Collectively secondary caregivers provide much less care than do primary caregivers. The amount of help they provide is influenced more by their own characteristics than by those of the elder. Findings indicate that coresidence of the primary and secondary caregivers is the most important predictor of the amount of help provided by secondary caregivers. Men and nonrelatives are more active in secondary than in primary caregiving roles; men as secondary caregivers provide more hours of help than women as secondary caregivers. Concentration of care within the family of the primary caregiver rather than distribution of care through the extended family is identified as an important trend with policy implications for potential formal service targeting interventions. The article is thorough in comparing study findings with those of previous caregiver studies.

Van Gelder, S., & Bernstein, J. (1986). Home health care in the era of hospital
    prospective payment: Some early evidence and thoughts about the future.
    Pride Institute Journal of Long Term Home Health Care, 5(1), 3-11.

This article presents some preliminary evidence of the impact of Medicare's prospective payment system (PPS) on the use of home health care, places this evidence into the
context of other dynamic factors affecting home health agencies, and draws some conclusions regarding the overall impact of Medicare hospital PPS and other factors on future
issues facing home health providers.

Vertrees, J. C., Manton, K. G., & Adler, G. S. (1989). Cost effectiveness of home
    and community-based care. *Health Care Financing Review, 10*(4), 65-78.

This article describes the Medicaid Section 2176 waiver programs in Georgia and
California and assesses the ability of each to meet the congressional condition that the
program diverts eligibles from nursing homes with a budget-neutral outcome or with no
additional cost to Medicaid. Statistical methods are described and analyses presented to
evaluate the programs' abilities to preserve budget neutrality. Neither program was assessed to be budget neutral, and the reasons for this are described.

Victor, C. R., & Vetter, N. J. (1988). Preparing the elderly for discharge from
    hospital: A neglected aspect of patient care? *Age and Ageing, 17*(3),
    155-163.

This study used a random sample of people aged 65 and over discharged from hospitals
throughout Wales to investigate the preparation the patients had received for their discharge while they were in the hospital. *Preparation for discharge* was defined as receiving notice of impending discharge and discussion with staff about the return home. With
a response rate of over 80%, the authors found that 39% of the sample received less than
24 hours' notice of discharge, and fewer than half reported that a member of the hospital
staff had discussed discharge with them during hospitalization. In contrast patients cared
for in geriatric medicine received much better preparation and discharge planning than
did patients seen by other specialties. The authors conclude that, with the exception of
geriatric medicine, discharge planning for the elderly is a severely neglected aspect of
patient care.

Wan, T. T. H. (1987). Functionally disabled elderly. *Research on Aging, 9*(1),
    61-78.

This study examined the relationship among health status, social support, and use of
services in a sample of 694 elders who had a functionally limiting condition. The sample
was drawn from a household survey of 2,146 noninstitutionalized elderly studied in the
1979 Statewide Survey of Older Virginians. This article presents (a) validation of theoretical domains of health status indicators; (b) causal analysis of six health variables in
explaining use of health and social services; (c) establishment of causal structural rela-

tions among health status, social support, and services use behavior; and (d) application of a clustering methodology to identify target subgroups for service intervention. The findings suggest that social support not only is an enabling factor for use of services but also is a buffering factor between poor health functioning and use of services. A targeting methodology for classifying health and social support users identified predictors of social services use. Performance on activities of daily living was the strongest predictor, followed by ADL rating, mental status rating (MSR), and living arrangements. The study concludes that some of the disabled elderly may use physician services for reasons other than physical health problems and points to an earlier analysis showing that approximately 7% of noninstitutionalized elderly who were severely impaired would benefit from ambulatory services but were not receiving them. This suggests the need to direct resources to this frail population and the need for further research to systematically identify functionally disabled elders with varying degrees of limitations to more accurately target policy and planning decisions.

Wan, T. T. H., & Arling, G. (1983). Differential use of health services among disabled elderly. *Research on Aging, 5*(3), 411-431.

This study examined the use of ambulatory services among the noninstitutionalized elderly (*n* = 772) who reported one or more activity-limiting chronic conditions in the 1979 Statewide Survey of Older Virginians. The study used multiple regression analysis of physician visits, hospital days, and use of social services to explore differential use of services according to predisposing, enabling, and need characteristics of the elderly. Findings are reported on the effects of these three factors, the combined effects of the three dimensions, the relationship between health and social services use, and major characteristics of users of physician services. The need characteristics appeared to have relatively greater effects on use of services than did the predisposing and enabling characteristics of the disabled elderly. Self-care limitations and physical functioning exerted a strong influence on the use of social but not physician services, while the number of psychological symptoms and illness episodes had a strong influence on the use of physician but not social services. Two distinct use patterns are hypothesized from these findings. One pattern involves those who have experienced moderate or severe functional incapacities that require supportive services (home health care, physical therapy, personal care, and so on). The second is a pattern of use by those who have experienced a number of physical and psychological problems. This analysis suggests that many disabled elders may have used physician services for reasons other than medical attention—particularly in response to psychological needs—raising questions about the appropriateness of the use of physician care. Physician visits were positively associated with the use of social services by the disabled elderly. Availability of a variety of social services may result in greater use of ambulatory care services in the community.

Wan, T. H., & Weissert, W. G. (1981). Social support networks, patient status and institutionalization. *Research on Aging, 3*(2), 240-256.

The research reported in this article studied the relationship of social support to patients' functional status and institutionalization. Multivariate analyses of data obtained from an experimental study of homemaker services and geriatric day care were performed to examine the role of social support networks as buffers between declines in physical functioning and the risk of institutionalization. Different dimensions of social support networks are examined to investigate the possibility of differential effects on the use of nursing homes. Findings indicate that social support plays an important role in mitigating the effects of deteriorative health status and thus reduces the risk of institutionalization; living alone was found to have a strong relationship to institutionalization. In addition those with stronger social support networks were most likely to improve in mental and physical functioning.

Wan, T. T. H., Weissert, W. G., & Livieratos, B. B. (1980). Geriatric day care and homemaker services: An experimental study. *Journal of Gerontology, 35*(2), 256-274.

   This article reports a randomized study comparing the impact on people who received geriatric day care, homemaker services, and both services combined with a control group who received none of these services. Outcomes showed significant differences for the day-care experimental group in physical functioning and activity level, for the homemaker group in physical functioning and contentment level, and for all of these outcomes for the combined services group. Increased use of services was associated with improved outcomes of care, particularly for continuing, even, and moderate amounts of care. Multivariate analysis of data identified factors other than the use of experimental services that were more effective in explaining variation in outcomes. For both the day-care and homemaker study groups, significant factors that affected all four outcome measures (ADL/physical functioning, contentment, activity level, and mental functioning) were primary diagnosis, impairment prognosis, and number of inpatient hospital days. Evidence suggests that use of these services can help the disabled elderly to sustain, if not improve, functioning and that these services helped to extend survivorship of patients, had a positive effect on physical and mental well-being, and a limited but positive effect on social activity. It is suggested that varying levels of intensity of day-care or homemaker services should be provided for different kinds of patients for maximum efficiency and benefits. The finding that these services do not replace institutional care needs for all patients causes the authors to recommend that policy recognize these services as additional rather than substitution services in the long-term care continuum.

Weissert, W. G. (1988). The national channeling demonstration: What we knew, know now, and still need to know. *HSR: Health Services Research, 23*(1), 175-187.

   This is an excellent review of the key findings of the channeling demonstration and a critique of how these findings fit into existing knowledge and future research in long-term care. The article emphasizes methodological issues as they relate to outcomes. It both identifies issues that undermined results of the project and realistically appraises its contributions. Three major results of the channeling demonstration are identified as (a) no difference between case management plus a few "gap-filling" dollars versus case management plus a long list of services, (b) surprisingly limited benefits to caregivers, and

(c) measurement of the magnitude of the formal for informal care substitution effect. The author extrapolates the contributions of these findings to policy formulation.

Weissert, W. G., & Cready, C. M. (1989). Toward a model for improved targeting of aged at risk of institutionalization. *HSR: Health Services Research, 24*(4), 485-510.

This article reports on a model featuring patient characteristics associated with institutionalization, nursing home bed supply, and a climate variable that together correctly classified 98.2% of cases residing in the community or a nursing home. The model was developed using a national sample of institutionalized and noninstitutionalized aged from the 1977 National Nursing Home Survey and the 1977 National Health Interview Survey. Factors that appear to be determinants of institutional residence for the elderly are physical dependency, degenerative disease and mental disorder, lack of spouse, being white, poverty, old age, unoccupied nursing home beds, and climate. It is suggested that effective targeting mechanisms may help increase the accuracy of predicting those at risk for institutionalization. Greater targeting accuracy may help to increase the cost-effectiveness of community-based programs.

Weissert, W. G., & Cready, C. M. (1989). A prospective budgeting model for home- and community-based long-term care. *Inquiry, 26,* 116-129.

This study subjected to break-even analysis 27 controlled experiments on home and community-based long-term care that were conducted in the past 30 years. To develop the break-even analysis, a weighted average use and cost experience of all patients studied in all projects was applied to compare 100 hypothetical treatment and control group patients. Health care costs for the treatment group averaged about 14% more than for the control groups across all studies and a similar amount among the subset of post-1980 studies that were evaluated. An analysis of the effectiveness of home and community-based long-term care services in reducing nursing home admissions and affecting hospital use and costs and other outpatient and treatment costs is presented. Across all analyses, community care increased net costs from 13.7% to 18.9%. To reduce community care costs, managers may be able to apply additional information to achieve specific performance goals; studies to date show that managers have had to rely on faulty information to set performance goals and costs. Break-even analysis identifies ways program managers may best expend cost-reduction efforts to gain maximum cost savings. Analysis indicates that the most effective ways to reduce net costs is for program managers to better target their services to those at risk for hospitalization and find ways to lower treatment costs. Targeting those at risk of nursing home placement or outpatient care use, and reducing inpatient admissions and length of stay, were less efficient but still useful ways to reduce costs. It is suggested that managers could use prospective performance targets and break-even data to judge performance and make adjustments on a monthly basis to operate more closely at break-even costs.

Weissert, W. G., Cready, C. M., & Pawelak, J. E. (1988). The past and future of home- and community-based long-term care. *The Milbank Quarterly, 66*(2), 309-388.

This is a review article that includes the results of home and community care studies conducted over the last several decades; 150 citations are incorporated in this article. All studies included in this review met five criteria: They were evaluation studies of community-based care in contrast with existing long- term care services, used an experimental design with a control group, included a minimum of 50 subjects in each study group, used the individual as the primary unit of analysis, and primarily served an older population. The article examines (a) the extent to which patients served in the studies reviewed were at risk of using a nursing home or hospital, (b) how much their institutional care use was reduced by using home and community care, (c) how much outpatient care use was reduced by home and community care use, (d) what the cost of new services was, (e) savings or losses resulting from changes in use of existing and new services, and 6) effects on various domains of health status. In addition to narrative discussion a variety of tables compare research results among various studies. This is a comprehensive review with a bibliography that includes many basic community care studies from the 1970s and 1980s.

Weissert, W. G., Elston, J. M., Bolda, E. J., Cready, C. M., Zelman, W. N., Sloane, P. D., Kalsbeek, W. D., Mutran, E. et al. (1989). Models of adult day care: Findings from a national survey. *The Gerontologist, 29*(5), 640-649.

This article characterizes a representative sample of 60 adult day-care centers nationwide in terms of three models of care. Each model is linked to a specific sponsor and serves a distinct population. Analysis of variance for participant characteristics was used to test the appropriateness of the model. Auspice Model I, based in a nursing home or rehabilitation hospital, accounts for 26.5% of the sample and provided care for 17.9% of study participants. Auspice Model II operated out of a hospital, freestanding unit, housing authority, senior program, or municipal or other sponsor and constituted 62.2% of the centers studied and 68.2% of the study participants. Special-purpose centers serving veteran, mental health, cerebral palsy, or blind populations constituted 11.2% of the day-care centers studied and cared for 13.6% of the study participants. Differences in staffing, activities, participant characteristics, costs, and other program features are compared among the three models. Model distinctions may be useful to policymakers by suggesting differences in how centers would be affected by changes in Medicaid reimbursement policy or availability of block grant funds as well as suggesting the types of needs day-care centers can meet. It is noted that, since the last study of this type a decade ago, Auspice Model II has broadened its mission to include more health-related activities and health care staff and is now serving a larger number of elders with mental disorders. Special-purpose centers are a new entity within the past decade. Little change in the economy of day care has occurred; it is regarded as a bargain for the number of hours of services, consumer satisfaction, and diversity of services provided.

Weissert, W. G., Wan, T. H., Livieratos, B. B., & Pellegrino, J. (1980). Cost-effectiveness of homemaker services for the chronically ill. *Inquiry, 17,* 230-243.

A randomized experimental approach was used to ask whether homemaker services would reduce institutionalization and improve or maintain physical functioning at levels as high as or higher than existing care options and to examine the effects of such services on use and cost of other Medicare services. The study assessed 630 Medicare-eligible individuals for need of homemaker services and then randomized them to control or experimental groups. The experimental group received an average of 368 hours of homemaker services as a Medicare Part A benefit (following three days of hospitalization); both groups retained eligibility for all regular Medicare services. A three-stage analysis of outcomes was conducted, controlling for various confounding problems. The most striking finding was that homemaker services significantly affected mortality but did not significantly affect physical functioning. Homemaker use did not have significant effects on institutionalization in nursing homes or on hospitalization; throughout all phases of the analysis the experimental groups using homemaker services had higher hospitalization rates, though not significantly so. It is conjectured that this may be the result of the homemaker acting as a monitor of the patient's health status and catalyzing prompt hospitalization when needed. Lower death rates and use of homemaker services are linked by this study. Medicare costs were 60% higher for the experimental than for the control group because homemaker services increased the use of existing services rather than serving as a substitute for them.

William, T. F., Hill, J. G., Fairbank, M. E., & Knox, K. G. (1973). Appropriate placement of the chronically ill and aged: A successful approach by evaluation. *Journal of the American Medical Association, 226*(11), 1332-1335.

This article reports the successful operation of a demonstration unit for comprehensive evaluation and appropriate placement of chronically ill and aged persons referred for nursing home placement. The Evaluation and Placement Unit (E-P unit) is staffed by a group of internists, public health nurses, social workers, and consultants in rehabilitation, psychiatry, and other areas, all with special interest and competence in the problems of aging. The patient spends about three hours in the evaluation unit clinic and receives a complete medical, social, functional, and mental status workup. One or more family members are asked to accompany the patient, and they are interviewed separately. A case conference held one week following the consultation workup includes the assessment team and other community professionals who have worked with the patient in the immediate past. The conference develops consensus on recommendations for further care and placement of the patient, and unit staff then assists the patient and family to implement the recommendations. After the first 30 months of operation, the study had evaluated 332 patients and provided follow-up for periods of 2 to 24 months. Initially referred for consideration for nursing home placement, 22% of patients seen by the E-P unit were enabled to remain at home, and only 35% were found to need nursing homes. An independent follow-up assessment found that 84% of the 332 patients were appropriately placed for their needs—an improvement of more than 20% over the degree of appropriateness of long-term care found in this community and in other studies. The article also provides

descriptive information about the patients' ages, diagnoses, and other attributes; discusses the fact that less than half had their own personal physician whom they saw regularly; and notes the importance of comprehensive medical evaluation for appropriate
determination of levels of care.

Wolock, I., Schlesinger, E., Dinerman, M., & Seaton, R. (1987). The posthospi-
    tal needs and care of patients: Implications for discharge planning. *Social
    Work in Health Care, 12*(4), 61-76.

This pilot study of hospital discharge planning after the implementation of DRGs focuses on the impact of social workers as discharge planners and the types of criteria that
most influence the selection of hospitalized patients for social work intervention. The
study followed 69 patients hospitalized for a serious illness and discharged to their own
or relative's homes for from 6 to 11 months after discharge. Interviews focused on
patient's posthospital needs, sources of help they received and how well they met needs,
and the extent to which hospital social work targets these needs in the discharge planning
process. Although the study included people as young as age 30, most of the subjects were
elderly, and all had substantial needs for care. Family members were the major care providers, with some use of formal services. Tables summarize the patients' posthospital
medical regimens, patient characteristics by receipt of postdischarge services, and information on the four most frequently used services: nursing, medical treatment such as
injections and physical therapy, homemaker services, and meal programs. Social work
intervention significantly affected the rate of formal service use; for the group of patients
who had no contact with hospital social work prior to discharge, the proportion using
community services was lowest (33%), followed by those who had received screening
services only (47%), and greatest for the patients receiving additional services (69%).
Social work contact was statistically significantly related to only two patient factors—
length of stay and whether or not the patient lived alone. Persons 70 years of age and older
were also more likely to be seen. The authors suggest that multiple prior hospital admissions, level of function, complexity of posthospital medical care needs, and predictors of
patient and family stress should be incorporated into new discharge screening systems to
more accurately target those who most need social work discharge planning interventions.

Wood, J. B. (1989). The emergence of adult day care as post-acute care agen-
    cies. *Journal of Aging and Health, 1*(4), 521-539.

This article reports the results of a study of the effects of the Medicare prospective
payment system on adult day-care centers (ADCC). The study followed 39 ADCCs over
three years in 12 communities in five states. Findings show that ADCCs are shifting their
services to meet the demands of heavier-care clientele leaving hospitals. ADCC care may
be offering "out-of-home home health care" when Medicare home health care benefits
terminate. Financing for ADCCs relies primarily on Medicaid and private pay, but the
increasing demand for medically related services for ADCC clients is prompting many
ADCCs to report a growing need for funding to cover the non-Medicaid eligible client;
Medicare is seen as the appropriate source for this coverage. In 1986 agencies also reported a shift to families of the frail elderly in responsibility for providing care. Mentally
ill clients with heavy care requirements (such as people with Alzheimer's disease) present

a challenge to ADCCs, which have neither the staff nor the facilities to accommodate this clientele while currently serving clients with postacute care needs as well as chronic care needs. ADCC responses to increased family requests for services such as respite at no additional cost have included establishing family support groups, providing patient education, and training family members. ADCCs in this study have experienced many of the effects of the Medicare prospective payment system that have been reported by other nonhospital service agencies. Clients are reported to be in a more disabled condition when the ADCCs receive them. The agencies interviewed described what they felt to be an increasing lack of coverage and increasing needs for service by the non-Medicaid-eligible older population. There are continuing reports of more requests for assistance on the part of family members caring for disabled older adults.

Wooldridge, J., & Schore, J. (1988). Effects of channeling on use of nursing home, hospitals and other medical services. *HSR: Health Services Research, 23*(1), 119-128.

This article summarizes the effects of the National Channeling Demonstration project, which was intended to reduce the use of acute and long-term medical services through the use of case management. Two case management treatment interventions were tested. In both models all clients received the core functions of outreach, screening and eligibility determination, assessment care planning and initiation of services, and monitoring and reassessment of service needs throughout their participation in the program. The Basic Case Management Model tested the premise that the major difficulty in getting long-term care in the community is lack of information about and ability to obtain and manage services in the existing system. Case management was intended to determine needs and arrange and coordinate services under the existing system of resources. Case managers had a small discretionary fund with which to purchase services to fill gaps. The Financial Control Model tested the premise that inadequate funding is responsible for inappropriate use of nursing homes. It was set up to alter access to services and use and still control costs through limits on average service expenditures and individual service expenditures as well as through cost-sharing by clients. Channeling found no treatment/control differences in nursing home use over time. Only the group that was in nursing homes at the time of eligibility screening for the study showed a decline in nursing home use. For this 2% to 3% of the total sample, both models of case management decreased nursing home days substantially—24% to 30% in the first year depending on the treatment group. Neither treatment model had any statistically significant effect on hospital use or on the use of medical and physicians' services.

Zarit, S. H., Todd, P. A., & Zarit, J. M. (1986). Subjective burden of husbands and wives as caregivers: A longitudinal study. *The Gerontologist, 26*(3), 260-266.

A two-year follow-up of 64 caregiver spouses of dementia patients was conducted to focus on factors associated with nursing home placement. Over half of those for whom status was determined were still at home, and only 11 patients were in nursing homes. Fifteen patients had died and, of these, about two thirds had spent some time in a nursing

home before their deaths. There were no gender differences in outcome except for a
higher death rate among male patients. A comparison of scores on burden scales and the
Memory and Behavior Problems Checklist was made. As hypothesized, caregivers' feelings of burden were associated with nursing home placement. The experience of greater
or lesser burden at any point in the patient's disease may be related to many factors, not
just severity of symptoms. The findings are consistent with general models of stress.
Caregivers feel burdened when the patient manifests deficits in behavior, caregivers react
differently to problem behaviors, and they vary in their skills for managing them. The
longitudinal analysis suggests that caregivers' ability to tolerate problem behaviors actually increases, even as the disease progresses. Subjective factors, especially caregivers'
perceived burden, were more strongly associated with nursing home placement than were
objective indicators of the severity of the dementia. Because of methodological issues,
the possibility that presence of specific symptoms led to institutionalization cannot be
ruled out. Availability of social supports was not found to be a factor in the placement
decision. Although wives initially reported more burden than husbands, no differences
were found at follow-up. A major implication of the findings is that carefully planned
interventions may effectively relieve caregiver burden. Programs that provide opportunities for respite and give special attention to early intervention with spouses may have
considerable impact on subjective burden.

Zawadski, R. T., & Eng, C. (1988). Case management in capitated long-term
    care. *Health Care Financing Review* (Annual Suppl.), pp. 75-81.

    The On Lok consolidated case management model is described and its impacts sum-
marized. The consolidated model of case management is defined as one in which a multidisciplinary team both assesses needs and provides the services ordered. Based in San
Francisco, On Lok provides comprehensive, interrelated services to a very impaired population using a multidisciplinary team of medical and nonmedical personnel who separately assess each client. Then the team develops a plan of care with the client and/or the
family and delivers the needed services. The team has access to an array of services that
they may adapt or create to meet clients' needs. On Lok differs from traditional long-term
care models in that it has total control over all service expenditures, is paid prospectively,
and assumes financial risk for the services it provides. Medicare is the single source of
payment for all services, and a full range of social and medical services are integrated
into a single program. The article summarizes the six working principles that underlie On
Lok's model and describes the composition and interrelationships of the multidisciplinary team. Community input is a key to external program accountability, and the multidisciplinary team provides an internal quality assurance process. Findings from the model
show that the most significant impact has been the reduction of high-cost hospital days.
Changes in use were found to be the result of reduction in both the number of hospitalizations and the lengths of stay. Nursing home days were also reduced. Community services have increased, offsetting some of the decrease in inpatient services. These changes
in service use are attributed in large part to On Lok's consolidated model of case management. Linking case management with service delivery increases the responsiveness of
the service system. The staff physician assumes total inpatient and outpatient primary

medical care responsibility and, through the multidisciplinary team process, has access to a broad array of services making it possible to find alternatives to expensive inpatient services. Capitation financing and provider assumption of financial risk give the multidisciplinary team the opportunity to create new, more cost-effective services not otherwise reimbursable in the fee-for-service system. In discussing alternate types of case management systems, the authors state that it is not a question of which model of case management is better but for what type of client, in what type of situation, is each model of case management most appropriate.

Zimmer, J. G., Groth-Juncker, A., & McCusker, J. (1984). Effects of a physician-led home care team on terminal care. *Journal of the American Geriatrics Society, 32*(4), 288-292.

In an effort to target populations for whom expanded home care programs would result in cost savings, this randomized controlled study tested the efficacy of a physician/geriatric nurse practitioner/social worker home care team that provides 24-hour on-call medical services in the home as needed. The goals of the team are to provide high-quality primary care to homebound chronically and terminally ill patients, maintaining them at home as long as they and their families wish, thereby reducing institutionalization and costs of terminal care. Health services use and estimated costs did not differ significantly for those patients who did not die while in the study. There was a higher death rate for patients who died at home, using considerably fewer days of hospital care and resulting in overall costs much lower than those of the controls. Of 21 team and 12 control patients who died but had at least two weeks of use experience in the study, team patients had about half the number of hospital days compared with controls during the terminal two weeks and had only 69% of the estimated total health care costs of the controls, even though they used more home care services. Evaluation demonstrated much greater satisfaction among team patients than among controls, especially among their caretakers. The study provides evidence for the effectiveness of a concerted effort to provide appropriate medical care for seriously ill and terminal patients by keeping them out of the hospital and enabling them to die at home. Unlike most hospice programs, which predominantly serve cancer patients, this study was effective in treating a mixed caseload of patients, about half of whom had other types of terminal diagnoses. Cost savings and consumer satisfaction indexes both support the viability of this model of care.

Zimmer, J. G., Groth-Juncker, A., & McCusker, J. (1985). A randomized controlled study of a home health care team. *AJPH, 75*(2), 134-141.

A team of a physician, social worker, and nurse practitioner delivered primary health care to homebound chronically or terminally ill elders who had been randomized to this treatment group. The team physician served as the primary physician for all care needs and was the attending physician for patients when they were hospitalized. Use of hospital and nursing home admissions was lower for the home care than for the control group, largely because the home care group members were more often able to die at home. The home care group used more in-home services and, although not statistically significant, their overall in-home care cost was lower than that of the control group. No significant differences in functional abilities were found between the two groups, but the home care patients and the informal home caregivers expressed significantly higher satisfaction with the care received. Patient and caregiver satisfaction were found to relate directly to health care use and cost reduction. The study shows that home care can be a cost-effective and desirable mode of treatment.

APPENDIX B

Research Agendas
Formulated at the NIA/AoA Conference

The NIA/AoA Invitational Conference on In-Home Health and Support Services was held in Bethesda, Maryland, in April 1990 to review the current state-of-the-art and to identify research gaps.[1] At the end of the conference, participants met in small groups to identify research priorities in three related areas: (a) home care in general, (b) respite care, and (c) board and care. As indicated in the following summaries, there is a need for better conceptualization of the service being offered. Other research topics identified were the need for care, use and supply of services, organization and delivery of care, effectiveness of care, definitions of quality of care and life, policy-relevant research, and innovative research designs. These reports constitute an excellent research agenda for the future.

Research Agenda on Home Care
(Group Rapporteur: A. E. Benjamin)

This subgroup addressed generic research needs in home care, cutting across all types of care. Research priorities were identified in four broad areas.

Need for Care

Better measures of and criteria for "need" for home care should be developed.

Attention should be given to distinctions between "unmet" and "partially met" needs. The "unmet" versus "met" dichotomy is inadequate.

Research is needed on variations in ADL measurement, specifically on the role of professional judgment and interpretation in the use of ADL measures.

Major work is needed on measuring preferences for care and examining the relationship of preferences to need.

There is a need for small-areas data on home care need and demand, including local, state, and regional data. Regional variations in use are well documented.

Because 25% of those with chronic disabilities are aged 45 to 64, research attention should be given to the needs and resources of this group.

Service Use

We know relatively little about the supply of home care services (volume, types). Attention should be given to unlicensed home health agencies and social services providers, about whom we have little data.

Descriptive studies of home care users are needed that profile and classify users in terms of needs and resources.

Longitudinal studies of chronic care service careers are needed, with specific attention to understanding factors affecting use and timing of home care and its relationship to other elements of long-term care services.

Research is needed that specifies and elaborates models of home care.

Organization and Delivery of Home Care

Much more research is needed on home care personnel—both research on home care worker careers and research on models of successful and satisfying work.

Research is needed on alternative approaches to or structures for organizing care, including various approaches to defining work roles (e.g., shared aide services).

We know very little about the uses of technology in home care—at a time when such use is mushrooming.

Comparative research is needed on models of care for younger, disabled ("independent living") populations and their relevance in terms of care for older persons.

More careful, controlled assessments are needed on the impact of adding formal case management to home care service packages.

Effectiveness of Home Care

Attention is needed to reconceptualizing home care outcomes, including adequacy and effectiveness of care. Better conceptualization will permit distinctions between unmet and partially met needs, for example. Outcomes need to be tailored to given home care models and populations. Attention also is needed on the role of autonomy and choice in understanding outcomes.

Research is needed on quality of care, the attributes of quality, and methods for identifying high-quality care. The impact of current QA approaches needs to be assessed.

Home care serves many subpopulations, and research is needed to specify the care needs of specific subpopulations and to understand who may be unsuitable for home care.

Research is needed on the impact of formal services on informal caregivers. More work is also needed on strategies to train informal caregivers at home.

Research Agenda on Respite Care
(Group Rapporteur: James A. Wells)

The Respite Care group determined that there were four areas needing further research. The group also identified two research designs to reduce the heterogeneity of the caregiver population.

Conceptualization of Respite Care

Definitions of relevant outcomes of respite are needed, especially those that lead to clear implementation of the forms of relief that might be provided to caregivers.

Research is needed to develop more sensitive measures of stress, burden, satisfaction, and other outcomes. This may require either new constructs or better instruments for measuring old constructs.

Research models need to be developed that clearly delineate the difference between the provision of services and the impact of those services on caregivers.

Designs need to ensure that provided services are carefully measured. Furthermore, when formal respite services are being evaluated, informal respite services should also be measured in both the treatment and the control groups.

Use and Supply of Services

Research is needed to document and describe the range of available services, the providers of the services, and the financing of the services.

Research is needed into how services are initiated and how they are delivered.

Research is needed to develop profiles of the users of respite services, especially how they vary in the need for respite care.

Perceptions and Evaluations of Respite Services by Caregivers Who Receive Them

Research is needed into how caregivers perceive formal versus informal services.

Research is needed into how caregivers evaluate the usefulness and quality of services.

Research is needed into how services fit into the caregiver's living arrangements.

Research is needed into the way respite services fit into the dynamics of networks of mutual obligation including kinship, friendship, and neighborhood networks.

Transitions and the Career of Caregiving

Research is needed to characterize the normal career of caregiving including how careers depend on the disease of the person for whom care is given, for example, Alzheimer's versus other diseases, or how careers vary by characteristics of the caregiver.

Research should address how stages in the career of caregiving can be effectively defined based on one or more dimensions of caregiving, for example, how long care has been given or the severity of illness of the person cared for.

Research is needed to address which respite services are needed and whether they are needed at different stages of the career.

Research should address how the stage of caregiving and the changing need for respite services relate to transitions such as initiation of formal care, home care, initiation of respite care, and transfer to nursing homes.

Research Designs

More effort needs to be put into research designs that eliminate heterogeneity in the population of caregivers.

The use of prospective studies should be encouraged, especially those sampling at the initiation of caregiving.

Studies may also be helpful that sample at the point of transition, for example, at the point when formal health care services come into the home. A mix of retrospective and prospective data collection may be used to characterize the impact on caregivers.

Research on Board and Care
(Group Rapporteur: Catherine Hawes)

This group primarily discussed topics or issues for a research agenda, with less attention devoted to methods. Compared with other types of care, especially little is known about board and care.

Models of Need, Demand, and Supply

Little is known about the "need" for the services and residential care provided by board and care homes, how need and other factors (e.g., SSI supplementation levels, nursing home bed supply, and readmission screening programs) contribute to demand for and use of board and care homes, and the relationship of supply to need and demand. Further, little is known about the factors that contribute not only to the overall supply of board and care beds but also to the supply of particular types of homes (e.g., large versus small, licensed versus unlicensed).

Definition and Measurement of Quality of Care and Life

Defining and measuring "quality" is not an easy task; however, such measures are essential to both descriptive and evaluative research.

The first task is finding the way to define *quality,* including the questions of who "ought" to define *quality* and how to address potential trade-offs among various aspects of quality, such as the issue of physical safety (e.g., ability of residents to exit a burning building); resident's financial well-being, safety, and quality of care (e.g., supervision of medications, provision of needed services or assistance); and quality of resident's life (e.g., autonomy and homelikeness of the environment).

Descriptive Studies

Both large-scale studies and smaller regional or local ones, as well as studies of board and care homes serving particular subgroups, are appropriate. Moreover it is important that studies capture the diversity of the population of the various types of board and care homes (e.g., large versus small, ownership, urban/suburban/rural) and the residents they serve (e.g., primarily private-pay versus SSI recipients, racial and ethnic subgroups). Studies were recommended on the following:

characteristics of the environment (e.g., homes, operators, staff, residents, services provided to residents, formal and informal, and quality of care)

extent and characteristics of unmet care needs among residents (this may be particularly pressing given trends in mortality and morbidity patterns and public policies that may be diverting impaired older persons from more intensive levels of care)

relationship of the board and care community (operators and residents) to other segments of the home and community-based long-term care system, including such issues as advocacy, placement referral, receipt of services, and so on

resident "transitions"—both from the community into and out of board and care homes and changes in status while in the home

owner/operator and staff "transitions" both into and out of the board and care industry and among licensed and unlicensed status

Evaluation of Services

A comprehensive description of the services actually provided is an essential element of evaluation studies.

Studies are needed that examine service need, service expectations, and service receipt. Services to be evaluated include those provided formally by the home; services formally provided by others (home health agencies, community mental health centers, physicians, case managers, advocates, and so on); and services provided informally by friends, family, and others.

Evaluations also are needed on the effect of board and care home services (and other services) on residents and operators and on cost (and, by implication, use of nursing homes), quality, health outcomes, transitions, satisfaction, and so on.

Policy-Relevant Research

There are a host of policy-relevant research topics that are especially important as pressure mounts for reforms in the way states and the federal government pay for and regulate board and care homes. Examples of these include the following:

the effect of current policies and regulations (e.g., payment levels and mechanisms, policies on nursing home bed supply, mental health policies, low-income housing supply, nursing home readmission screening) on the supply and use of board and care homes

effect of case management of various types on resident placement, referral, transitions, and well-being

patterns of changes in regulation and factors generating such changes

effect of trade association characteristics and activities on the regulatory and payment systems

effect of changes in regulation on supply, quality, cost, and the nature of the industry

Demonstrations and Evaluations

Demonstrations can provide valuable information on:

training and/or other technical assistance for operators

linking the community-based care system and board and care homes more closely, including service providers and case managers

provision of support groups (and possibly respite care) for operators of small board and care homes

the closing of a large board and care home and shifting residents to smaller homes

Note

1. For a copy of the conference agenda and list of participants, contact the cochairs, Dr. Marcia G. Ory or Dr. Alfred P. Duncker.

Index

About the Authors

A. E. Benjamin (a.k.a. Ted), (Ph.D., M.S.W.) is Associate Professor in the Department of Social and Behavioral Sciences, and Associate Director, Institute for Health & Aging, in the School of Nursing at the University of California, San Francisco. He received an M.S.W. in 1971 and a Ph.D. in political science and social work in 1977 from the University of Michigan. His research has analyzed variations across states in benefits for vulnerable populations, especially the elderly; the politics of resource redistribution to the elderly and children; overarching themes and issues in the provision of long-term care services to the chronically ill, particularly to the elderly and to persons with AIDS; and home and community-based services for the functionally dependent.

Alfred P. Duncker (Ph.D.) is the Director of the Division of Research and Demonstrations, Administration on Aging, which supports an array of research and demonstration projects focused on ways to improve in-home care and support services for the elderly. He joined the federal government in 1970 as a staff assistant to the 1971 White House Conference on Aging. He holds a Ph.D. in public law and government from Columbia University.

J. Kevin Eckert (Ph.D.) received his Ph.D. in anthropology from Northwestern University with specialization in social gerontology and medical anthropology. Prior to coming to the University of Maryland Baltimore County in January 1987, he was at Case Western Reserve

University. Currently he is Professor in the Departments of Sociology and Anthropology and Associate Vice-President for Graduate Studies. His current research examines the health and social adjustments of older people living in unregulated board and care homes and their caregivers. He is widely published in anthropology and gerontology.

Mary S. Harper (Ph.D., R.N., F.A.A.N.) is Coordinator, Long-Term Care Programs, Mental Disorders of Aging Research Center, National Institute of Mental Health. Her areas of specialty are psychogeriatric nursing and long-term care. She has written extensively on mental health services for older people. She is currently at the Administration on Aging, serving as Associate Director for Research and Development for the 1993 White House Conference on Aging.

Marie R. Haug (Ph.D.) is Professor Emerita of Sociology and Director Emerita of the University Center on Aging and Health. She received her Ph.D. in sociology from Case Western Reserve University in 1968, where she taught medical sociology, aging, and research methods until her formal retirement in 1984. She remains actively involved in aging research, publishing widely on a variety of aging and health care topics and taking a leadership role in professional organizations. She has recently received the prestigious NIH Merit award for her NIA research on the effects of stresses and strains on older people's physical health.

Susan L. Hughes (D.S.W.) directs the Program of Research in Gerontological Health at the Center for Health Services and Policy Research and is Associate Professor in the Department of Community Health and Preventive Medicine at Northwestern University Medical School. She received her Ph.D. in social policy and planning in health from the Columbia University School of Social Work in 1981 and has since conducted several studies of the cost effectiveness of community-based long-term care. She is the author of numerous research articles on community-based and long-term care options. She is also currently investigating musculoskeletal-related functional impairment in the elderly and its association to health care use and cost.

Stephanie M. Lyon (M.A.) received her M.A. in sociology with a specialization in social gerontology from the University of Maryland. She is a doctoral student in policy sciences at the University of

Maryland with a concentration in aging policy. She is currently Project Director for research in board and care homes in the Baltimore area and has cowritten several articles on the health and living arrangements of older people.

Rhonda J. V. Montgomery (Ph.D.) is the Director of the Institute of Gerontology and Associate Professor of Sociology at Wayne State University in Detroit, Michigan. For the past 10 years her research has focused on public policies and family relations among older adults. She has conducted several studies of families providing care to the elderly, which aimed at assessing the feasibility, costs, and benefits of alternative programs for supporting these families in their caregiving efforts. Currently she is studying the utility, design, and delivery of respite services for families caring for persons with Alzheimer's disease.

Marcia G. Ory (Ph.D., M.P.H.) is Chief, Social Science Research on Aging, Behavioral and Social Research Program, National Institute on Aging, National Institutes of Health, Bethesda, Maryland. She holds a Ph.D. from Purdue University and a M.P.H. from the Johns Hopkins University. She is very active in professional organizations and serves on several national task forces and advisory boards dealing with aging and health issues. Her main areas of interest include aging and health care, health and behavior research, and gender differences in health and longevity. She has published widely on these topics.

Meryl B. Rappaport (M.S.W., L.C.S.W.) is a doctoral candidate in the Department of Social and Behavioral Sciences, University of California, San Francisco (UCSF). She received both her Masters and Bachelor's degrees in social welfare from the University of California, Berkeley. Concurrent with her full-time doctoral program, she is the Director of Education and Research for the California Association for Health Services at Home. Her professional interests include the impact of high-technology home care on patients and caregivers, caregiver stress, home care licensure, certification and quality issues, home care as part of a community-based continuum of care for the elderly and chronically ill, and methods for building interdisciplinary teams in health care settings.

James G. Zimmer (M.D., D.T.P.H.) is currently Associate Chairman in the Department of Community and Preventative Medicine and Director of the Master of Public Health program at the University of Rochester School of Medicine and Dentistry. He received his B.A. from Cornell University, his M.D. from Yale University School of Medicine, and his Diploma in Tropical Public Health from the London School of Hygiene and Tropical Medicine. His activities have led to many national presentations and a number of publications on quality assessment and assurance and other aspects of nursing home care.